"On Pérez Rosario's brilliant reconstructio
the sting of her own legacy. She also glov
ignited in Latin American artists who foun
de-territorialized nowhere or utopia of New York. From that same fraught city, where
heritage identities and trajectories become burdens akin to the Holy Grail, this book
brings a major poet and activist into focus as incitement to read more and to write
bravely."

—*Doris Sommer, author of* The Work of Art in the World:
Civic Agency and Public Humanities

"*Becoming Julia de Burgos* is a smart and original study of this important poet and
cultural figure. Vanessa Pérez Rosario is an astute and insightful reader of Burgos's
poetry, letters, and journalism. Pérez Rosario is also a talented cultural historian: in
addition to [offering] readings that yield political and aesthetic dimensions of Burgos's
writing, Pérez Rosario also contextualizes Burgos's life transnationally, placing her at
the center of debates among Puerto Rican intellectuals about gender, colonialism, and
cultural identity. An important study from an exciting and talented new critical voice."

—*Farah Jasmine Griffin, author of* Clawing at the Limits of Cool:
Miles Davis, John Coltrane, and the Greatest Jazz Collaboration Ever

"In this beautifully written and thoroughly researched study, one of the most important
artistic and literary icons of the Nuyorican and Latino diaspora finally gets her due.
Vanessa Pérez Rosario gives us the most current and definitive resource to understand not
only Julia de Burgos's extensive body of work, but also the expansive cultural movement
that continues to find inspiration in her legacy."

—*Arlene Dávila, author of* Culture Works:
Space, Value, and Mobility across the Neoliberal Americas

"*Becoming Julia de Burgos* makes a truly significant contribution to multiple fields as
it demonstrates the commitment and attention to local histories and locations, set into
larger contexts, that marks the best work in Puerto Rican and Caribbean Studies."

—*Elizabeth Rosa Horan, co-editor of* This America of Ours:
The Letters of Gabriela Mistral and Victoria Ocampo

BECOMING JULIA DE BURGOS

published with a grant
Figure Foundation
where the road wind poet

BECOMING
JULIA DE BURGOS

The Making of a
Puerto Rican Icon

VANESSA PÉREZ ROSARIO

UNIVERSITY OF ILLINOIS PRESS

Urbana, Chicago, and Springfield

Library of Congress Control Number: 2014950831
ISBN 978-0-252-03896-9 (hardcover)
ISBN 978-0-252-08060-9 (pbk.)
ISBN 978-0-252-09692-1 (e-book)

To my parents,
Carmen and Frank Pérez

"The voice of an epoch is in the words of its poets."
—Victor Hernández Cruz

CONTENTS

ILLUSTRATIONS

Figures

Color plates, following page 126

ACKNOWLEDGMENTS

One of the most enjoyable parts of working on this project has been the opportunity to sit with many of the writers and artists of the Nuyorican community and beyond who have inherited Julia de Burgos's legacy and continue to extend it in interesting and meaningful ways: Jack Agüeros, Andrea Arroyo, Caridad De La Luz, Marcos Dimas, Martín Espada, Sandra María Esteves, Yasmín Hernández, Aurora Levins Morales, María Teresa (Mariposa) Fernández, Belkis Ramírez, Sonia Rivera-Valdés, Bonafide Rojas, Fernando Salicrup, Juan Sánchez, Luz María Umpierre, Manny Vega, Chiqui Vicioso, Emmanuel Xavier, and the members of Taller Boricua. Without them, Julia de Burgos would not be the icon she is today.

This project has undergone many transformations on its way to becoming the book you now hold in your hands. I am grateful for the institutional support I have received along the way from the Chicana/Latina Research Center at the University of California, Davis, the Faculty Fellowship Publication Program at City University of New York, the American Association of University Women American Fellowship and Publication Grant, the Library Fellowship from the David Rockefeller Center for Latin American Studies at Harvard University, the Postdoctoral Fellowship from the Center for Puerto Rican Studies, and the Career Enhancement Fellowship from the Woodrow Wilson Foundation.

The many conversations that I have had with friends, conference panelists, colleagues, librarians, archivists, and research assistants have helped shape the book. Thank you to Emilio Bejel, Yarimar Bonilla, Arnaldo Cruz-Malavé, Arlene Dávila, Juan Flores, Pedro Juan Hernández, Inés Hernández-Ávila, Elizabeth Horan, Regine Jean-Charles, Neil Larsen, Laura Lomas, Helvetia Martell, Jorge Matos, Edwin Meléndez, Oscar Montero, Joan Morgan, Frances Negrón-Muntaner, Crystal Parikh, Riché Richardson, Consuelo Saez Burgos, Virginia Sánchez-Korrol, Doris Sommer, Maritza Stanchich, Salamishah Tillet, and Arlene Torres. A special thanks goes to all of the staff at the Center for Puerto Rican Studies library and archives and to the *Centro Journal* for granting permission to publish a version of "Julia de Burgos' Writing for *Pueblos Hispanos*: Journalism as Puerto Rican Cultural and Political Transnational Practice" (25.2 [Fall 2013]: 4–27) in chapter 3.

Thank you to my editors at the University of Illinois Press, Larin McLaughlin and Dawn Durante, who believed in the project from the very beginning. Both have been helpful and generous with their time. Thank you to my readers at the press for their careful and detailed comments.

I am especially grateful for my family for being supportive, loving, and patient through the writing process.

BECOMING JULIA DE BURGOS

INTRODUCTION

In the early morning hours of 5 July 1953, two New York City police officers spotted a figure on the ground near the corner of Fifth Avenue and 106th Street in East Harlem. As they approached, they saw the body of a woman with bronze-colored skin. Once a towering woman at five feet, ten inches, she now lay in the street, unconscious. They rushed her to Harlem Hospital, where she died shortly thereafter. The woman carried no handbag and had no identification on her. No one came to the morgue to claim her body. No missing person's case fit her description. She was buried in the city's Potter's Field. One month later, the woman was identified as award-winning Puerto Rican poet Julia de Burgos. Her family and friends exhumed and repatriated her body.[1]

When I began writing about Julia de Burgos, I hesitated to mention her notorious death, seeking to move away from the narratives of victimhood that have shrouded her life for more than half a century. I wanted to focus on her poetry, her activism, and her legacy. Most Puerto Ricans already know her story, and many both on the island and in New York have been captivated by her life. However, I soon realized the importance of recounting even the most difficult details as I introduced her to new audiences. Her migration experience and her death on the streets of New York capture the imaginations of readers everywhere. *Becoming Julia de Burgos* builds on recent approaches to her work that focus on movement, flow, and migration.[2] This book proposes a new way of reading Burgos's work, life, and legacy, focusing on the escape routes she created to transcend the rigid confines of gender and cultural nationalism.

In Puerto Rico, the Generación del Treinta (Generation of the 1930s) writers created cultural works that responded to Antonio S. Pedreira's *Insularismo* (1934), an influential account of the shaping of Puerto Rican culture

Figure 1. Julia de Burgos, ca. 1934–38. Miriam Jiménez Collection, Archives of the Puerto Rican Diaspora, Center for Puerto Rican Studies, Hunter College, City University of New York.

and character, which asks, "¿Cómo somos y qué somos los puertorriqueños globalmente considerados? [How and what are we Puerto Ricans globally considered?]." The writers of this generation were obsessed with totalizing genres that they believed would heal the wounds of colonialism. They rooted Puerto Rican national identity in the land. Puerto Rican studies scholars have noted that the literary canon created and imposed by the *treintistas* (1930s writers) in a colonial society has taken the place of a national constitution and compensated for the lack of an independent nation-state.[3] Lyric poetry was demoted and assigned marginal status.[4] For the 1930s writers, the pleasure and eroticism of such poetry constituted an excess that threatened the nation. With her imagery of waterways, routes, and pathways, Burgos creates a dynamic subject that could not be fixed or contained, placing her among the historical *vanguardias*.[5] She attempts to create escape routes as a liberatory strategy, but in the end she confronts similar patriarchal structures abroad, suggesting that migration is not a liberatory strategy. She satisfied her quest for freedom through the imagination. While themes of Puerto Rican independence and U.S. imperialism cut across her work, other important motifs include the rights of women and their struggle to assert themselves in a patriarchal society.

The escape routes in Burgos's poetry, in her prose, and in her creatively productive life in San Juan, Havana, and New York helped her write herself out of the nation, challenge the work of the *treintista* writers, and provide routes for other island-based writers who chose to work from a position of exile. These routes allowed her to write herself out of a nation that consigned her—a working-class woman of African descent—to the role of a housewife and mother.[6] Her deployment of paths, routes, and journeys is not limited to her poetry. These themes permeate her prose, her letters, and her life. Juan Gelpí notes that Burgos creates a nomadic subject in her poetry.[7] Gilles Deleuze and Félix Guattari suggest that the nomadic subject develops in open spaces, in environs without horizons, such as the steppe, the ocean, and the desert. While the migrant moves from one destination to the next, for the nomadic subject, "every point is a relay and exists only as a relay."[8] Rosi Braidotti extends Deleuze and Guattari's work to suggest the possibilities of nomadism for feminist agency. The basis of a feminist nomadic consciousness can be found in the various maps through which feminists exit phallocentrism. According to Braidotti, "Nomadic consciousness is a form of political resistance to hegemonic, fixed, unitary, and exclusionary views of subjectivity."[9] The routes that Burgos creates to escape the heteropatriarchy of the Generación del Treinta nation builders also create spaces in which gay, lesbian, Nuyorican, and Puerto Rican writers on the margins can have fruitful interactions and encounters. In life and in the literary works of many of these writers, Burgos becomes a figure of sexile, a person who migrates because of his or her gender or sexuality. Braidotti notes that "nomadic shifts endorse a creative sort of becoming; they are a performative metaphor that allows for otherwise unlikely encounters, and unsuspected sources of interaction, experience and knowledge."[10]

Burgos's death is the stuff of legend. Gossip shrouded her life, but her death made her the subject of great storytelling, myth, and speculation. Edward Said notes that prominent intellectuals are often symbolic of their time: "In the public consciousness they represent achievement, fame, and reputation which can be mobilized on behalf of an ongoing struggle or embattled community."[11] Burgos became a symbol of her time. In the only biography of her to date, Juan Antonio Rodríguez Pagán highlights the creation of Burgos as a cult figure: "Se va tejiendo en torno a su persona una leyenda . . . que la rescata para siempre de la muerte y del olvido [A myth is woven around her life . . . which saves her eternally from death and oblivion]."[12] Among critical scholars on the island, her life often symbolizes the nation; she is remembered as "la expresión de la conciencia nacional puertorriqueña ante la crisis de identidad que representa ser absorbidos por la cultura norteamericana [the expression of Puerto Rican national consciousness faced with assimilation into North American culture]."[13] Puerto Rican literary critic José Emilio González writes that her intensity "era el grito herido de nuestra conciencia nacional en la soledad de nuestra noche política [was the wounded cry of our national conscience reflecting the solitude of our darkest political hour]."[14]

It is not surprising that many people see Burgos as symbolizing the nation. Her life dramatizes a series of sociohistorical problems that define an important era in Puerto Rico's history—from the 1917 signing of the Jones Act, which extended U.S. citizenship to Puerto Ricans, to the 1952 status change under which the island became a free associated state. Although Burgos was born in 1914, her birth year is often cited as 1917, coinciding with the Jones Act. The origin of this confusion is unclear, but a 1917 birth date reinforces her status as a symbol of this defining moment.[15] Burgos's death in 1953, just a year after the island became a free associated state, represents the idea that Puerto Rican culture (supposedly) died at the time of the island's absorption into a politically ambiguous relationship with the United States. As with other historical figures who represent their nations, some observers seek to sanitize Burgos's story and legacy. As time passes, her story is co-opted and serves the nation as well as the diaspora. Yet understanding Burgos's life and works requires understanding her struggle against hegemony and her enduring belief that political action will enable radical democratic principles of social justice and equality to shape a better world.

During the first half of the twentieth century, many island-based writers, musicians, and artists scripted Puerto Rican migration as both tragedy and cultural contamination.[16] Rafael Hernández's classic *jíbaro* (peasant) song, "Lamento borincano" (Puerto Rican Mourning, 1929), and René Marqués's play, *La carreta* (*The Oxcart*, 1953), are salient examples. Written in New York (most likely in East Harlem, where Hernández lived), "Lamento borincano" decries the social and economic conditions that led so many to migrate in search of work.[17] The characters in Marqués's play leave their rural Puerto Rican town in search of the American Dream in New York City. However, the culture shock of incompatible values and the city's dehumanized modernity and hostility traumatize the matriarch, Doña Gabriela, and her family. Their only hope is to return to their former peasant lives. Puerto Rican scholar Juan Flores notes that in the play, "the entire migration experience is presented as a process of abrupt moral and cultural deterioration."[18] *La carreta* was celebrated both in Puerto Rico and internationally for more than a generation as the classic literary interpretation of recent Puerto Rican history.[19] To many observers, Burgos embodies the *carreta* of Marqués's canonical play. She becomes a metonym for the island itself, her life a version of the narrative of migration as tragedy. She is consumed by the city, just as the island is consumed by U.S. imperialism.

Puerto Ricans in New York who came of age in the 1970s remembered Burgos's migration experience differently than did those on the island. Participants in the social movements of the 1960s and 1970s saw her experiences of isolation, financial hardship, and delegitimized existence as illustrating the need for solidarity, coalition, and community. Burgos's life story reminds Nuyorican poet Sandra María Esteves of her mother, her Titi Julia, and "all those families who came to the United States with dreams expecting to find work and a better life, but instead encountered a different reality."[20] Burgos's life evokes the experiences of those migrants who faced discrimination and criminalization because of their linguistic and cultural differences, race, class, and gender. Her poetry binds the experiences of Puerto Rican women, energizing and legitimizing collective emancipatory strivings for many Puerto Ricans in New York. In her final poems, written in English in the months before her death, Burgos wrote of the loneliness, despair, and anguish that shroud the migrant's experience. In theme and emotional inflection, her work and her life inspired the work of a generation of Puerto Rican diaspora writers who came into their own during the 1970s.[21]

The way in which artists and writers have deployed Burgos is important to her legacy. The final two chapters of this book explore Burgos's influence and presence in the contemporary public imaginary as captured in the work of writers and visual artists. In New York in particular, writers and artists pick up on Burgos as an early figure of sexile and on what I refer to as the feminist nomadic subject in her poetry. The cultural production of Puerto Rican writers and artists in New York exceeds the narrowly defined cultural nationalism of the *treintista* writers and cannot be reconciled within the boundaries of Pedreira's *Insularismo*.[22] The intellectual who writes from exile "does not respond to the logic of the conventional but to the audacity of daring, and to representing change, to moving on, not standing still."[23] While Burgos's legacy has in some cases been used to symbolize tragedy, this book explores those writers and artists who invoke her memory to "always move away from the centralizing authorities towards the margins, where you see things that are usually lost on minds that have never traveled beyond the conventional and the comfortable."[24] These writers and artists redefine and expand the boundaries of Puerto Rican identity beyond the geographical border of the nation.

Nuyorican and U.S. Latino/a diasporic poets and performers summon the memory of Burgos as a way to perform, manifest, transmit, and reinvent Puerto Rican and Latino/a diasporic identities. Remembering Burgos activates memory circuits across Puerto Rican communities on the island and in New York as well as among members of Latino/a communities who share these New York neighborhoods. Dominican poet Sherezada (Chiqui) Vicioso and Mexican visual artist Andrea Arroyo, among others, learned of Burgos as they participated in the cultural life of East Harlem. El Barrio, experiencing rapid gentrification, is the historically Puerto Rican neighborhood where Burgos once lived. In *Cities of the Dead*, Joseph Roach argues that social processes of remembering and forgetting are performances that reveal, convey, and reinvent culture. Performances that reinvent are particularly relevant in what Roach describes as the circum-Atlantic world, focusing on "the centrality of the diasporic and genocidal histories of Africa and the Americas, North and South, in the creation of the culture of modernity."[25] Roach argues that the relationship between memory, performance, and substitution, or what he calls surrogation, plays a critical role in the way culture reproduces itself. The surrogate, however, is never exact, either falling short of its precedent and thereby creating a deficit or exceeding the space and thus creating a surplus. The three-part relationship—memory, performance, and surrogation—becomes most visible in funereal rituals. As public spectacles and occasions for organizing, funerals honoring a consequential member of the community offer an opportunity for re-creating communal affiliations. United around a corpse, community members reflect on loss and renewal of shared bonds, which the deceased symbolically embodies. This process of succession through performance creates a place, an "invisible network of allegiances, interests, and resistances that constitutes the imagined community. In that place also is a breeding ground of anxieties and uncertainties about what that community should be."[26] In other words, in the act of memorializing Burgos, Latino/a writers and artists explore cultural, political, and economic dynamics influencing popular notions of *Latinidad*. The concept of *Latinidad* has been partially defined by the way that mass culture and the media homogenize all Latinos into one group, erasing national origins, histories, race, class, and gender differences that exist under this umbrella term.[27] Sites of memory, vigils, performances, and parades are cultural exchanges that reinvent, re-create, and restore.

In contrast to dominant narratives invested in myth and legend, *Becoming Julia de Burgos* strives to release Burgos from the limited nationalist narratives that are often used to define her. Although Burgos remained committed to political nationalism in her writing and her life, she resisted the narrow cultural nationalism of her 1930s contemporaries in Puerto Rico. Even now, when her story has been sanitized and "purified," her refusal to be co-opted by totalizing narratives lives in her work and in the work of those writers and visual artists who keep her memory alive.

Julia de Burgos's Life

Julia Constanza Burgos García was born on 17 February 1914 in the town of Carolina, Puerto Rico, the eldest of Paula García de Burgos and Francisco Burgos Hans's thirteen children. Julia was intimately familiar with struggle, hardship, and death. She watched six of her younger siblings die of malnutrition and other illnesses associated with poverty. In 1931, she graduated from the University of Puerto Rico High School and entered the University of Puerto Rico, receiving a teaching certification two years later. In 1934, she married Rubén Rodríguez Beauchamp and took a job with the Puerto Rico Emergency Relief Administration, distributing milk and food to children at a milk station. In 1935, she began a short career as a teacher—one of the few professions open to working-class women—in the rural town of Barrio Cerro Arriba in Naranjito. During this time, she wrote her first collection of poetry, *Poemas exactos a mí misma* (Poems to Myself), which she later considered juvenilia and never published. She published her first poem, "Yo quiero darme a ti" (I Want to Give Myself to You), in *Alma Latina*, a magazine edited by Graciany Miranda Archilla. Miranda Archilla was a poet, journalist, essayist, and cofounder of a new Puerto Rican poetic movement, Atalaya de los Dioses (Watchman of the Gods), which came to be known as Atalayismo. In those early years, she also wrote "Río Grande de Loíza," which became one of her most well-known works and was later included in her first published collection, *Poema en veinte surcos* (Poem in Twenty Furrows, 1938). She most likely met her friend and mentor, Luis Lloréns Torres, one of the leading poets of the time, at a *tertulia* (literary salon) that met at a restaurant, El Chévere. As her work became more known, she met several of the other writers of the time, including Luis Palés Matos, Evaristo Ribera Chevremont, and Francisco Matos Paoli.[28]

Julia de Burgos's teaching career was short-lived. Although she had completed a two-year teaching degree, she, like many women of her social class, lacked the financial means to pursue an advanced degree that might offer more stable employment. Like many of these women, Burgos went to work as soon as possible to help support her family.[29] Indeed, throughout her life, Burgos sent money to her family, as she mentions in several letters to her sister from New York and Cuba.[30] She never realized her dream of completing a doctoral degree.[31]

In 1936, she left her teaching position and moved to Old San Juan, where she published her work in local newspapers and magazines. That same year, a nationalist weekly, *La Acción*, published her poem "Es nuestra la hora" (Ours Is the Hour), a cry for Puerto Rican independence. With this poem, her voice joined the nationalist cause, demanding independence from U.S. imperialism and occupation. She continued to support the Nationalist Party through writings in the San Juan newspaper *El Mundo*, with her poetry, and by attending rallies until her 1940 departure from Puerto Rico. This poetry became the primary work for which she is remembered.

Burgos also wrote some important essays in Puerto Rico and in New York that have received little critical attention.[32] During the 1930s, she wrote a series of six educational stories for children to be broadcast on Puerto Rican radio as part of a U.S. educational campaign, the Escuela del Aire (School of the Air). She also wrote an essay to support a 1936 nationalist rally in Puerto Rico and kept a journal while hospitalized in New York.[33]

The year 1938 would prove important for Burgos. She not only published *Poema en veinte surcos* but also met Dominican intellectual Juan Isidro Jimenes Grullón. A medical doctor, Jimenes Grullón was in Puerto Rico lecturing on his book, *Luchemos por nuestra América* (We Fight for Our America), at the Ateneo Puertorriqueño, the island's premier cultural institution. Jimenes Grullón had spent nearly two years in prison for organizing a coup against Dominican dictator Rafael Trujillo before receiving amnesty and being exiled in 1935. Jimenes Grullón shared Burgos's commitment to anticolonialism and anti-imperialism as well as her passion for freedom from reactionary governments. The two quickly developed a romantic relationship, and her marriage to Rodríguez Beauchamp ended.[34] However, her relationship with Jimenes Grullón, who came from a prominent Dominican family and had his eye on his country's presidency, challenged and defied the Old World hierarchies that separated two people of their social positions. As a divorced woman in a conservative Catholic society, Burgos found that gossip, speculation, and vicious rumors undermined her respectability.[35] Burgos wrote and published her second collection of poetry, *Canción de la verdad sencilla* (Song of the Simple Truth), in 1939.[36] On 13 January 1940, she left for New York, where she stayed briefly with Jimenes Grullón. The following June, she joined him in Cuba, where she lived until November 1942. At that time, she returned to New York alone, her relationship with Jimenes Grullón severed permanently. In a 25 September 1940 letter to her sister, Burgos wrote that she was at work on a new book, *El mar y tú* (The Sea and You), but lacked the funds to publish it.[37] The book was published posthumously in 1954. When Julia's sister, Consuelo, arranged the volume's publication, she added a final section, "Otros poemas" (Other Poems), that included works Burgos had sent to family members while she was in Cuba and New York.

From late 1942 until her death, Burgos lived in various neighborhoods in Harlem, where she struggled to make a living as a writer. She wrote for the Spanish-language weekly *Pueblos Hispanos* from 1943 to 1944, further developing her political voice. Many observers, including Burgos's biographer, Rodríguez Pagán, have argued that Burgos's move to New York without family and friends was the result of a self-destructive, suicidal impulse.[38] However, her journalism shows her political commitment to radical democracy and the struggle for immigrant and Puerto Rican rights and her advocacy of solidarity with Harlem's African American community. In addition, these writings as well as her poetry reveal her understanding of cultural identity as fluid and unbound by national territory.

In 1943, Burgos married Armando Marín, a Puerto Rican musician who had lived in New York for many years. Both of them had difficulty finding work, and they subsequently moved to Washington, D.C., where Marín had a job possibility. During their nine months there, they felt isolated as a consequence of their separation from the New York Puerto Rican community. As Burgos wrote to her sister on 14 May 1945,

> Sobre todo nos aniquila la distancia de nuestro propio pueblo que teníamos tan cerca en Nueva York. Estoy loca por encontrarme de nuevo en mi segunda casa, que es como considero a esa llamada ciudad de hierro después de pasar casi un año de vaciedad en esta capital del silencio.

> The hardest part of all of this is being away from our own community that we lived among in New York. I am eager to return to my second home, as that is how I now see that city of steel, after living almost a year secluded in this capital of silence.

In Washington, Burgos worked as a secretary in the government office of the Coordinator of Inter-American Affairs but was fired after FBI officials asked about her writing for *Pueblos Hispanos*, which the report described as the Puerto Rican nationalist organ and mouthpiece in New York. She responded, "*Pueblos Hispanos* has become too Communist. I just want to see Puerto Rico be independent and free." Later that day, she was asked to take her things from the office and not to return to the building. Soon thereafter, she and Marín returned to New York.[39]

From 1947 on, she had difficulty finding steady work and held a series of unsatisfying jobs in factories and dental offices. Her physical state deteriorated as she battled depression and alcoholism. She spent her last years in and out of Harlem Hospital and Goldwater Memorial Hospital on Welfare Island (now Roosevelt Island) in the East River. Her split with Marín may have led to her first hospitalization. While confined, she intermittently kept a journal: one of the entries provides her recollections of the breakdown that prompted her first stay at Harlem Hospital in 1948:

> En la calle con lo que llevo puesto por todo equipaje, con los síntomas de mi enfermedad, sin trabajo, sin equilibrio, con mi más preciada propiedad: mis libros y mis versos, abandonados en un sótano por no tener donde llevarlos. Me ví esa tarde al borde de desterrarme definitivamente de la vida del modo más violento.[40]

> I was on the street with all of my belongings on my back, suffering from the symptoms of my illness, with no job, no sense of stability, and with my most prized, worldly possessions, my books and my verse, abandoned in a basement for lack of anywhere to store them. I found myself on the verge of banishing this earth in the most violent way.[41]

A fiercely independent woman, Burgos likely found it unbearable to be an object of study and to be dependent on doctors and nurses. Her diagnosis apparently was not clear to her at first, and she felt humiliated while enduring tests. Doctors talked around her but not directly to her. She felt isolated and longed for visitors.[42] Confinement to a wheelchair frustrated her:

> ¿A dónde me llevan? Y por qué en sillón; arrastrada por una muchachita de apenas cien libras, cuando puedo moverme por mis propios pies?

> La primera sensación es de bochorno y humillación.[43]

> Where are they taking me? And why in a wheelchair; pushed around by a girl who barely weighs one hundred pounds, when I can stand on my own two feet?

> The first emotions are shame and humiliation.

The staff watched her constantly and examined her blood, urine, brain waves, and liver function. The nurses and patients remarked on her physical racial difference: "Todo el mundo comenta sobre mis cabellos erizados y empastados [Everyone comments on my coarse, bristly hair]."[44] Filling out her hospital intake form, Burgos listed her occupation as writer; hospital staffers crossed out her words and replaced them with "suffers from amnesia."[45] These details circulated among the Nuyorican community in the 1970s, resonating with members' longing for recognition and experiences with criminalization and discrimination.[46]

Burgos spent long periods, sometimes months, at Goldwater Memorial Hospital between 1950 and 1953. She was ultimately diagnosed with cirrhosis of the liver and upper respiratory disease, both consistent with chronic alcoholism. Her journal describes nonspecific injections that sedated her. Aware of

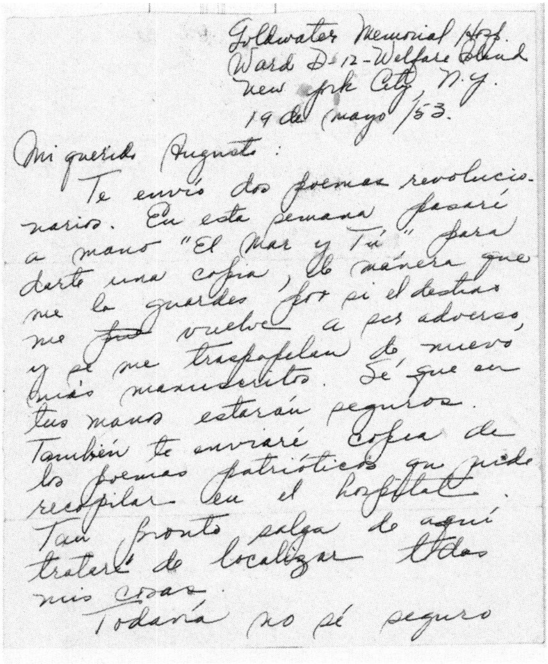

Goldwater Memorial Hosp.
Ward D⁰ 12 - Welfare Island
New York City N.Y.
19 de mayo /53.

Mi querido Augusto:

Te envío dos poemas revolucionarios. En esta semana, pasaré a mano "El Mar y Tú", para darte una copia, y la manera que me la guardes, por si el destino me vuelve a ser adverso, y se me traspapelan de nuevo más manuscritos. Sé que en tus manos estarán seguros. También te enviaré copia de los poemas patrióticos que pude recopilar en el hospital. Tan pronto salga de aquí trataré de localizar todas mis cosas.

Todavía no sé seguro

Figure 2. Julia de Burgos to Augusto Calderón, 19 May 1953. In this letter, she refers to her poems as "revolucionarios" and "patrióticos" (revolutionary and patriotic). Sandra Rodríguez Papers, Archives of the Puerto Rican Diaspora, Center for Puerto Rican Studies, Hunter College, City University of New York.

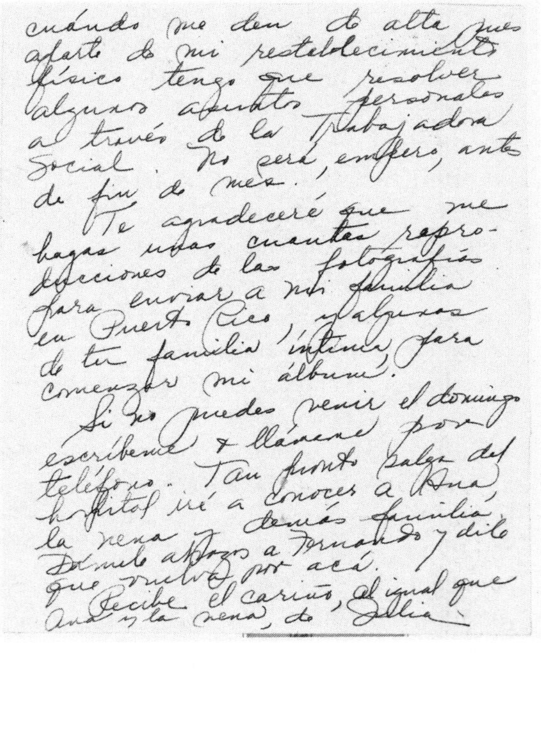

cuándo me den de alta pues aparte de mi restablecimiento físico tengo que resolver algunos asuntos personales a través de la Trabajadora Social. No será, empero, antes de fin de mes.

Te agradeceré que me hagas unas cuantas reproducciones de las fotografías para enviar a mi familia en Puerto Rico, y algunas de tu familia íntima, para comenzar mi álbum.

Si no puedes venir el domingo escríbeme y llámame por teléfono. Tan pronto salga del hospital iré a conocer a Ana, la nena, y demás familia. Dale mis abrazos a Fernando y dile que vuelvo por acá.

Recibe el cariño, al igual que Ana y la nena, de Julia

her deteriorated physical and emotional state, her family and friends in Puerto Rico begged her to return. With her life spinning out of control because of her financial instability, her alcoholism, and her precarious living situation, Burgos regularly mailed her poetry to her sister and other relatives for safekeeping. While in the hospital, she wrote her two final poems in English, "Farewell in Welfare Island," and "The Sun in Welfare Island," describing the condition of exile and her sense of seclusion and desolation. These poems can be read as precursors to the literature of Nuyorican and U.S. Latina/o writers of the 1970s in both theme and emotional intonation. In the end, her health problems, poverty, loneliness, and alcoholism led to her decline and death.

Overview

Burgos's writing and legacy can be conceived in two parts, her writing on the island and her work and legacy in the diaspora. Chapter 1, "Writing the Nation: Feminism, Anti-Imperialism, and the Generación del Treinta," describes the development of Burgos's social, political, and creative consciousness on the island during the 1930s. It focuses on her first poetry collection, *Poema en veinte surcos*, where she creates images of routes, travel, and water as a way to escape containment. Chapter 2, "*Nadie es profeta en su tierra*: Exile, Migration, and Hemispheric Identity," examines Burgos's migratory routes from Puerto Rico to Havana and New York by looking at her second and third poetry collections as well as her little-studied letters to her sister. This chapter extends the term *sexile*, usually used to describe queer migration, to heterosexual women whose sexuality appears excessive in Caribbean morality, contributing to their departure from the island. Chapter 3, "*Más allá del mar*: Journalism as Puerto Rican Cultural and Political Transnational Practice," looks at the significance of New York's Spanish-language press—specifically the weekly newspaper, *Pueblos Hispanos: Semanario Progresista* (Hispanic Peoples: Progressive Weekly, 1943–44). It explores how Puerto Ricans employed journalism as a form of cultural and political transnational practice. Chapter 4, "Multiple Legacies: Julia de Burgos and Caribbean Latino Diaspora Writers," studies the work of Puerto Rican, Dominican, and Cuban writers in the diaspora who inherited and extended Burgos's legacy in the contemporary public imaginary. Chapter 5, "Remembering Julia de Burgos: Cultural Icon, Community, Belonging," highlights the multiple ways in which Burgos's legacy extends into visual culture and El Barrio neighborhood in East Harlem. Finally, the conclusion examines how *Latinidad* and *Latino* are umbrella terms that have come to represent consumer ethnicities while erasing histories, race, class, and gender differences. By remembering and claiming Burgos, artists and writers push back on these homogenized images of *Latinidad*, as she often comes to represent the most vulnerable members of society.

Burgos's writing creates the nomadic and migratory subjects as a way to escape narrowly defined notions of identity and has inspired later generations of Puerto Rican and Latino/a writers both on the island and in the diaspora. This book highlights the enduring contributions Burgos's writing has made to women's, gender, and sexuality studies by articulating a more fluid diasporic identity not tied to geographic borders. More than sixty years after Burgos's death, the United States is simultaneously beginning to recognize the large and fast-growing Latino/a minority's cultural legacy and introducing new forms of criminalizing brown-skinned migrants. The current celebrity status of a few Latino/as masks the racism, economic, and political disenfranchisement of most members of the community. Since the 1960s, however, writers and artists have remembered, reinvented, and riffed off Burgos in their efforts on behalf of inclusion, recognition, and equal rights.

1

WRITING THE NATION

Feminism, Anti-Imperialism, and the Generación del Treinta

In December 1938, at the age of twenty-four, Julia de Burgos self-published her first collection of poetry and traveled around Puerto Rico selling copies. She was raising money to help cover the cost of her mother's cancer treatments. This story, like many others about her, circulated for decades and contributed to the myths shrouding her life. Traditionally read as a story of daughterly devotion, it can also be seen as an example of Burgos's ambition, self-promotion, and determination to establish herself as a writer. Burgos's praxis and writing during the early part of her career reveal her savvy ability to fashion herself as a writer and to seize opportunities.

This chapter explores the creation of a feminist nomadic subject in Burgos's first poetry collection, *Poema en veinte surcos* (Poem in Twenty Furrows, 1938), written during the height of the Puerto Rican nationalist movement. While committed to the idea of political nationalism throughout her life, Burgos nonetheless employed a feminist nomadic subject in her poetry, aligning her with the Puerto Rican literary *vanguardias*, that allowed her to find points of departure from the phallocentric and patriarchal Puerto Rican cultural nationalist project of the 1930s. This subject subverts conventions and anticipates her later departure from the island. As developed in her poetry, nomadism refers to a "critical consciousness that resists settling into socially coded modes of thought and behavior."[1]

Various literary trends and currents circulated in Puerto Rico during the 1920s and 1930s. The members of the Generación del Treinta were committed to articulating a sense of Puerto Rican cultural identity in the face of U.S. colonialism. The result was a paternalistic literary canon that was written primarily by men, concerned with nation building, and characterized by the metaphor of colonialism as illness. The *treintista* writers privileged totalizing genres such as the novel and the interpretive essay as varieties that could heal the wound of

colonialism. They sought to define a national identity or "essence" character-
ized by the natural landscape and geography of the island. Antonio S. Pedreira,
Tomás Blanco, Luis Palés Matos, Vicente Geigel Polanco, Manrique Cabrera,
Luis Muñoz Marín, and Enrique Laguerre are some of the canonical writers
and intellectuals of this generation whose works defined and dominated Puerto
Rican letters at least until the 1970s.[2] In his famous essay, *Insularismo* (1934),
Pedreira expressed the need to define Puerto Rican identity as tied to the is-
land's geography. Images of the land dominated poems and novels of the time,
exemplified by Enrique Laguerre's *La llamarada* (1935). The lyric and poetry
were considered inferior genres.

This national or cultural identity emerged from the myth of the *jíbaro*,
scripted by the novelists of the 1930s as a peasant farmer of European descent
who embodies traditional values of fraternity and brotherly love. Although this
identity stands in direct contrast to U.S. colonialism and imperialism, it is also
fraught with contradictions.[3] Rooted in linguistic purism that recognized Spain
as the motherland, the *jíbaro* is grateful to Spain for the island's "noble" heri-
tage. The *jíbaro*-based national identity fails to acknowledge the centuries of
Spanish colonialism, the struggles for independence from Spain, and the legacy
of slavery on the island. While many of these writers called for a return to the
land, most of them lived in the city. This nostalgic identity shuns modernization
and urbanization while rejecting U.S. imperialism. The idealization of the *jíbaro*
ignored the island's labor movement as well as the problems associated with
poverty, such as poor hygiene, disease, malnutrition, and lack of education.

The 1920s and 1930s also produced another group of writers, primarily poets,
whose words may have been less widely read but nevertheless challenged and
rebelled against the balanced and harmonious world depicted by the *treintista*
writers, providing counternarratives. The Latin American *vanguardias* have
been defined by their search for something new, the redefinition of art, the
creation of manifestos published in small magazines, experimentation, and the
autochthonous. Their work explores the present and the future, the urban, and
a hybrid and fragmented world.[4] During this era, Puerto Rico featured no fewer
than fifteen "isms," including *pancalismo*, *panedismo*, *diepalismo*, *euroforismo*,
ultraista, *noísmo*, *los seis*, *atalayismo*, *integralismo*, *transcendentalismo*, and
Grupo Meñique.[5] Periodicals published by these movements included *Faro*
(1926), *Vórtice* (1926), *hostos* (1929), and *Indice* (1929–31). Among the im-
portant literary *vanguardias* were Evaristo Ribera Chevremont, Jose de Diego
Padró, Luis Palés Matos, Graciany Miranda Archilla, and Clemente Soto Vélez.
Vicky Unruh notes that the *Atalayistas* "supported the incipient Puerto Rican
nationalism and separatism being disseminated by Pedro Albizu Campos."[6]
The *vanguardias'* activity was marked by autochthonous concerns, a focus on

nationalist and Antillean cultural affirmation, African cultural influences, and an Americanist continental orientation.[7] The various writers participated in men-only *tertulias* (literary salons) that did not welcome Burgos. Diego Padró recalled that he and the other leading poets of the era "gozábamos la alegría de vivir y no emancipábamos por completo de las formas pesadas y asfixiantes de la civilización. . . . Era una bohemia de solitarios que no admitía ni de broma el elemento femenino [rejoiced in the joy of life and emancipated ourselves completely from the heavy and asphyxiating forms of civilization. . . . It was a solitary bohemia that did not admit the feminine element even as a joke]."[8]

Technological advancements shifted American poetry traditions. Lesley Wheeler notes that "technologies of presence—especially radio broadcast in the early part of the twentieth-century—altered the cultural role of poetry recitation in American life."[9] Prior to these technological developments, poetry recitations had been displays of interpretation by someone other than the poet, but they increasingly became "spectacles of authority" that would "manifest the authentic presence of the poet for audiences."[10] In the 1920s and 1930s, the practice of poets reading, reciting, and performing their own work was novel, but it would become an important source of income and prestige.[11] Julia de Burgos was working at the edge of this cultural shift as a *declamadora* (someone who recites and interprets poetry) and was exploring the possibilities of radio's potential to unify and socialize. From 1936 to 1937, Burgos had a contract with the Department of Public Instruction's Escuela del Aire, a radio education program for children that sought to combat illiteracy and share public information on social and economic problems as well as daily events.[12] Her husband, Rubén Rodríguez Beauchamp, was a broadcast journalist and may have helped her get the contract to write for Escuela del Aire.[13] During the summer of 1936, Burgos recited her poetry for *La casa del poeta* (House of the Poet), an extension of a literary salon hosted by poet Carmen Alicia Cadilla that aired on a local radio station at nine in the evening.[14] Both the literary *vanguardias* and technological developments played a role in the development of Burgos's literary voice.

In *Poema en veinte surcos*, Burgos experimented with various styles of writing prevalent among Puerto Rican writers of the time, including *telurismo* and *neocriollismo*, the *negrista* poetry of Luis Palés Matos, and the eroticism of Luis Lloréns Torres. These styles influenced her work and contributed to the development of her unique lyrical voice. Political activity on the island informed Burgos's life and her commitment to poetry, but her nomadic subject championing freedom and justice fundamentally and ideologically distinguishes her work and aligns her with the *vanguardias*. Burgos always speaks for oppressed sectors of the population, those excluded from the dominant national identity of the time. The nomadic subject becomes a "form of political resistance to hegemonic, fixed, unitary, and exclusionary views of subjectivity."[15] Burgos also distinguished herself from her contemporaries stylistically, focusing not on the land, as the *neocriollistas* did, but instead on waterways, the sea, paths, and the open space of the cosmos.[16] Her primary image, the fluidity of the sea (which isolates the island in Pedreira's work) connects Puerto Rico to other islands and nations in Burgos's poetry.

A close look at Burgos's points of convergence and divergence from the intellectuals of the time reveals that through her poetry, she attempted to define Puerto Rico as a heterogeneous place steeped in history. Because she understood identity as fluid and unbound by geography, her poetry is still read today by Puerto Ricans and Latino/as in the United States and on the island. The Afro-Antillean ideas expressed in Burgos's poetry make her work a precursor to later island writers such as Mayra Santos Febres as well as 1970s writers of the Puerto Rican diaspora in New York and 1990s U.S. Latino/a writers.

The Mighty River of Loíza

Many critics have noted the importance of the poem "Río Grande de Loíza" in Julia de Burgos's work. Most often, however, critics read it as a *neocriollista* poem or a love song to the river of her childhood and a tribute to Puerto Rico's natural landscape. In this poem, Burgos creates a premodern world in which humans and nature exist in harmony. As with much of her work, critics have read this poem as a way to understand her biography.[17] Poetry conventions changed over the twentieth century, emphasizing the presence and authenticity of the poet in an increasingly modernized world. In many ways, Burgos's writing moves away from modernists' theories of impersonality and takes up the self, authenticity, and intimacy as topics. Burgos invents her own origin myth and cosmology in this poem. In the final stanzas, she lays bare the violent wounds of history, refusing to mask the traumas of time.[18] The *treintistas* focused on the land; Burgos focuses on the river, using it to create a nomadic subject that, like water, cannot be contained.

The poem opens with the speaker employing the rhetorical figure of apostrophe—the calling out to an inanimate thing—and in the speech act turns the river into an interlocutor through the power of language. As a figure of speech, apostrophe involves addressing a dead or absent person, an animal, a thing, or an abstract quality or idea as if it were alive, present, and capable of understanding. In Burgos's poem, the river appears as a man/river throughout, and the speaker invokes a pantheistic river god. In awakening the river, the speaker and the river fuse; subject and object become one. Where pleasure and eroticism constitute excess for the nation builders, these stanzas reveal pantheistic ideas and the eroticizing of nature. In the next stanza, the influence of the *vanguardias* is felt as Burgos personalizes the poem and unveils her own cosmology. She reveals her origins and describes herself as if she were born from the natural landscape of the world. The *vanguardias* create images that "embody connections between personal and cosmic beginnings" and take place not in a specific sociohistorical context but in "a mythical time-out-of-time and in the imaginary spaces of human and universal origins."[19]

¡Río Grande de Loíza! . . . Alárgate en mi espíritu
y deja que mi alma se pierda en tus riachuelos,
para buscar la fuente que te robó de niño
y en un ímpetus loco te devolvió al sendero.

Enróscate en mis labios y deja que te beba,
para sentirte mío por un breve momento,
y esconderte del mundo y en ti mismo esconderte,
y oír voces de asombro en la boca del viento.

Apéate un instante del lomo de la tierra,
y busca de mis ansias el íntimo secreto;
confúndete en el vuelo de mi ave fantasía,
y déjame una rosa de agua en mis ensueños.

¡Río Grande de Loíza! . . . Mi manantial, mi río,
desde que alzóme al mundo el pétalo materno;
contigo se bajaron desde las rudas cuestas,
a buscar nuevos surcos, mis pálidos anhelos;
y mi niñez fue toda un poema en el río,
y un río en el poema de mis primeros sueños.

Llegó la adolescencia. Me sorprendió la vida
prendida en lo más ancho de tu viajar eterno;
y fui tuya mil veces, y en un bello romance
me despertaste el alma y me besaste el cuerpo.[20]

Río Grande de Loíza! . . . Undulate into my spirit
And let my soul founder in your rivulets,
To seek the fountain that stole you as a child
And in mad haste returned you to the path.

Wind into my lips and let me drink you,
To feel you mine for a brief moment,
And hide you from the world in myself
And hear voices of fear in the wind's mouth.

Come down for an instant from the earth's spine,
And look for the intimate secret of my longing;
Confounded in the sweep of my bird fantasies,
Drop a water rose in my dreams.

Río Grande de Loíza! . . . My source, my river,
After the motherly petal raised me into the world;
With you went down from the rough hills
To seek new furrows, my pale desires,
And all my childhood was like a poem in the river,
And a river was the poem of my first dreams.

Then came adolescence. Life surprised me
Fastening to the broadest part of your eternal voyage;
And I was yours a thousand times, and in a beautiful romance,
You woke my soul and kissed my body.[21]

In these stanzas, the speaker sees herself as a part of the natural world. The river, the flower, and the natural landscape create and inspire her. The speaker's oneness with the river evokes a primordial world. She travels and visits distant lands, creating new avenues for exploration.

At the close of the poem, Burgos cannot deny the island's violent history of colonialism and slavery. She abandons the concept of a harmonious world suspended outside of time and acknowledges the complexity and heterogeneity of the modern world and of Puerto Rico.

¡Río Grande de Loíza! . . . Azul. Moreno. Rojo.
Espejo azul, caído pedazo azul de cielo;
desnuda carne blanca que se te vuelve negra
cada vez que la noche se te mete en el lecho;
roja franja de sangre, cuando bajo la lluvia
a torrentes su barro te vomitan los cerros. (14)

Río Grande de Loíza! . . . Blue. Dark. Red.
Blue mirror, fallen blue fragment of sky;
Nude white flesh that turns you black
Every time night goes to bed with you;
Red band of blood, when under the rain
The hills vomit torrents of mud.[22]

The three isolated words, "Azul. Moreno. Rojo," follow the invocation of the river to reference the blue sky, brown river, and red earth. The lines that follow these three words recall the island's history of slavery and widespread miscegenation. This stanza suggests the importance of the process of creolization and syncretism in defining the Americas and the Caribbean. As the river runs red, the closing lines of this stanza highlight the violence and bloodshed deeply entrenched in the island's history of colonization, the slaughter of the indigenous population, and the legacy of slavery.

Although the Río Grande de Loíza was important in Burgos's childhood experiences, it also played a significant role in the history of the region and by extension the island. According to anthropologist Edward Zaragoza, Loíza Aldea, a coastal village fifteen miles east of San Juan, is in many ways a microcosm of Puerto Rican history. The Taíno Arawak Indian village of Loíza is where the Spanish first landed on the island. In the early decades of the conquest, the Taínos and later enslaved Africans mined the Loíza River for gold. In the nineteenth century, Loíza Aldea became a sugar-producing area. African customs, carnivals, and religious rites are still practiced there, as they are elsewhere in Puerto Rico.[23] By evoking the image of the river and this region as a metonym for the island, Burgos affirms the importance of the African presence on the island and in the Americas.

In the poem's final stanza, Burgos continues to conjure the pain and violence the river has witnessed over the centuries:

> ¡Río Grande de Loíza! . . . Río grande. Llanto grande.
> El más grande de todos nuestros llantos isleños,
> . si no fuera más grande el que de mí se sale
> por los ojos del alma para mi esclavo pueblo. (14)

> Río Grande de Loíza! . . . Great river. Great tear.
> The greatest of all our island tears,
> But for the tears that flow out of me
> Through the eyes of my soul for my enslaved people.[24]

By juxtaposing the phrases *Río Grande* (great river) and *Llanto grande* (great tear), she suggests their interchangeability. The river, composed of tears, has witnessed vicious history. Burgos decries the enormity of the pain, love, and anguish she carries in her heart for her native land and its "enslaved people," claiming that her pain is as great as the collective weeping reflected in the river. The poet mourns the lost unity of the world but knows it can only exist outside of time. The lines suggest the suffering and violence of colonialism, simultaneously denoting the present condition of U.S. colonialism. Through this modern image of a heterogeneous and fragmented world, her prayers for the people and island of Puerto Rico continue to resonate strongly today. The Río Grande de Loíza opens into the Atlantic Ocean in the town of Carolina, a rural area at the time Burgos wrote the poem. Today, Carolina is surrounded by metropolitan San Juan and as a result is overdeveloped and devastated by crime and poverty. The persistently high unemployment rate and lack of local industry not only here but throughout the island give new meaning to her words "enslaved people."

Anti-Imperial and Anticolonial Poetry

The 1930s literature is historically linked to the landowning class, whose decline in power began with the 1898 U.S. military invasion of the island. The Spanish estate owners who would have governed had the island gained independence rapidly lost control, and their heirs went on to create the Puerto Rican literary canon, using it to impose their version of cultural nationalism.[25] This paternalistic literary canon has taken the place of a national constitution and compensated for the lack of an independent nation-state. The canon therefore resembles—but should not be confused with—the controlling and unifying mechanism provided by the state.[26] Paternalism suggests a hierarchical relationship in which some subjects are considered superior to others. The paternalistic person views himself as a father figure, figuratively subordinating other members of society to the role of children. The rhetoric of paternalism employs the family as the central metaphor for the nation.[27] This model permeates all aspects of the nation, from politics to religious and cultural traditions, gender roles, and the construction of literary texts and canons. In the literary realm, the patriarchal hierarchy privileges certain literary forms and writers. Burgos, however, has a different response to the wound of colonialism, replacing totalizing narratives with solidarity and attachments consistent with a nomadic politics that is "a matter of bonding, of coalitions, of interconnections."[28] The ability to form connections based on a transgressive and transitory nomadic identity counters the great familial narrative. Burgos rejects the paternalism and nostalgia of the *hacendado* class and substitutes solidarity. She argues that the first step in achieving a sense of Puerto Rican identity is the independence of the island.

Burgos's biography no doubt influenced her stance. Whereas most of the era's writers and political leaders were descendants of the landowning gentry, Burgos's working-class family (and many other such families) moved to Carolina in search of employment. She had further contact with members of the island's less privileged community during her stint as a teacher at a rural school in Barrio Cerro Arriba in Naranjito. This direct contact with the poverty of the island undoubtedly shaped her determination to speak out against oppression.

Puerto Rico's chronic poverty became more acute during the 1930s as a consequence of the Great Depression. Unemployment grew and per capita income fell around 30 percent between 1930 and 1933.[29] People demanded relief efforts and jobs, and laborers in the needle, tobacco, and sugar industries struck for better wages.[30] After beginning in Caguas, protests spread to Santurce, San Germán, and Mayagüez. An August 1933 strike in Caguas involved seven thousand tobacco workers, five thousand of them women. The same month, women working in the needle industry struck in Lares, San Germán, and Mayagüez, where more than two thousand workers from close to seventy different shops walked off the job and at least one woman striker was killed. Of the 838 workers reported to be on strike in Santurce the following September, 600 were women. Later in the month, a protest against the United Porto Rico Sugar Company resulted in the death of another striker in Gurabo. In January 1934, sugar workers launched a general strike.[31] The first significant federal intervention came with the creation of the Puerto Rico Emergency Relief Administration, which employed thousands, including Julia de Burgos, to distribute food and basic necessities.[32]

After teaching for a year in Naranjito, Burgos moved to Old San Juan with her husband. In 1936, she joined the Frente Unido Femenino Pro Convención Constituyente de la República de Puerto Rico (Women's United Front for the Constitutional Convention of the Republic of Puerto Rico), an auxiliary of the Nationalist Party. As the organization's general secretary, she wrote press releases for several years and delivered a speech, "La mujer ante el dolor de la patria" (Women before the Challenges of the Homeland), in support of the Nationalist Party. In her writings for the Frente Unido Femenino, Burgos espoused the traditional rhetoric of the Nationalist Party, much of it in contrast with the more inclusive ideology expressed in her poetry, which was appearing regularly in San Juan literary magazines by 1938. Other women intellectuals on the island at the time struggled to enter public life without testing the underlying racist and classist ideology established by their male counterparts. Burgos, however, was more open about challenging these views.[33]

Between 1935 and 1938, Burgos strove to articulate her own ideals, experimented with language and stylistics, and paid homage to nationalist rhetoric, aligning her with the *vanguardias*. Throughout her life, Burgos battled social norms and stereotypes of gender, race, class, and ethnicity. While she longed to establish herself as a serious writer, addressing concerns of national and international significance, she felt constrained by the conservative roles embraced by many of the women intellectuals of her generation. The *vanguardias'* political activism was dominated by progressive or leftist causes, and Burgos's strong political poetry made her one of the few women writers associated with that category.[34]

On 12 September 1936, *La Acción* published Burgos's poem, "Es nuestra la hora" (Ours Is the Hour), a call for workers to unite, organize, and fight against U.S. imperialism. Burgos implores the *campesino* (peasant) to join the nationalist cause. She acknowledges the specter of disease and poverty that afflicted the exploited workers on the island.

> Ya se acerca el grito de los campesinos
> y la masa
> la masa explotada despierta.
> ¿Dónde está el pequeño que en el "raquitismo" deshojó su vida?
> ¿Dónde está la esposa que murió de anemia?
> ¿Dónde está la "tala" que ayudó a sembrarla, la que hoy esta muerta?
> ¿Dónde está la vaca?
> ¿Dónde está la yegua?
> ¿Dónde está la tierra?[35]

> Already the peasants' battle cry approaches
> and the masses
> the exploited masses awaken.
> Where is the little one who "in rickets" leaves his life behind
> Where is the wife who died of anemia?
> Where is the vegetable patch she helped plant, the one that is dead
> today?
> Where is the cow?
> Where is the mare?
> Where is the land?

In this stanza, she lists the diseases that afflicted the population, diseases intensified by rampant poverty and malnutrition. She uses agrarian symbols such as *vaca*, *yegua*, and *tierra* and responds to these queries in the poem's next stanza, holding the United States accountable for the loss of this agrarian world: "Campesino noble / tu desgracia tiene sólo una respuesta: / El Imperialismo de Estados Unidos [Noble peasant / your disgrace has but one response: / The imperialism of the United States]."[36] In response, Burgos advocates hemispheric unity based on the ideas of José Martí as a way to confront U.S. expansionist policies. She proposes taking up arms against the U.S. forces and closes the poem with a call for Puerto Rican independence: "Una patria libre se unirá al concierto / de los pueblos grandes, / en Hispano América [A free country will join the concert / of great nations, / in Hispanic America]."[37] The connection, solidarity, and action she puts forward as a response to U.S. colonialism differ greatly from the nostalgia and the totalizing metaphors of many *treintista* writers.

Her early political poetry contains numerous images of workers and their connections to the land. However, Burgos never articulates a mythologized *jíbaro* and rejects nostalgia for an idealized past. In "Desde el puente de Martín Peña" (From the Martín Peña Bridge), for example, she responds to the threat of colonialism by inspiring the workers to unite. The poem opens with the phrase "Tierra rota [Broken land]," evoking an image that resonates throughout the poem.

> Tierra rota. Se hace el día
> el marco de la laguna.
>
> Un ejército de casas
> rompe la doble figura
> de un cielo azul que abastece
> a un mar tranquilo que arrulla. (56)
>
> Broken land. The dawn becomes
> the frame of the lagoon.
>
> An army of houses
> breaks the double figure
> of a blue sky that feeds
> a tranquil sea, cooing.

In a striking alternative to the metaphor of the hacienda and the idea of the great Puerto Rican family, the image of the houses in this poem is combative—an "army of houses" disrupts the tranquil horizon. Throughout the poem, Burgos repeats the phrase "Un ejército de casas [An army of houses]," not only countering the mythologized, peaceful hacienda but also suggesting an interruption of nature's peace.

> Hacha del tiempo cortando
> carne de siglos de ayuna.
> Adentro la muerte manda.
> Afuera el hambre murmura
> una plegaria a los hombres
> que al otro lado disfrutan
> de anchos salarios restados
> a hombres obreros que luchan. (57)
>
> The axe of time cutting
> flesh of centuries of fasting.
> Inside death governs.
> Outside hunger murmurs
> a prayer to the men
> that on the other side enjoy
> wide salaries subtracted
> from struggling working men.

Here, she recognizes U.S. economic infiltration and exploitation of workers in the sugar industry. Rather than mythologize the *jíbaro*, she underscores the hunger, disease, poverty, and death prevalent on the island and calls for workers to unite, acknowledging the reality of life for the working-class population. This solidarity with the workers' movement appears not only throughout Burgos's first poetry collection but also in her later writings from abroad.[38] Her intellectual trajectory resembles that followed by anarchist Luisa Capetillo, another nomadic Puerto Rican intellectual.[39]

Poema en veinte surcos contains several poems that display this support for the workers' movement. "Amaneceres" (Dawnings) opens with a call for spiritual and mental awakening through self-reflection and self-awareness: "¡Amaneceres en mi alma! / ¡Amaneceres en mi mente! [Dawnings in my soul! / Dawnings in my mind!]" (22). A movement inward leads to heightened consciousness: "Cuando se abre la puerta íntima / para entrar a una misma, / ¡qué de amaneceres! [When the intimate door is opened / to enter oneself / what dawnings!]" (22). The poem calls on workers to unite, seize the hour, and participate in the present, suggesting that progress can be made by leaving behind imitation and passivity: "y que cuelgue todas las canciones de rumbo burgueses, / y rompa sus segundos en un millón de himnos proletarios [and let hang all the songs of bourgeois ways / and break its seconds into a million proletarian hymns]" (22). In this poem, she refers to "true" and "false" selves, a split that reappears in her more personal and intimate poems such as "A Julia de Burgos" (To Julia de Burgos), in which the "false" self is socially constructed and gendered. In "Amaneceres," Burgos uses this split to address a socially constructed, bourgeois self. The bourgeois man is concerned with money, tradition, social customs, and race—what the poem considers false constructions.

> La otra,
> la dimensión social
> la tradición,
> la raza,
> el capital.
>
> El hombre aburguesado
> de cuerpo,
> de mente
> y de energía.
>
> El hombre desviado
> huyendo ferozmente de sí mismo. (23)

The other,
the social dimension:
tradition,
race,
capital.

Bourgeois man
of body,
of mind
and energy.

Man derailed
fleeing ferociously from himself.

The "bourgeois self" in "Amaneceres" is disconnected from its instincts and therefore disconnected from nature itself—the problem of modern humans who are alienated from their true selves. Burgos critiques the social trappings of the Old World aristocracy by refusing to mythologize the *jíbaro* as a simple peasant with not a care in the world.

El hombre tierra,
hecho a dos dimensiones violentas.
La dimensión común:
cinco sentidos,
y un cuerpo y una mente.

El hombre todo. Él. (23)

Man earth
made in two violent dimensions.
The common dimension:
five senses,
and one body and one mind.

The whole man. Him.

She goes on to describe "true" persons as tied to the land, not necessarily in an agricultural sense but rather by recognizing that they are part of nature and in touch with their natural instincts. Burgos suggests that ideas emanate from the *campo* (countryside). According to Burgos, the strength to confront any form of oppression or socially imposed identity comes from within, not from a movement, cause, or political affiliation. Burgos offers a powerful counternarrative to the blood ties and hierarchical structures inherent in the paternalistic rhetoric of her generation, creating for herself and others a way out of the nation.

Early Twentieth-Century
Feminism in Puerto Rico

The rhetoric of paternalism on the island infantilized women, the working class, and Afro-descendants. Early twentieth-century women struggled for inclusion and for more meaningful public roles. Hispanic-affiliated women asserted moral superiority to distance themselves from poverty and blackness. Elite Puerto Rican feminists articulated their own moral vision of elite egalitarian marriages and their rights to intellectual and sexual freedoms. Their desire for distance from what they perceived as "disreputable" darker-skinned women prevented them from mounting significant challenges to the liberal project of the family.[40] A working-class movement did challenge liberal notions of respectability and the "great national family" with ideas of free love. Male labor leaders also dreamed of their version of male dominance, enclosing working-class women in an idealized, circumscribed domesticity. Plebeian women who challenged this vision were effectively marginalized. A racially charged, sexual demonization of working-class women was the primary means of a repressive colonial campaign, with bourgeois women playing an important role in the surveillance and control of their poorer sisters: "Long-standing practices of informal neighborhood surveillance" made women of higher status "invaluable allies in the thrust to eradicate female promiscuity."[41] Eileen Suárez Findlay notes that "in the eyes of conservative male elites and colonial officials, activities such as [surveillance], as well as the 'ladies' intervention into working-class family life, were vastly preferable to their increasing demands for female suffrage."[42]

Burgos's speeches, press releases, and other writings for the Frente Unido Femenino repeated the parochial rhetoric of the Nationalist Party, although she contradicted that rhetoric in her poetry, in her letters to her sister, and in the way she lived her life. Lícia Fiol-Matta has examined how Gabriela Mistral variously hid from and revealed her ambiguous sexuality through a variety of public masks that at times challenged and at times affirmed reductive and confining social roles for women.[43] Burgos, too, began to create a public persona that shadowed the more radical ideas expressed in her poetry. In 1938, she stopped using her married name, Julia Burgos de Rodríguez, to sign both personal letters and Frente Unido Femenino documents, abandoning the project of constructing a socially acceptable image in favor of living her life according to her own ideas of freedom and social justice. This change in approach contributed to her departure from the island.

The Frente Unido Femenino was committed to fighting for Puerto Rican sovereignty. On 7 July 1936, the newspaper *El Mundo* printed a press release written by Burgos in her capacity as the organization's general secretary. She announced that the group's official constitution had been accepted at the Convención Nacional de Mujeres Portorriqueñas (National Convention of Puerto Rican Women) in San Juan on 28 June. Poet Trina Padilla de Sanz, known as la Hija del Caribe (the Daughter of the Caribbean), had been named honorary president, and Martha Lomar had been elected acting president. The press release encouraged women across the island to organize local chapters.

During the 1910s and 1920s, Puerto Rican women fought for suffrage, demanding enfranchisement in the political and public sphere. These changes would disrupt the gender system established by the ruling class. Magali Roy-Féquière notes that "creole women's search for voice and empowerment was initially facilitated by a pragmatic and selective adherence to suffragist praxis." According to Roy-Féquière, elite creole women had contradictory effects on *hacendado* hegemony, challenging the system to allow them to participate in public life while supporting the existing race and class structure.[44] Nationalist Party leader Pedro Albizu Campos and others accused these feminists of failing to support Puerto Rican men in their fight for independence from U.S. imperialism and of putting personal concerns before those of the nation. In "Feminismo y la independencia patria" (Feminism and National Independence), published in *El Mundo* in 1930, Albizu Campos reproached feminists who had fought for suffrage in a 1926 colonial election. He believed that the only worthy goal was the creation of a sovereign Republic of Puerto Rico, arguing that no one had rights under colonial rule. In his view, therefore, women suffragists were attempting to benefit from and support U.S. imperialism.[45]

Elite creole women had limited access to cultural capital. As caretakers of the home, women taught children and were the bearers of Puerto Rican culture. Some education among this class of women was therefore welcomed and in fact deemed essential to the development of a strong nation. Access to higher education led to various opportunities for women of the middle and upper classes. By the early twentieth century, unprecedented numbers of women had become teachers, and they became important to suffrage struggles. These teachers came not only from well-to-do-families but also from among small landholders and artisans. Some, like Julia de Burgos, were of working class and/or of African descent. These women often supported their families and experienced more tenuous working conditions.[46] Moreover, these women had only limited opportunities because they could not afford to travel abroad to further their education or obtain professional degrees in areas such as medicine, law, or pharmacy.

Burgos and the other members of Frente Unido Femenino publicly backed the Nationalist Party and its leaders and seemed willing to subordinate themselves to the party's men. On 13 July 1936, *El Mundo* published a note by

Burgos announcing a special mass to be held the following day dedicated to the health of Juan Antonio Corretjer, who was to be tried for treason, and to the "restablecimiento de la paz y justicia pública [return to peace and justice]." The notice also explained that the women of Frente Unido Femenino had sent a cablegram to the Pope requesting his intercession on behalf of both Corretjer and Albizu Campos, who was also in jail:

> Su Santidad, Ciudad Vaticana, Las Mujeres de Puerto Rico humildemente ruegan a Su Santidad interceda excarcelación poeta patriota Corretjer, archivo proceso contra liderato nacionalista, presidencia Albizu Campos católico.

> His Holiness, Vatican City, the women of Puerto Rico humbly beg Your Holiness to intercede on behalf of the patriot and poet Corretjer, for his release, and intercede also in the lawsuit filed against the leadership of the National Party president, the Catholic Albizu Campos.

In another press release published in *El Mundo* on 21 July 1936, Burgos expressed Christian beliefs not found elsewhere in her work: "Mujeres portorriqueñas, que representáis la fuerza latente de nuestra nacionalidad, por decreto de la infinita voluntad de Dios Omnipotente; que hizo de cada mujer un símbolo divino, ofrendándole la gracia de la maternidad [Puerto Rican women, you represent the latent strength of our nation, by decree of the infinite will of the Almighty God; who has created every woman to be a symbol of divinity, through the gift of maternity]." She repeated her plea to God and asked the women to continue to pray for Corretjer and Albizu Campos before closing with an appeal for a regional sense of identity, recalling the names of all those who had fought for freedom and democracy in the Americas. In these lines, she suggests a transnational partnership, a theme found elsewhere in her work. She articulates a hemispheric identity that builds alliances across borders and stands in opposition to U.S. imperialism, following the tradition of José Martí.[47]

> Cumplamos el mandato de nuestra condición de mujeres cristianas; oremos con devoción y fe solemne para que la tranquilidad vuelva a reinar en nuestra patria intervenida y para que se haga justicia con esos patriotas nacionalistas, en quienes se está procesando también a Bolívar, a Sucre, a Martí, a Washington y a todos los libertadores del mundo.

> Let us fulfill our mandate as Christian women; let us pray with solemn devotion and faith for peace to reign again in our occupied country and for justice to be done for our nationalist patriots, in whom you are also prosecuting Bolívar, Sucre, Martí, Washington and all the liberators of the world.

Burgos repeated this idea of solidarity with other Latin American nations in countless poems written from abroad, among them "Ibero-America resurge ante Bolívar" (Ibero-America Resurges before Bolívar), "Canción a los pueblos

hispanos de América y del mundo" (Song to the Hispanic People of America and
the World), and "Saludo en ti a la nueva mujer americana" (I Greet You the New
American Woman). She also wrote a poem that denounced Dominican dictator
Rafael Trujillo ("Himno de sangre a Trujillo" [Hymn of Blood to Trujillo]) and
wrote a song in support of the Dominican people ("Canto a la ciudad primada
de América" [Canto to the Oldest City in America]). These works express ideas
of hemispheric unity that invite other Latin Americans to identify with Burgos
and see her as a champion for Latino/a unity.[48]

The women of the Frente Unido Femenino met with U.S. government of-
ficials to plead their case and express allegiance to the Nationalist Party. When
Senator William H. King, a Utah Republican, came to visit the island on 15
August 1936, the women met with him, although he refused to meet with Albizu
Campos or other party representatives.[49] According to a report by Burgos,

> Le indicamos al señor King que era nuestro criterio que él no había sido introducido
> a las personas que representan los verdaderos sentimientos y aspiraciones legíti-
> mos del pueblo de Puerto Rico; que sólo había sido introducido a los azucareros y
> capitalistas, que confabulados con el régimen, explotan al pueblo de Puerto Rico.[50]

> We told Mr. King that in our view, he had not met the people who represent the
> true feelings and legitimate aspirations of the people of Puerto Rico. He had only
> been introduced to those involved in the sugar industry and the capitalists who, in
> cahoots with the regime, exploit the people of Puerto Rico.

The women went on to express their disdain for the U.S. regime on the island
and called for the immediate departure of U.S. colonial officials: "Replicamos
que en nombre de la mujer puertorriqueña queríamos decirle que odiamos el
régimen norteamericano en Puerto Rico y que si ellos tenían las intenciones
de evacuar nuestro territorio, deberían hacerlo inmediatamente [We wish to
say, on behalf of the women of Puerto Rico, that we hate the North American
regime in Puerto Rico and if they intend to evacuate our land, they should do
so immediately]." The women asked King to meet with Albizu Campos, but
the senator responded that he did not talk to murderers and that since he was
a capitalist and the United States was a capitalist country, it made sense that
he would meet only with capitalists. It is unlikely that the women expected
King to sympathize with their cause, but the letter carried great symbolism
and received much publicity.

However, Burgos's poetry also clashed with her nationalist prose, particularly
when she wrote about women's roles and exalted the island's Spanish ancestry.
On 23 September 1936, the Frente Unido Femenino members commemorated
the 1868 Revolt of Lares with a demonstration in that town. Burgos delivered a
powerful, persuasive, and poetic speech, "La mujer ante el dolor de la patria."
She articulated views consistent with *albizuismo* by claiming the Spanish women

who had fought in the Spanish Civil War as Puerto Rico's heroic ancestry and by encouraging Puerto Rican women to take up arms, as Spanish women had, and join the fight alongside their men.[51]

> Que estamos dispuestas a ir al sacrificio que la libertad impone, para demostrarle al mundo la herencia de nuestra tradición heroica, que en estos momentos ha florecido en las valientes mujeres españolas que marchan, fusil en mano, junto a los hombres, a defender una causa que ellas creen justa y noble.[52]

> We are willing to make the sacrifices required to achieve our freedom, to show the world the heritage of our heroic tradition, which now blossoms in the brave Spanish women marching, rifle in hand, along with the men, to defend a cause they believe to be just and noble.

Later in this speech, she embraced more traditional gender roles and espoused the conservative discourse of *marianismo*, an ideology prevalent in Latin American countries.[53] Also known as the cult of Mary, *marianismo* teaches that women are semidivine, morally superior to and spiritually stronger than men. Burgos advocated *marianismo* qualities, including the expectation that women should sacrifice their own desires for others and should uphold ideal feminine characteristics such as moral strength and superiority.

> Las elecciones partidistas sólo han servido para dividir la familia puertorriqueña. La mujer ha sido creada por Dios como símbolo de la unidad sagrada de la vida, que fecundiza en la maternidad. Ella es el centro del hogar, que irradia su amor, su abnegación y su ternura a todos lados. Pero no olvidarse de los principios de confraternidad humana; que hacen de la nación la familia común, que hacen de la Patria el hogar común. Así mismo debe ser ella el centro de la patria, irradiando su amor y su verdad por todas partes. Por lo tanto, no debe ella contribuir a dividir la patria, porque con ello está dividiendo su propio hogar. Se está faltando el respeto a sí misma y a la gracia divina que creó en ella la pureza de la maternidad.[54]

> Partisan elections have only served to divide the Puerto Rican family. Woman was created by God as a symbol of the sacred unity of life, which finds its origin in motherhood. She is the center of the home, which radiates her love, her unselfishness and her tenderness to all. We cannot forget the principle of human brotherhood; it makes the nation the common family, which makes the country the common home. Each woman should also be the center of the homeland, shining love and truth everywhere. Therefore, she should not contribute to the splintering of the country, because in doing so, she fragments her own home. She disrespects the integrity of the home and the divine grace that lies at the center of motherhood.

Burgos thus defined the national role of women as that of the traditional wife and mother. These ideas align with the religious tone she adopted in her newspaper and party writings and reflect the conservative feminism of elite *criollas*

such as Mercedes Solá, a suffragist leader and schoolteacher who help[
feminist thought on the island during the 1920s. Solá developed her ideas ˙ᴏ᷇
of fear that radical feminism, favored by many working-class feminists, might
gain popularity in Puerto Rico."[55] Consequently, she and other middle-class
women developed a brand of feminism that did not pose a threat to the status
quo, presenting themselves as collaborators in the nationalist project.[56] How-
ever, Burgos's poetry and letters described marriage as confining and expressed
resentment toward the limited roles available to women.

Reading Race and Gender

The *treintista* version of cultural nationalism remains dominant today, but dis-
sident versions of culture were expressed as early as the 1930s. Burgos's early
poetry, including "Río Grande de Loíza" and "Ay ay ay de la grifa negra" (Oh
My, Oh My, Oh My, of the Nappy-Haired Negress, 1938), counters the idealized
jíbaro by remembering slavery's painful legacy on the island. Rather than my-
thologizing the *jíbaro*, she recognizes the exploitation of both men and women
living in poverty. This depiction set her apart from many other writers of the
time, although not all writers of this generation denied the African presence
on the island. Palés Matos's collection of *negrista* poetry, *Tun tun de pasa y
grifería* (Tom-Toms of Kinky Hair and All Things Black, 1937), for example,
celebrates Puerto Rico's African heritage.[57] The Afro-Antillean poetry of Luis
Palés Matos, for example, challenges Hispanism and Pedreira's *Insularismo*.
Burgos, too, affirms a mixed-race construction of Puerto Rican culture not only
in "Río Grande de Loíza" but also and more notably in "Ay ay ay de la grifa
negra."[58] These literary works are highly experimental and constitute a deliberate
reclaiming of the African presence on the island as an autochthonous tradition.
Vanguardia works commonly were framed in broader Americanist contexts
and affirmed explicitly Americanist positions. This discourse "celebrated the
continent's humanism, energy, 'ancestral' spirit, and radical newness as powerful
antidotes to European cultural exhaustion."[59]

By the mid-1930s, the debate over the blackness of Puerto Rican culture was
in full swing. On 13 November 1932, Palés Matos published the essay "Hacia
una poesía antillana" (Toward an Antillean Poetry) in *El Mundo*.

> En un sentido general, el hecho de que las Antillas hayan sido colonizadas y pobladas
> por la raza hispánica, no significa que después de cuatrocientos años, que repre-
> sentan multiples generaciones, continuemos tan españoles como nuestros abuelos.
>
> El negro vive física y espiritualmente con nosotros y sus características, tamizadas
> en el mulato, influyen de modo evidente en todas las manifestaciones de nuestra
> vida popular. . . .

Su vitalidad, su dinamismo, su naturaleza primitiva . . . nos da su pasión, su verbosismo exuberante, su elasticidad de actitudes y su extraño magnetismo, que adquiere en el mulato una especie de fuerza mística arrolladora.

. . . Yo diría que el antillano es un español con maneras de mulato y alma de negro.[60]

In a general sense, the fact that the Antilles has been colonized and populated by the Hispanic race does not signify that after four hundred years, which in itself represents multiple generations, we remain as Spanish as our grandfathers. . . .

The black man lives physically and spiritually with us, and his characteristics, scattered in the mulatto, are quite evident in the manifestations of our popular life. . . .

His vitality, his dynamism, his natural primitiveness . . . it gives us his passion, his exuberant verbosity, his elastic attitudes and his strange magnetism, which acquires in the mulatto a form of resounding mystical strength.

. . . I would say that the Antillean is a Spaniard with mulatto manners and the soul of a black.

Here, Palés Matos echoes the search for Americanists and national concerns of the literary vanguards of his time. His *negrista* poetry had caused a stir among the reading public, and Tomás Blanco's "Elogio de la plena: Variaciones boricuas" (In Praise of the Plena: Boricua Variations, 1934) attempted to reconcile Puerto Rico's creole elite identity with the island's racial heterogeneity.[61] Creole intellectuals of the time insisted almost unanimously that Puerto Rico was the whitest island of the Caribbean. Intellectuals such as Blanco, Emilio Belaval, and Margot Arce divorced popular forms of African expression found in Puerto Rico from their cultural origins. The *mulata* appears as the favored fantasy sex object in Blanco and Belaval's writings and in other literature of the time.[62]

"Ay ay ay de la grifa negra," first published in 1938, is one of Burgos's best-known poems. The racial awareness articulated in this poem is more explicit than that found in her other poetry. In "Ay ay ay" she demonstrates a racial awareness rare among writers of the time, with Palés Matos one of the few exceptions.

Ay, ay, ay, que soy grifa y pura negra;
grifería en mi pelo, cafrería en mis labios;
y mi chata nariz mozambiquea.

Negra de intacto tinte, lloro y río
la vibración de ser estatua negra;
de ser trozo de noche, en que mis blancos
dientes relampaguean;
y ser negro bejuco

que a lo negro se enreda
y comba el negro nido
en que el cuervo se acuesta.
Negro trozo de negro en que me esculpo,
ay ay ay que mi estatua es toda negra. (52)

Oh my, oh my, oh my, I'm nappy-haired and pure black:
kinks in my hair, on my lips Kaffir,
my nose so flat it Mozambiques.

Black of pure tint, I lament and laugh
at the pulsings of being a black statue;
a mass of night in which my white
teeth lightning;
a black vine
winding round all is black,
gives curve to the black nest
in which the raven lies.

Black mass of black in which I form myself,
oh my, oh my, oh my, my figure is all black.[63]

The woman in these opening stanzas is described in dehumanizing stereotypes and has no agency. She does not speak; rather, she is described as a statue, and neither her feelings nor her humanity are ever revealed to the reader. Her hair is "grifería," her lips are "cafrería," and her nose is "chata," while the whiteness of her teeth is so bright, its contrast to her black skin is a lightning flash, "relampaguean." Palés Matos, one of the first poets to write in this style and typical of the *negrista* poets of the period, creates similar images in his poetry. George Robert Coulthard and more recent critics such as Magali Roy-Féquière have noted the stereotypical qualities and lack of humanity afforded to the Africanist figures created in much of the early *negrista* poetry, though Afro-Cuban poet Nicolás Guillén stands out as an exception. His poetry transcends the stereotypical representations and thereby poignantly articulates African humanity within the racist cultural context of the 1930s.[64]

Like Palés Matos, Burgos insisted that the experiences of Afro-descended peoples were critical to Caribbean and more specifically Puerto Rican life. Although Burgos expressed a racial identity in stereotypes, she also created a split between the master and the enslaved race in this poem. The speaker rejects any association with the colonizing power and clearly locates herself among the enslaved race, claiming an African heritage and rejecting any affiliation with the race of the ruling power.

Dícenme que mi abuelo fue el esclavo
por quien el amo dio treinta monedas.
Ay ay ay que el esclavo fue mi abuelo
es mi pena, es mi pena.
Si hubiera sido el amo,
sería mi vergüenza;
que en los hombres, igual que en las naciones,
si el ser el siervo es no tener derechos,
el ser el amo es no tener conciencia. (52)

They tell me that my grandfather was a slave
for whom the master paid out thirty gold coins.

Oh my, oh my, oh my, that that slave was my grandfather
is my sorrow and my grief.
If he had been the master,
it would have been my shame:
for in men, as in nations,
if to be a slave implies one has no rights,
to be a master implies one has no conscience.[65]

Although tracing her heritage to slavery can account for much of her sorrow, the speaker says she prefers this heritage to the master's lineage, which lacks a conscience. She also suggests the history of rape and miscegenation forming part of the legacy of slavery and acknowledges the exploitation and subjugation of black women's bodies.[66]

Ay, ay, ay, los pecados del rey blanco
lávelos en perdón la reina negra.

Ay, ay, ay, que la raza se me fuga
y hacia la raza blanca zumba y vuela
a hundirse en su agua clara;
o tal vez si la blanca se ensombrará en la negra.

Ay, ay, ay, que mi negra raza huye
y con la blanca corre a ser trigueña;
¡a ser la del futuro,
fraternidad de América! (52–53)

my, oh my, oh my, wash the white King's sins away
in the black Queen's forgiveness.

Oh my, oh my, oh my, that race is on the run
and toward the whites it buzzes and it flies,

to sink in their pure water;
or possibly whiteness will be darkened by the black.

Oh my, oh my, oh my, my black race flees
and merges with the white, becoming bronze,
to be the race of the future,
of America's fraternity!

In the penultimate stanza, Burgos refers to the concept of *mestizaje*, or racial whitening, a process promoted throughout Latin America by nation-building elites to breed out undesirable African and indigenous qualities. One of the most well known proponents of whitening was Mexican politician and writer José Vasconcelos, author of *La raza cósmica* (The Cosmic Race, 1925). Burgos turns this idea on its head when she suggests that the white race could be eliminated or "improved" through racial mixing. She exalts a mixed racial identity as the race of the future, one that will unite the Americas. In so doing, she expresses an Americanist concern common among Latin American *vanguardias* of the time, as they "forecast an energetic new day, a potent new human species, and a powerful new art."[67] Although this concept of *mestizaje* is problematic, the poem wrestles with Puerto Rico's racial heterogeneity, a reality that the *criollo* elite of the time refused to acknowledge. The poem's speaker is a woman of African heritage, allowing Burgos to challenge and subvert the idea of nation as family. Island writers as well as diaspora writers in New York later picked up this important part of Burgos's legacy, writing about blackness as a political identity.

Fashioning the Self
in Burgos's Feminist Poetry

While many of Burgos's early poems display characteristics of nomadism, her poems of self-definition best exemplify the feminist nomadic subject. In them, she reveals her feelings of frustration with the insular and parochial island culture. She criticizes the bourgeois society of the Ateneo Puertorriqueño, the institution of marriage, and the limited opportunities available to women. These frustrations, along with the island's changing political climate, ultimately lead her to abandon her homeland, never to return.

In her poem "A Julia de Burgos," she reveals a split, or double consciousness, suggesting postmodernist ideas of identity as performance. The socially constructed self performs femininity. The speaker dramatizes the conflict between her socially acceptable constructed identity and her inner voice as a woman artist, and she wants to rid herself of this "other" Julia de Burgos. The artist/ poet Julia speaks to the socially constructed Julia, revealing an internal battle between a "true" and a "false" self that she is unable to reconcile. This poem echoes the works of other great early twentieth-century women artists of the Americas, including Frida Kahlo's *Las dos Fridas* (1939), Gabriela Mistral's "La otra" (1954), Anne Sexton's "Her Kind" (1960), and Sylvia Plath's "Three Women: A Poem for Three Voices" (1962). In these poems and artwork, the artists stage a confrontation between two warring aspects of themselves, the "true" artist self and a "false" socially constructed self. These two selves are irreconcilable; one must ultimately destroy the other.

"A Julia de Burgos" not only preceded these other works but is unique in that the "true" poet self is the speaker and the victor. In the other poems, the socially accepted "false" self speaks and kills off the "true" self. Revealing what I call a poetics of presence and authenticity, the poet/speaker in Burgos's poem rejects and criticizes the bourgeois woman. The opening lines set the stage for these two conflicted selves. The poet is aware that her "true" self is a threat to the social woman: "Ya las gentes murmuran que yo soy tu enemiga / porque dicen que en verso doy al mundo tu yo [Already the people murmur that I am your enemy / because they say that in verse I give the world your me]" (9). The poet/speaker is dangerous, the enemy, because she unveils her innermost thoughts—those things that should remain unspoken, such as her political convictions and her sexual desire. The poet/speaker then asserts herself and clarifies her position, rejecting the words of others and suggesting that the exterior "false" self must be killed off.

> Mienten, Julia de Burgos. Mienten, Julia de Burgos.
> La que se alza en mis versos no es tu voz: es mi voz;
> porque tú eres ropaje y la esencia soy yo;
> y el más profundo abismo se tiende entre las dos. (9)

> They lie, Julia de Burgos, they lie. They lie, Julia de Burgos.
> The one that rises in my verse is not your voice: it's mine.
> You're only the clothing; the essence, though, is me;
> and the deepest chasm yawns between the two.[68]

She establishes the divide in this stanza, and from this point on, the speaker describes the two incompatible parts of herself, revealing that identity is a performance. Burgos expresses the struggles and challenges faced by woman artists in this society. The "false" self is described as *ropaje* (clothing), *fría muñeca de mentira social* (a bloodless mannequin of social lies), *miel de cortesanas hipocresías* (a honey of courtly hypocrisies), *egoísta* (an egoist), *grave señora señorona* (an imperious grand dame), *te rizas el pelo y te pintas* (curling its hair and painting its face), *dama casera, resignada, sumisa* (a housewife, resigned, submissive), and *flor de artistocracia* (an aristocratic blossom). The false self is associated with artificial social constructs, appearances, and ego. She is the ideal woman, knowing how to dress properly and observe decorum. The "true" self in this poem is the poet, the life force that has hidden behind the mask of social decorum. She describes this aspect of herself as *esencia* (an essence), *viril destello de la humana verdad* (a virile starburst of the human truth), *la vida, la fuerza, la mujer* (life, strength, woman). She is truth and substance. She is not a *señora*, a term that indicates social class and marital status, but rather a *mujer*—a woman.

As a bourgeois outsider, the speaker allows herself to offer an incisive critique. The greatest challenge the "false" self faces in this poem is the lack of control over her decisions and her destiny. The performance of femininity is guided and manipulated by the patriarchal society in which she lives. Her life is not her own. Her husband is her keeper, and she is subject to his desires: "tú eres de tu marido, de tu amo [you belong to your husband, your master]." Her life is dictated from the outside, and she lacks the ability to make her own choices:

> Tú en ti misma no mandas; a ti todos te mandan;
> en ti mandan tu esposo, tus padres, tus parientes,
> el cura, la modista, el teatro, el casino,
> el auto, las alhajas, el banquete, el champán,
> el cielo y el infierno, y el qué dirán social. (10)

> You in your self rule not; you're ruled by everyone;
> in you your husband rules, your parents, relatives,
> the priest, the dressmaker, the theater, the casino,
> the car, the jewels, the banquet, the champagne,
> the heaven and the hell, and the what-will-they-say.[69]

In contrast to this performance of womanhood, which is dictated by the fashions of the time—the priest, the husband, and all that makes up the world of social aristocracy—the speaker of the poem espouses the poetics of presence, struggles to live her own life and remain authentic. Around the same time in 1938 when this poem was published, Burgos dropped her married name; rather than reverting to her maiden name, she inserted *de* before her father's last name, which in Spanish indicates marital status or possession. She thus became Julia de Burgos, symbolically taking possession of herself.

In "A Julia de Burgos," the speaker asserts that she has always remained true to herself and to her inner voice, making clear that the "true" self is the poet: "la que se alza en mis versos no es tu voz: es mi voz [Who rises in my verses is not your voice. It is my voice]." She lays bare her soul in her poetry—"en todos mis poemas desnudo el corazón [in all my poems I undress my heart]"—and struggles to remain true to herself: "en todo me lo juego a ser lo que soy yo [I gamble everything betting on what I am]." The poet controls her destiny and makes her own decisions: "en mí manda mi solo corazón, mi solo pensamiento; quien manda en mí soy yo [in me only my heart governs, / only my thought; who governs in me is me]." She goes on to say, "yo de nadie, o de todos, porque a todos, a todos, en mi limpio sentir y en mi pensar me doy [I belong to no one, or everyone, because to everyone, to everyone / I give myself in my clean feeling and in my thought]." The speaker here defines her vocation as a poet, understanding that a poet's obligation is to speak truth. This poem is concerned with authenticity and illuminating the voice of the poet, ideas that were at the forefront of early twentieth-century poetic trends.[70]

Burgos clearly conveys her commitment to her craft as a writer. In the last two lines, the speaker/poet addresses the "false" self, expressing her commitment to rebel against it and all imposed social restrictions. She also evinces her determination to combat all other forms of injustice and inhumanity when she says, "contra ti, y contra todo lo injusto y lo inhumano, / yo iré en medio de ellas con la tea en la mano [against you and against everything unjust and inhuman, / I will be in their midst with the torch in my hand]." These themes permeated Burgos's work throughout her writing career. She persistently struggled for the rights of the oppressed. Here, she strips away all that clutters the self, arriving at a place of self-knowledge and self-understanding regarding her calling as a poet, a woman, and an artist.

Burgos's "Pentacromia" (Pentachrome) is another well-known and widely read poem that appears in the first collection. It is recalled mostly because of the controversial ending and her explicitly articulated desire to be a man. This poem was first published in *El Imparcial*, a nationalist newspaper, on 4 December 1937. In it, she conveys her longing for freedom to travel and explore. In the opening stanza, the woman speaker wishes to be "Don Quijote o Don Juan o un bandido / o un ácrata obrero o un gran militar [Don Quijote, or Don Juan, or a bandit / or an anarchist worker, or a great soldier]" (25). She repeats the opening phrase, "Hoy, quiero ser un hombre [Today, I want to be a man]," in the next six stanzas. This desire implies the opportunities not available to her because of her gender. She wants to be an active participant in the world, not a passive bystander. In the final stanza, she articulates her rage and her desire to rebel.

> Hoy, quiero ser un hombre. Subir por las tapias,
> burlar los conventos, ser todo un Don Juan;
> raptar a Sor Carmen y a Sor Josefina,
> rendirlas, y a Julia de Burgos violar. (26)

> Today, I want to be a man. Scale adobe walls,
> the convents mock, I would be a Don Juan;

abduct Sor Carmen and Sor Josefina
conquer, and ravage Julia de Burgos.

The reference to Don Juan highlights the way that men's sexuality and virility are glorified throughout literary history. The women in this poem live in a convent and are denied their sexuality. The juxtaposition of Don Juan and the sisters in the convent magnifies the socially accepted double standard regarding men's and women's sexualities. The positioning of the women in the poem suggests women's disempowerment and active exclusion from the world. The final line of the stanza is the most shocking, disclosing Burgos's feelings of vulnerability and lack of power in a patriarchal society. The fact that the rapes occur in a convent also constitutes an affront to the Catholic Church.

Burgos's commitment to her craft as a writer is apparent in this first collection of poetry. Many of these poems reveal the verbal experiments and thematic inquiries into language that characterized the works of the *vanguardias*. They were particularly concerned with a search for aesthetic legitimation, with affirming artistic power by identifying with the initial formation of language, and with the idea of re-creating language from the void.[71] In "Se me ha perdido un verso" (I Have Lost a Verse), Burgos expresses many of the frustrations that artists experience when cultivating their craft. Poetry is described as a tangible object. The words are a sculpture that the poet must form. She expresses frustration with the mystery of inspiration, which is present and then quickly disappears. Words and poetry have a life of their own.

> Partió calladamente, deforme y mutilado,
> cargando en su mutismo el vago sentimiento
> de haber vestido en carne gastada de palabras
> para exhibir mi entrada a un intento poético. (18)

> It left quietly, deformed and mutilated,
> carrying in its silence the vague sentiment
> of having dressed in flesh worn of words
> to exhibit my entry into a poetic intent.

She further anthropomorphizes poetry here by addressing it in a second-person singular direct speech act, "¡Tú! ¡Verso! [You! Verse!]." This repeated direct address suggests a present, living object. This form has been used for centuries in a poetic tradition to bring inanimate objects to life. In a final attempt to define poetry, Burgos writes,

> Ya puedo definirte. Traes ímpetu de idea,
> y vibra en tus palabras el ritmo de lo nuevo.

Eres el hoy del mundo; la afirmación; la fuerza.
¡Revolución que rompe las cortinas del tiempo! (19)

Now I can define you. You bring an impetus of idea
and in your words the rhythm of the new vibrates.

You are the world's today; the affirmation; the strength.
Revolution that shatters the curtains of time!

Her definition of poetry here echoes the notion of a poetics of presence and authenticity found in "A Julia de Burgos." Poetry is an expression of the present, a life force. Finally, in poetry she defines herself by finding her voice: "me he encontrado yo misma al encontrar mi verso [I find myself when I find my verse]." As such, the attempt to define poetry is an attempt to define the self. The self is in a symbiotic relationship with poetry. The artist and the art object become one. The poet/self gives shape to poetry; poetry gives shape to the self. The two cannot be defined separately. Poetry, addressed as an exterior object outside the self earlier in the poem, has merged with the poet's existence. Burgos returns to this theme in her third collection of poetry, *El mar y tú* (The Sea and You). Burgos affirms her presence by attempting to give form and structure to her words and ideas. Her ability to poignantly and effectively express her frustration as a woman artist revolutionizes the lyric. Poetry, writing, and art have often been described as a lifeline for women artists and as a vehicle for self-discovery and self-expression. Although Burgos did not give birth to these ideas, the explicit expression of her relationship to her art is part of her legacy to subsequent generations of women artists.

Burgos continues to create escape routes throughout the poetry in *Poema en veinte surcos*, but the speaker increasingly escapes into the imagination because the avenues to freedom in the physical world are not open to her. For example, in "Intima" (Intimate), she expresses her desire to escape this world and leave behind her human form. In "Mi símbolo de rosas" (My Symbol of Roses), the poet feels trapped. She looks inside to her own subjectivity and imagination for sustenance. Her inability to reconcile herself with the world leads her to turn inward. This work is enigmatic and obscure. The primary image here is of forty open roses that symbolize her heart. The poet feels trapped and in pain, but she does not find a way to escape. Unable to free herself from her social situation, she looks for a space inside, in her imagination, to sustain her. She writes of the "triunfo de la imaginación [triumph of the imagination]" and "mi vida en fuga continua hacia adentro [my life in pursuit continues to turn within]" (58).

In "Mi alma" (My soul), Burgos reveals a fragmented and disconnected self, suffering in alienation, a state she compares to the experience of exile, anticipating her departure from her homeland. The speaker's mental state is fragile, and she wants to rebel, to move away from all that is imposed on her.

> La locura de mi alma
> no puede reclinarse,
> vive en lo inquieto,
> en lo desordenado,
> en el desequilibrio
> de las cosas dinámicas,
> en el silencio
> del libre pensador, que vive solo,
> en callado destierro. (65)

> The madness of my soul
> cannot rest,
> it lives in the unsteady,
> in the disorder,
> in the instability
> of the dynamic,
> in the silence
> of the freethinker, who lives alone
> in quiet exile.

Burgos calls on the metaphorical space of exile, suggesting that the intellectual and freethinker lives in this space. In "Intellectual Exile: Expatriates and Marginals," Edward Said notes that the idea of the intellectual as outsider is "best exemplified by the condition of exile, the state of never being fully adjusted, always feeling outside the chatty, familiar world inhabited by natives, so to speak, tending to avoid and even dislike the trappings of accommodation and national well-being. Exile for the intellectual in this metaphysical sense is restlessness, movement, constantly being unsettled, and unsettling others."[72] The intellectual stands for freedom and knowledge and thus always remains on the margins, refusing to be co-opted.

The final poem is the collection's most salient example of a nomadic subject, also exemplifying the *vanguardias'* search for the new. In "Yo misma fui mi ruta" (I Am My Own Path), the speaker creates her own path in life. She describes how she had attempted to be what society dictated, a wife and a woman who adhered to social norms: "Yo quise ser como los hombres quisieron que yo fuese: / un intento de vida; / un juego al escondite con mi ser. [I longed to be what men desired: / a spark; / that played hide and seek with my soul]" (70). She concludes that she cannot be that woman but instead must forge a new trajectory. She sees herself as the promise and hope of the new. She must leave the past and find a new way.

> Pero yo estaba hecha de presentes,
> y mis pies planos sobre la tierra promisora
> no resistían caminar hacia atrás,
> y seguían adelante, adelante,
> burlando las cenizas para alcanzar el beso
> de los senderos nuevos. (70)
> [. . .]
> cuando ya los heraldos me anunciaban
> en el regio desfile de los troncos viejos,
> se me torció el deseo de seguir a los hombres,
> y el homenaje se quedó esperandome. (71)

> But I was firmly in the present,
> with my feet planted on the promissory earth
> refusing to retract,
> they moved onward and forward,
> eluding the ashes to reach the embrace
> of uncharted paths.
> [. . .]
> when heralds announced my arrival
> among the royal promenade of the old guard,
> thwarted within me was any desire to follow,
> their homage for me waited in vain.

The speaker here is resolute and prepared to break with the past, expressing a desire that is consistent with Said's notion of metaphysical exile. As a model for the intellectual, exile means that the intellectual cannot follow a set path. The state of always being marginal should be experienced by the intellectual not as a "deprivation and as something to be bewailed, but as a sort of freedom, a process of discovery in which you do things according to your own pattern, as various interests seize your attention, and as the particular goal you set yourself dictates."[73] While the exile is often defined as a person who moves from one point to the next, Said defines the metaphysical exile differently and in a way that is more consistent with the nomadic trajectory, which resists commonly accepted moral codes of behavior and thought.

During the 1930s, Burgos developed her social, political, and creative consciousness. Her first collection of poetry includes many of the themes that she continued to explore in her writing throughout her life. From 1935, when she wrote "Río Grande de Loíza," until 1938, when she published *Poema en veinte surcos*, Burgos embarked on the path she would follow throughout her life. She abandoned the social mask she constructed during her marriage to Rodríguez Beauchamp and in her writing for Frente Unido Femenino. Her poetry critiqued Puerto Rico's oppressive social norms while she remained committed to the island's political independence. In her first collection of poetry, Burgos began creating escape routes, and her search for the new tied her to the literary vanguards. She continued to use images of water and other forms of movement and fluidity to create pathways and avenues in search of the new. The flights, migrations, and exiles in her poetry anticipate her physical departure from the island. These itineraries opened up the possibility of finding a home elsewhere, outside the restrictive confines of the insular, colonial, and patriarchal nation.

2

Exile, Migration, and Hemispheric Identity

When Julia de Burgos embarked for New York on 13 January 1940, she was twenty-five. She had already written three collections of poetry and published two. She had been married and divorced. Stigmatized by Puerto Rico's conservative culture because of her divorce, Burgos left, with no plans to return. "I want to be universal," she exclaimed in a letter to her sister, Consuelo, shortly after her arrival in New York. Burgos's decision to leave the island and spend the remainder of her life abroad generated much criticism, romantic speculation, and gossip among those who believed her departure from the island set in motion a series of events that resulted in her death. In Puerto Rican literature and expressive culture of the 1940s and 1950s, the narrative of migration as tragedy prevails. Burgos subsequently became a symbol of this tragedy in the collective imagination of many Puerto Ricans both on the island and in New York.[1] However, Burgos's migration experience can also be read as an escape from victimhood. This chapter follows her migratory routes to New York, to Havana, and back to New York in the larger context of Puerto Rican migration. By reading her second and third collections of poetry, *Canción de la verdad sencilla* (Song of the Simple Truth, 1939) and *El mar y tú* (The Sea and You, 1954), and her understudied letters with attention to gender, her experience of migration no longer appears as victimization; rather, Burgos emerges as an early figure of sexile.

Political and economic factors have often been taken into account when studying the reasons for migration from Latin America and the Caribbean to the United States. In recent years, Lawrence La Fountain-Stokes and other scholars have explored the causal link between sexuality and migration.[2] Theorist Manolo Guzmán coined the term *sexile* to refer to "the exile of those who have had to leave their nations of origin on account of their sexual orientation."[3] This chapter extends the definition of *sexile* to include heterosexual women who have been excluded and displaced because they are deemed sexually transgressive within patriarchal, heteronormative discourses.[4] Using this term to refer to women brings to mind Puerto Rican anarchist Luisa Capetillo, who is remembered as one of the most important writers and union organizers for the cigar industry, a *lector* who worked as a labor organizer and a woman's rights activist in Puerto Rico, Tampa, and New York. Today she is celebrated as an early Puerto Rican feminist and is famous for getting arrested for wearing pants in public in Havana.[5] Written on the eve of her departure for the United States, Capetillo's *Mi opinión sobre las libertades, derechos, y deberes de la mujer* (My Opinion on the Freedoms, Rights, and Duties of Women, 1911) was the first Puerto Rican book dedicated exclusively to questions of gender and women's rights.[6] From Tampa, she significantly revised and expanded this work to write about the condition of women more generally, publishing the new edition from Florida in 1913.[7] Lisa Sánchez González notes that Capetillo left the island after being "harassed by both colonial regimes she had experienced in Puerto Rico and becoming discontented with the workers' movement" there.[8] As an early feminist who left the island in search of greater freedoms from a patriarchal society, her work anticipates later generations of writers who hoped that migration would be a liberatory strategy from oppression because of gender and sexuality.[9] Literary works abound with Caribbean women characters whose sexuality is seen as transgressive or deviant and who are ostracized by their communities. Although Burgos's sexual orientation is not in question, it is important to understand the role that gender played in her decision to leave the island and in her inability to make a home for herself in Cuba or New York. Social circumstances beyond her control repeatedly thwarted her ambitions.

In "Female Sexiles?: Toward an Archeology of Displacement of Sexual Minorities in the Caribbean," literary critic Yolanda Martínez-San Miguel argues for a definition of *sexile* that refers to two simultaneous and complementary definitions of displacement: as misfits within Caribbean patriarchal discourses and as a negotiated and temporary exclusion for fulfillment of divergent sexual desires. She proposes the script of sexile as it has been used in queer Caribbean studies to "think about the configuration of alternative communal identities based on recent narratives that go beyond the heteronormative and homonormative matrixes." She stretches the meaning of sexile as "a negative notion that motivates collective action to include the relationship between nonsovereign nations of the insular Caribbean and the role of sexual minorities in the constitution of other narratives of collective identification."[10] The control of women's sexuality and queer sexual minorities shares a common structure, as both are excluded from the nation because they are deemed excessive and transgressive.

Burgos's assertiveness, outspokenness, divorce, affair, and bohemian lifestyle resulted in substantial gossip and prejudice on the island. One New York–based

Figure 3. Julia de Burgos and Juan Isidro Jimenes Grullón, ca. 1939–42. General Collections, Archives of the Puerto Rican Diaspora, Center for Puerto Rican Studies, Hunter College, City University of New York.

friend, Emelí Vélez de Vando, remembered that the women of San Juan's cultural circles accepted Julia de Burgos the poet but could not be associated with Julia de Burgos the woman.[11] Burgos's rejection of marriage and traditional roles for women, her poverty, and her race all factored into her conflicted relationship with her home country and significantly influenced her decision to depart. Burgos continued to create migratory and nomadic subjects in *Canción de la verdad sencilla* to escape being fixed into the racist and elitist imagination of the national project.[12] Shortly after publishing this book, she left the island. In her final poetry collection, *El mar y tú*, we see the culmination of her nomadic subject, which uses death and abjection to escape containment. Later Puerto Rican gay and lesbian émigré writers picked up this image of sexile, realizing the metaphor and turning Burgos into a lesbian fictional character who is expelled from the nation because of her exorbitant sexual desires (see chapter 4). This phenomenon highlights the links that exist between Burgos's affirmation of her sexuality and her nontraditional choices and the sexual liberation movements that defined the lesbian, gay, bisexual, and transgender movements of the 1970s.[13]

Canción de la verdad sencilla

Julia de Burgos wrote *Canción de la verdad sencilla* shortly after meeting Juan Isidro Jimenes Grullón, and he later recalled having "witnessed the birth of all those poems." Jimenes Grullón said that when he went to bed, Burgos "would stay up to write and in the morning she would show me what she had written during the night, always love poems."[14] Yet a close reading of this collection reveals that these poems are more than simple love poetry. Burgos further develops a nomadic subject that imagines flights, travel, and bodily transformations as a way to escape containment. While much of the poetry deals with the theme of love, the speaker must leave behind the world and undertake imaginative journeys through which she becomes one with nature and her lover. The collection highlights the thrust to break down barriers, remove limitations, and transgress boundaries. Although the canonical literature of the time is concerned with nation building and perpetuating the myth of the *jíbaro* (peasant) and the nation as the great Puerto Rican family, the nomadic subject finds a way to escape that world.

The collection is characterized by its sensual lyric poetry that draws on the tradition of *erotismo* (eroticism) to elude the island's narrowly constructed gender roles for women and affirm female sexuality. Although eroticism was a popular style of writing at the time, especially for women writers, the *treintistas* viewed eroticism, pleasure, and the lyric as an excess and dissipation that threatened the national family.[15] Eroticism circumvents the procreative function of sex, defying the circumscribed role of women in the nation as wives and mothers. The poems included in this collection are about intimacy, silence, solitude, and isolation, all of which were perceived as threats to the community, family, and nation. If the literature of the time was concerned with advancing the national project and defining the Puerto Rican personality, Burgos's poems challenged the national canon, revealing how women often remained outside of the construction of the nation.

Women writers across Latin America—among them, Juana de Ibarbourou, Alfonsina Storni, and Clara Lair—cultivated an erotic lyric style in response to the suppression, denial, and demonization of their sexuality. Burgos certainly was familiar with their work, and in "Cinco poetisas de América (Clara Lair, Alfonsina Storni, Gabriela Mistral, Juana de Ibarbourou, Julia de Burgos)," published in the 13 November 1937 issue of *Puerto Rico Ilustrado*, Luis Lloréns Torres explicitly compared the five women.[16] Expressing physical desire in writing was liberating for women writers in a way that it was not for men, whose virility had for centuries been glorified in literature and art. Eroticism was a way for women to take control of their bodies and their sexuality, as Burgos did in "Alta mar y gaviota" (High Sea and Seagull), where she describes the female body in landscape imagery.

> En ti aquieto las ramas abiertas del espacio,
> y renuevo en mi arteria tu sangre con mi sangre.
>
> ¡Te multiplicas!
>   ¡Creces!
>
>   ¡Y amenazas quedarte
>   con mi prado salvaje![17]

In you I quiet the open branches of space,
and I renew in my artery your blood with my blood.

You multiply!
                    Grow!
                                    And you threaten to possess
                                    my wild meadow!

These lines suggest an erection that will penetrate the woman's "meadow." Erotic poetry expresses a disjunction between sexuality and procreation, defining sexuality purely in terms of pleasure and thus constituting a revolutionary and empowering expression for women.[18] After the sexual revolution of the 1960s, eroticism took on a new form of countercanonical, liberatory poetic discourse. Eroticism is tied to a specific historical period when women sought to reclaim control over their bodies and assert their sexuality through a poetics of intimacy.

In this collection, Burgos reveals a world where harmony is restored through the union of two lovers outside of the social trappings imposed by the family and the nation. The poems move from isolation to connection with the cosmos, a connection that is often mediated through union with the lover. The final poems in the collection reveal a frightening (or liberating) loss of ego and submission to the love object.[19] In the first poem, "Poema detenido en un amanecer" (Poem Detained at Daybreak), the speaker parallels the awakening of her senses to the dawn. She begins by describing a sense of alienation and isolation, repeating "Nadie [Alone]" three times in the first stanza. She is unique, isolated, and separated from the world.

Nadie.
Iba yo sola.
Nadie.
Pintando las auroras con mi único color de soledad.
Nadie. (9)

Alone.
I wander in seclusion.
Alone.
Sunrises painted in my solitary shadows.
Alone.

In the fifth stanza, a sudden shift occurs, and the speaker awakens. Her phrases are shorter, punctuated with exclamation marks to denote life and energy. The world is animated.

Madrugadas de dioses
maravillosamente despertaron mis valles.
¡Desprendimientos!
¡Cauces!
¡Golondrinas! ¡Estrellas!
¡Albas duras y ágiles! (9)

Glorious mornings
wondrously creep into my valleys.
Flights!
Riverbeds!
Swallows! Stars!
Hard and agile dawns!

Burgos draws a parallel between the sun bringing life to the world and her personal awakening to a wholeness that embodies truth in the poem. "Todo en ti: / ¡sol salvaje! / ¿Y yo? /—Una verdad sencilla para amarte . . . [Everything in you: / savage sun! / And I? /—Loving you, a simple truth . . .]" (10). Her love poems to nature and the cosmos are some of the strongest in the collection, intricately weaving love, nature, and eroticism.

In this poetry, silence implies a void with infinite possibilities that may not be available in real life but that can be accessed through poetry, imagination, and travel. The collection's travel theme is exemplified by "Viaje alado" (Winged Voyage), where the speaker escapes the cluttered and noisy artificial world through imaginative flight:

Por encima del ruido de los hombres
una larga ilusión se fue rodando,
[. . .]
Como corola al viento
todo el cosmos abrióseme a mi paso, (19)

Over the clatter of man
an outstretched fancy unfolded,
[. . .]
Like a garland in the wind,
the cosmos unfurled before me.

In these poems, love lies outside of social pretenses, formalities, and expectations. In "Canción desnuda" (Naked Song), her love is characterized as pure because it is not clothed, bound, or burdened by social norms: "Me solté a la pureza de un amor sin ropajes / que cargaba mi vida de lo irreal a lo humano,

/ y hube de verme toda en un grito de lágrimas [I freed myself to the purity of unclothed love / that carried me from the unreal to the human, / and I was to see all of myself in a scream of tears]" (28).

Images of walking, paths and roads prevail in the nomadic subject's first incarnation in *Poema en veinte surcos* (Poem in Twenty Furrows, 1938). In this second incarnation, the nomadic subject escapes containment through imaginative flights, as in "Transmutación" (Transmutation). The speaker is still and quiet as she leaves behind the world: "me he desgarrado el mundo de los hombros, / y he quedado desierta en mar y estrella, [the world was rent from my shoulders, / and I have been deserted by sea and star]" (14). By so doing, the speaker inhabits a space that is limitless—without boundaries, restrictions, or borders. The poem ends not with a period but rather with open-ended ellipses.

> Aquí no hay geografía para manos ni espíritu.
> Estoy sobre el silencio y en el silencio mismo
> de una transmutación
> donde nada es orilla . . . (14)

> No geography here for hands, for spirit
> Above silence and in quietude
> transmutation
> there is no shore . . .

The nomadic subject created here resists settling into socially coded ways of thinking and behavior. While at this point in her life, Burgos had not literally traveled beyond the island, she creates a subject in her poetry that subverts conventions and exists outside prescribed social norms. The nomad inhabits other spaces and imagines new possibilities. The creative promise of union, love, and nature in this poetry attests to the nomadic subject's capacity to free "the activity of thinking from the hold of phallocentric dogmatism, returning thought to its freedom, its liveliness, its beauty."[20]

Letters Home: Developing a Latin American Sense of Identity in New York and Cuba

If we expand the definition of *sexile* to include the expulsion of women from the immediate family of the nation because they do not conform to traditional gender roles, we can see how the term applies to Julia de Burgos. Her first two collections of poetry attest to her desire to break social norms for women. Burgos's personal letters reveal that she saw Jimenes Grullón as a means of escaping island politics and fulfilling her dream of becoming a world-renowned poet. While her exile certainly brought her isolation, loneliness, and despair, traveling abroad also gave her opportunities to grow as a writer and provided her with alternative perspectives. She crossed borders in both her writing and her personal life.

Though the lovers she created in her poetry unite beyond boundaries and social constraints, her relationship with Jimenes Grullón violated social norms. His parents strongly opposed the relationship because of Burgos's social background, lifestyle, and reputation, and Jimenes Grullón ultimately bowed to their wishes. In *Julia de Burgos: Vida y obra* (Julia de Burgos: Life and Work, 1966), Yvette Jiménez de Báez referred to Jimenes Grullón, who was still alive at the time, as Señor X (Mr. X) in an effort to protect his identity, suggesting the scandalous nature of his relationship with Burgos even in the 1960s. In addition, the omission of his name may have increased the mystery, speculation, and gossip surrounding Burgos's life. In 1994, Jimenes Grullón remembered that his parents "sought out information about Julia and were told that, yes, Julia was a great poet, but she was not a woman attached to the traditional values of home and family. She had a tendency to dipsomania, and as was to be expected (my parents were good bourgeois), they opposed the relationship."[21] Jimenes Grullón left Puerto Rico in November 1939 after his parents demanded that he end the relationship, but Burgos joined him in January 1940. Burgos's letters demonstrate that she was well aware of the criticism engendered by her nontraditional lifestyle.

Burgos left Puerto Rico on 13 January 1940 aboard the *San Jacinto* and arrived in New York City five days later.[22] She was excited at the possibilities that this new life might afford her. On the day of her arrival, she wrote to her sister,

> Lo que importa en este momento es que se enteren cuanto antes que ya estoy en mi destino, al lado del que siempre sigue siendo el amado tierno, y para ustedes el hermano cariñoso. En verdad estoy maravillada. Hice una travesía muy feliz, llena de sorpresas. Mi emoción y mi sensación eran sorprendidas, unas veces por corrientes maravillosas de algas amarillas en pleno Atlántico, y otras veces por fantásticos cruceros hechos de nubes en el horizonte. Cerca de Nueva York cayó una lluvia de nieve preciosa. Desembarqué.

> What matters now is that you know I am fulfilling my destiny beside the one who will always be my tender beloved and to you a loving brother. I am in awe. I had a pleasant journey full of surprises. My emotions and senses were captivated, at times by wonderful currents of yellow algae in the Atlantic, and at other times by fantastic clouds on the horizon shaped like cruise ships. Approaching New York there was a beautiful snow shower. I disembarked.

When Burgos arrived in New York City in 1940, she settled in the bustling Puerto Rican enclave in East Harlem, with its movie houses, theaters, social and political clubs, restaurants, and bodegas. Her first letters from the city convey a sense of excitement, adventure, awe, and enthusiasm. El Barrio featured a vibrant music scene that included composers Rafael Hernández, Pedro

Flores, Pedro Ortiz Dávila (known as Davilita), and Francisco López Cruz, all
of whom had moved to New York in the 1920s. During the following decade,
the American big band model was fused with Latin music, and Puerto Rican
musicians such as Juan Tizol, Fernando Arbello, Ramón Usera, and Ralph
Escudero explored the expanding universe of jazz while playing or arranging
for Duke Ellington, Fletcher Henderson, and others. The 1930s and 1940s
were also the golden age of Puerto Rican trios and quartets, as compositions
by Hernández and Flores had become part of the popular musical repertoire
across Spanish-speaking America.[23]

New York City had long been a point of confluence for writers, artists and
political exiles from Latin America and the Caribbean, and by 1940, several
politically engaged *vanguardia* writers and intellectuals, among them Clemente
Soto Vélez and Graciany Miranda Archilla, resided there.[24] Puerto Rican migra-
tion during World War II and the persecution and dismantling of the Puerto
Rican Nationalist Party made the city the last stop for the *vanguardias*.[25] Soto
Vélez, who was imprisoned with Pedro Albizu Campos in 1936, settled in New
York after his release and worked with Harlem congressman Vito Marcantonio's
American Labor Party.[26]

Writing to her sister on 30 January 1940, just a few days after arriving in
New York, Burgos described her excitement and awe. Her sense of adventure
highlights the differences between rural Puerto Rico and the metropolis. She
marveled before the expansive city and the modern forms of public transporta-
tion. She used the English words *bus* and *subway* in this letter, the beginning
of a process by which the language—which she had learned as part of her
education under the U.S. colonial system—increasingly infused her writing
while she lived abroad. As in her poetry, Burgos's letters and other writings
from New York emphasize walking and movement, though she highlighted
the cityscape rather than the rural landscape. These letters are examples of a
nomadic consciousness that paralleled the rejection of fixed forms of identity
expressed in her writing.

Aquí cada día abre nuevos horizontes, y cada paso dado es una maravilla en el
apretado haz de las sensaciones. He caminado bastante por la ciudad, y me he
perdido varias veces. Esta manía de atreverme a todo me ha hecho a los dos días de
estar aquí, tirarme sola a caminar en "bus." Los medios de comunicación son muy
complicados aquí. Imagínate nueve millones de habitantes en el radio de la ciudad,
la mayoría caminando—pues aquí es muy poca la vida familiar—empujándose unos
a otros en las guaguas, en las tiendas, en los cafés, etc. Para todo este público tiene
que haber tranvías y subways y trenes elevados, de manera que en cada esquina
cambian de dirección, y hay que ser experto en su telaraña. Y yo que a los dos días
de llegar, muy segura de mí misma me fui a caminar en una guagua de dos pisos, fui
a parar sin saberlo a Long Island, una parte de la ciudad bastante distante, separada

por un enorme puente. . . . A los dos días fue en el subway que me perdí. Caminé algunas calles por debajo de la tierra, en las grandes avenidas subterráneas de NY hasta dar con mi tren. Así es como se aprende, y no tengo miedo de ir a cualquier sitio sola. Como yo sé inglés, me es fácil salir.

Este es un pueblo verdaderamente organizado. En las esquinas en vez de policías, hay luces rojas y verdes, que automáticamente indican a los carros y el público el momento de pasar. En los automáticos, especie de cafés, se sirve uno mismo la comida, con bandejas y todo.[27]

Every day opens new horizons and every step is a marvel of new sensations. I explored quite a bit of the city and I got lost several times. This fervor I have for daring to try everything led me after being here for only two days to venture out alone by "bus." The systems of communication are very complicated here. Imagine nine million inhabitants in the radius of the city, most on foot, as there is very little family life here. People push each other on the buses, in shops, in cafes, etc. For all these persons there must be trams and subways and elevated trains that change direction at each corner and one must be an expert in this complicated web. After having been here for only two days, feeling very sure of myself, I went for a ride on a double-decker bus and I ended up unknowingly in Long Island, a part of the city that is quite remote and separated by an enormous bridge. . . . Two days later, I got lost riding the subway. I walked among some of the large underground NY avenues to find my train. That's how you learn, and I have no fear of venturing out alone. Since I know English, it's easy for me to maneuver the city.

This is a truly organized town. On the street corner, instead of police, there are red and green lights that automatically indicate to the cars and the pedestrians when it is their turn to cross. In the cafeterias, a kind of café, you serve yourself, with trays and all.

As Burgos's letters illustrate, Puerto Rican migrants to New York encountered not only a new culture but also an urban metropolis that was startlingly different from rural life on the island. Even if migrants came from San Juan, as she did, the contrast with New York City was striking.

Burgos's letters provide a rare look into the life of an early Puerto Rican working-class woman migrant to New York City. Most other accounts of Puerto Rican women in New York from this era describe life for women of a different social class. Burgos's impressions and responses to the grandeur of the buildings, the modern architecture, and cultural life offered by the city contribute to the historical record.

He visto los dos edificios más altos del mundo: El Empire State Building, de 108 pisos, y el Kreisler [sic] de 90. El "Radio City," de Rockefeller, es una especie de ciudad pequeña compuesta por varios edificios en el corazón de la ciudad. Maravilla arquitectónica. Arte completamente moderno, sobrio y lleno de ángulos. Es casi todo de mármol. "Times Square" es una cuadra llena de luces fantásticas, que asombra de luz y color. Ayer visité con Juan y unos amigos el Museo de Arte

Moderno. Juan, que sabe mucho de arte, me fue explicando todo maravillosamente.
He aprendido mucho.

En cuanto a diversiones iremos a la Opera, a Ballets y a Music Halls, novedades
para mí en este continente. El Parque Central, que es más grande que San Juan, está
ahora desierto, con árboles sin hojas y lagos helados. Se patina y se corre en trineos.

I have seen the two tallest buildings in the world: the Empire State Building, with
108 floors, and the Kreisler [*sic*] with 90. Rockefeller's "Radio City" is a kind of small
town that consists of several buildings in the heart of the city. It is an architectural
wonder. It is thoroughly modern art, sober, and geometrical. It is almost entirely
of marble. "Times Square" is a block full of fantastic lights that astounds you with
its brilliance and color. Yesterday I visited with Juan and some friends the Museum
of Modern Art. Juan, who is knowledgeable about art, explained everything to me
marvelously. I learned a lot.

As for entertainment, we will go to the Opera, Ballet and Music Halls, all novelties
for me in this continent. Central Park, which is larger than San Juan, is now deserted,
with leafless trees and frozen lakes. People skate and ride sleds in the park.

Her experiences in New York informed her writing and enabled her to connect
to a public that extended beyond Puerto Rico. At the Museum of Modern Art,
which had moved to its current International Style building at 11 West 53rd
Street in 1939, Burgos would have seen works by Pablo Picasso, including
Guernica (1937), the artist's protest against the bombing of the Basque town
by that name by German planes flying for the Fascist side in the Spanish Civil
War. She might have also seen José Clemente Orozco's *Zapatistas* (1931) and
works by Diego Rivera. Jimenes Grullón greatly admired Mexican art and cul-
ture, dedicating *Luchemos por nuestra América* (We Fight for Our America,
1936) to the Mexican Revolution and the Mexican minister of education, José
Vasconcelos, who wrote the book's preface. Jimenes Grullón highlights Rivera's
art as authentically expressing the reality of Latin America without imitating
Europe. Later that year, the Museum of Modern Art featured *Twenty Centuries
of Mexican Art*, the largest exhibit of its kind at the time in the United States.
The exhibition showcased not only pre-Hispanic art but also works that captured
the horrors of war and the Mexican Revolution. Rosi Braidotti considers muralist
art to be "nomadic art par excellence, and its space is neither public nor private,
neither entertainment nor information—it visits the places in between and it
keeps on moving in space and in time."[28] Rivera's *Kneeling Dancer* (1939) and
Frida Kahlo's *The Two Fridas* (1939) were part of the exhibit.[29]

During this period, Burgos was optimistic about her intellectual and cultural
endeavors, telling her sister on 30 January 1940, "Estoy progresando en mis
relaciones culturales. Venderé libros y daré recitales. La semana que viene
trataré de enviarles algo para la casa [I am making progress with my cultural
relationships. I will sell books and give readings. Next week I will try to send

recital poetico
de la genial poetisa puertorriquena

julia de burgos

LONGWOOD CASINO   VIERNES 10 de MAYO de 1940

867 Longwood Ave.   Bronx, N.Y.   A las 8 P. M.

Figure 4. Flyer for poetry reading by Julia de Burgos, 10 May 1940. Pura Belpré Papers, Archives of the Puerto Rican Diaspora, Center for Puerto Rican Studies, Hunter College, City University of New York.

something for the home]." And in fact, she did make great progress in her literary endeavors and her networking during the first half of 1940. On 24 February, the Master Theater featured a recital of her work. On 7 April, the Association of Puerto Rican Journalists and Writers hosted a public homage to Burgos and Antonio Coll y Vidal.[30] On 10 May, she held a poetry reading in the Bronx. The photograph included in the program shows Burgos holding a copy of *Poema en veinte surcos*.[31] She may have met folklorist, writer, and librarian Pura Belpré at this event. Belpré, like Burgos, was an important member of the city's Puerto Rican community. She made the New York Public Library branch at 115th Street in Harlem a center for the Spanish-speaking community from 1929 on.[32] Burgos was involved in other cultural activities as well, giving her an opportunity to grow and develop as a writer and thinker.[33] Among the Puerto Rican and Latino/a intellectuals she met were Emelí Vélez de Vando and her husband, Erasmo Vando, both of whom were involved in the theatrical community as well as active on behalf of Puerto Rican rights.[34]

Jimenes Grullón left for Cuba in April 1940, and Burgos joined him in Havana the following June. While there, she wrote to family members of her excitement at traveling and exploring the world, expanding her horizons and further developing her craft as a writer. Living in Cuba gave her the opportunity to meet and share her work with Latin American writers and intellectuals such as Juan Bosch, Pablo Neruda, Raúl Roa, Nicolás Guillén, and Spanish émigré Juan Ramón Jiménez. On 27 June, she explained to her sister that one of her reasons for traveling to the island was to develop as a writer.

> Aunque tú no lo creas, yo estoy en Cuba, la hermosa tierra de Martí. ¡Quién hubiese pensado hace tres años que iba yo a recorrer tierras de América! Todo se lo debo a Juan, mi eterno amado. Sabía que al seguirle, me iba a seguir yo misma por todas mis más íntimas ambiciones, y ya ves que se están realizando. . . .
>
> ¡Consuelín, por primera vez he pisado tierra libre de América Indo-hispánica! Es algo grandioso. Invoqué a Martí, y recordé tanta sangre puertorriqueña vertida en Cuba por la causa de la Independencia. ¡Dónde estarán esos hombres hoy! La bandera Cubana, tendida por todos los horizontes, me produjo una enorme sensación de tristeza. Es tan parecida a su hermana, la nuestra. Sin embargo, esa última ondula solamente en unos cuantos corazones puros, que han sabido guardarla del ventarrón fatal que ha arrancado la vergüenza a la mayor parte de nuestro pueblo.[35]

> You will not believe it. I am in Cuba, the beautiful land of Martí. Who would have thought three years ago that today I would travel across the Americas! I owe everything to Juan, my eternal beloved. I knew that in following him, I would be following my innermost ambitions, and as you can see, they are becoming a reality. . . .
>
> Consuelín, for the first time I have set foot on the land of independent Indo-Hispanic America! It is a grandiose thing. I invoked Martí, and I remembered how much Puerto Rican blood was shed in Cuba in the struggle for Independence. Where are these men today? The Cuban flag, waving on all horizons, produced in me a tremendous sense of sadness. It is so like its sister, ours. However, the latter undulates only in a few pure hearts who have managed to keep her safe from the fatal gale that has destroyed the pride of most of our people.

Burgos was in the process of developing a hemispheric identity based on José Martí's notions of *nuestra América* (our America), and Havana played an important role in that process. She sought to make connections and establish alliances beyond Puerto Rico on behalf of the island's independence. Her close friendship with Bosch during those years may have influenced her ideas. Bosch, along with Jimenes Grullón and others, was in Havana organizing the Dominican exile community into a revolutionary party that would fight the Trujillo regime and restore peace to the country, efforts that led to the creation of the Dominican Revolutionary Party in 1942.[36]

Bosch, a Dominican writer, intellectual, and revolutionary, was living in exile at the time and would become one of his country's most influential twentieth-century political figures.[37] According to Lorgia García Peña, Bosch's creative writing and political thought featured "a distinctive style that sought to challenge the margins of the nation and the rhetoric of oppression imposed by the various U.S. military occupations of the twentieth century and the Trujillo regime." Influenced by the ideas of unity and solidarity put forth by nineteenth-century ideologists Eugenio María de Hostos and José Martí, Bosch was "one of the first thinkers to articulate and promote the creation of a transnational *dominicanidad* that could exist outside the geographical borders of the nation." He did so by believing in alliances among Dominicans living abroad and by "allowing the voices of the diaspora to insert themselves in the national dialogue, interpellating history and complicating notions of national frontiers."[38] These ideas resonate with Burgos's work.

In 1994, Bosch recalled the encounter between Neruda and Burgos:

> He met her at my house, that's where he met her, at 107 Joveyar. Neruda came there to lunch with me. Jimenes Grullón was there, and Julia, naturally. Nicolás Guillén brought him over, since it was Nicolás Guillén who had told me that Neruda wanted to meet me. So I invited him to lunch, him and Neruda. . . . That is when he met Julia, when he first knew Julia's poetry. I had asked Julia to copy some of her verses so that he could read them. Neruda read them. The next day he had a reading in Havana, at the Municipal Hall. I went to the recital, so did Julia and Jimenes Grullón—the three of us went, and there I asked him what he had thought of Julia's verses; and he said that Julia was called to be one of the greatest poets of the Americas.[39]

Roa, a Cuban intellectual, diplomat, and professor, was a leftist who was imprisoned in 1931 for his antigovernment activities and who participated in the 1933 strike that ousted Gerardo Machado.[40] In a July 1940 letter to Consuelo, Julia described meeting Roa:

> Él está encantado con mi obra, y me llama superior a la Ibarbourou. Yo sabía que saliendo de Puerto Rico el mundo cambiaría para mí. Juan Bosch opina lo mismo que Roa, y dondequiera se me presenta como la mejor poetisa de las Antillas. Yo estoy por creerlo, ¡ja, ja! En verdad cada día me siento más satisfecha de mi obra y descubro nuevas fuerzas en mí. Me alegra por Puerto Rico, pues doquiera que vaya seré puertorriqueña.

> He is pleased with my work, and says that it is superior to Ibarbourou's. I knew that by leaving Puerto Rico, the world would change for me. Juan Bosch agrees with Roa and wherever I go I am introduced as the best poet of the Antilles. I am about to believe it, ha, ha! Truthfully, every day I feel more satisfied with my work and I discover new resolve within. This is also a victory for Puerto Rico, because wherever I go, I will always be Puerto Rican.

Although Burgos's relationship with Jimenes Grullón did assist her in meeting other Latin American intellectuals outside of Puerto Rico, Bosch remembered that Jimenes Grullón did not help Burgos advance her career as much as he could have and possibly even hindered and discouraged her ambitions as a poet. According to Bosch, Burgos never became one of the greatest poets of the Americas, as Neruda and Lloréns Torres had predicted, "for one simple reason: because she didn't publish, she didn't publish. Not even Jimenes Grullón got interested in that, in her publishing. He never made any effort to make Julia's verses known in Cuba. He did nothing; that was probably a part of his jealous nature."[41]

As a Caribbean writer and intellectual, Bosch emphasized the importance of leaving home and publishing abroad. Reminded that Burgos had published her work in Puerto Rico, Bosch clarified,

> Yes, but Puerto Rico is a very limited space from that point of view. The Puerto Rican intellectual that never left the island never became known, like the Dominican; that's why Julia never became known. But Julia had those exceptional qualities, and one has to realize that this was forty-five years ago, that is, when Gabriela Mistral was the fashion as a woman poet. Gabriela Mistral's poetry is a poetry closely bound to the poetic formulas of the time, its beauty notwithstanding, because she did it with great beauty, but Julia did not allow herself to be influenced by her.[42]

In *Julia de Burgos: La canción y el silencio* (Julia de Burgos: The Song and the Silence), Ivette López Jiménez explores Burgos's writing in the context of contemporary Latin American women writers Mistral, Delmira Agustini, and Alfonsina Storni, all of whom faced such challenges as alienation, isolation, extreme poverty, and oppression in a society that undermined women artists and intellectuals.[43] Burgos's words in a 27 October 1940 letter to her sister express the frustration she felt as she reached for her goals: "Ya te lo he dicho, mi vida es un continuo sube y baja, inexorablemente mi ambición de altura me lleva al sueño, para atropellarlo mi destino contra la realidad [As I said, my life is a continuous rise and fall. My high ambition inexorably leads me to dream, only to find it shattered against reality]."

Gender Migration: Home as a Site of Resistance and Conflict

Burgos had a conflicted relationship with her native island. She loved it and always supported its independence, but she also was frustrated with Puerto Rico's conservative society. Family poverty had required her to work hard and make sacrifices, and even her relationship with Jimenes Grullón was not easy. Although home and family remained sites of strength and resistance, Burgos was not interested in returning. She recounted the pain, hurt, and resentment she felt toward those on the island who criticized, judged, and condemned her life choices. In July 1940, when Burgos was living in Havana with Jimenes Grullón, she received the literature prize from the Instituto de Literatura Puertorriqueña for *Canción de la verdad sencilla.*[44] On 17 July, she told her sister of her disbelief at winning the award:

> En verdad Consuelín, esa ha sido la sorpresa más grande de mi vida. . . . Te aseguro que había perdido todas las esperanzas, máximo cuando me encontraba ausente. Además, desde la innumerable fila de enemigos gratuitos en todos los órdenes que dejé en casa, nunca pensé que me fuera a hacer justicia.

> Consuelín, this has really been the biggest surprise of my life. . . . I assure you I had lost all hope, especially now that I find myself absent. Moreover, because of the countless enemies on all fronts that I left at home, I never thought I would be judged fairly.

She was amazed that the judges had looked past her personal life and judged her poetry objectively. Regarding the award, she wrote, "nadie es profeta en su tierra [no one is a prophet in their homeland]," revealing the conflicted emotions she felt toward her homeland. Edward Said describes the condition of exile as "strangely compelling to think about but terrible to experience. It is the unhealable rift forced between a human being and a native place, between the self and its true home: its essential sadness can never be surmounted."[45]

Burgos found the island's poverty and hunger less painful than its hurtful gossip. On 9 July 1940, she wrote to Consuelo,

> No quisiera ir a Puerto Rico por muchos motivos de índole moral, que tú bien conoces. No quiero encontrarme con ciertas personas a quienes he tronchado de mi existencia, gracias a la distancia. De volver a encontrarlas surgirían los viejos rencores y agrias actitudes mentales, y quisiera conservar mi vida limpia de toda sombra pasada.

> I do not want to return to Puerto Rico because it will affect my morale, as you well know. I do not want to cross paths with some of those people who I have pruned from my life, thanks to the distance. Encountering them again, old resentments would emerge and I would once again have to contend with their bitter mental attitudes. I want to keep my life free of past shadows.

She explained further on 12 September,

> Me emocionó tu cartita pues me recordó de mis días de práctica en la Universidad. Aquellos días llenos de ilusión que ya no volverán nunca, días solamente heridos por el hambre y la miseria, pero no por la calumnia y la crueldad.

> I was thrilled because your note reminded me of my practicum days at the university. Those days were filled with dreams that will never return, happy days that were pierced only by hunger and misery, but not by calumny and cruelty.

Social control over women's sexuality occurred in ways that resembled the control of sexual minorities—gossip and rumor. La Fountain-Stokes notes that displacement of sexual minorities often occurs because of "social intolerance, discrimination, harassment, and persecution."[46] Many of the early studies on Burgos paint her decision to leave the island as the fulfillment of a self-destructive impulse.[47] However, her letters reveal her conscious decision to leave behind the island's condemnation and exclusion, though that decision brought her sadness. On 16 December 1940, she wrote,

> No quiero ir a Puerto Rico. Cada día me aleja más de su superficie para encontrarme en su entraña, en lo más hondo de su corazón, en su bendita tierra donde hoy descansa nuestra Santa con nuestras almas apretadas de eterno amor. Es lo único por lo cual algún día me decida volver en viaje de pájaro a mi patria: a besar la tierra que la guarda y a llorar sobre ella mis lágrimas más tiernas. Por lo demás, espero verlos a todos en el extranjero.

> I do not want to go to Puerto Rico. Every day I find myself farther away from her shores, only to find myself deep within her womb, in the depth of her heart, in this holy land where the soul of our Saint [their mother] now rests eternal. If I decide to return one day, it will be only to kiss the earth that surrounds her and water it with my tender tears. Otherwise, I hope to see you abroad.

While Burgos and Jimenes Grullón were passionately attracted to each other, the dissolution of their relationship was equally heated. At the beginning of 1941, Jimenes Grullón's parents traveled to Cuba from the Dominican Republic to visit their son. It is unclear whether they knew beforehand that Burgos had joined him in Havana, but while there, they renewed their pressure on him to end the relationship. Burgos at first remained optimistic that the relationship would prevail, writing to her sister on 7 January,

> He escrito los poemas más trágicos de mi vida, y he tenido días negros en los que he pensado hasta en el suicidio. Los padres . . . no le han hablado todavía de mí, pero tiran puyitas a los amigos . . . Pero estoy triunfando. Ellos quedan todavía en La Habana, y yo me voy al lado de Juan.

> I have written the most tragic poems of my life, and I have had dark days when I contemplated suicide. His parents . . . have not yet spoken of me, but they make scathing comments to our friends. . . . But I'm winning. They are still in Havana, and I'll leave with Juan.

Burgos and Jimenes Grullón subsequently traveled to Santiago de Cuba, on the southeastern part of the island, and he apparently placed her in a Catholic boardinghouse for single women. Their relationship soon deteriorated, and on 14 July, she wrote to her sister,

Hago una vida más puritana que la más puritana de las momias femeninas. Paso el día cosiendo, oyendo la radio y hablando con las damas, que me rodean en la casa de huéspedes; la noche, sentada rígidamente en una reunión formal, comentando las inaptitudes de las sirvientas, manteniendo mi posición de *"esposa"* prejuiciada y mojigata; y en cualquier momento inesperado, por la calle, Juan se encuentra con un amigo de la familia, y me presenta como *amiga*. ¡Qué te parece Consuelín! Te juro que a veces es horrible. ¡Y tan sola que me siento, tan indefensa, sin atreverme a dar un paso! Adoro a Juan; él me adora a su manera, pensando en primer lugar en su familia, que le ha dicho que se suicidará si se casa conmigo.

I live a more puritanical life than the most puritanical of female mummies. I spend the day sewing, listening to the radio, and talking to the ladies around me in the guest house. At night, we sit rigidly in a formal meeting room, commenting on the unsuitability of the servants. I play the role of the prudish "wife" and if at any unexpected moment walking down the street, Juan meets a family friend, he introduces me as a *friend*. Imagine it, Consuelín! I swear sometimes it's horrible. And I feel so alone, so helpless, not daring to take a step! I love Juan, and he loves me in his own way, always thinking first of his family, who tell him that marrying me would be suicide.

Burgos was keenly aware of Jimenes Grullón's weaknesses and limitations. Although he was a public champion for truth, freedom, and equality who wrote about the importance of social justice, he did not uphold those values in his personal life. Burgos understood her precarious position, and after returning to the Cuban capital, she sought to protect herself by enrolling once again in courses at the University of Havana. On 22 April 1942, she told Consuelo,

De todo hemos hablado, y he recibido golpes tremendos, que nunca esperé. Mi único refugio ahora es el estudio. A él me he aferrado con verdadera fiebre. Ante una negación social, hija de lo ficticio, una afirmación intelectual, hija de la valoración propia. Seré doctora, Consuelito, en todas las carreras que me he propuesto terminar. Mis diplomas serán tremendas bofetadas, para los eternos perseguidores. En ellos, en su obtención, solamente estaré yo, mis facultades innatas, más nobles y aristócratas que las herencias huecas.

We talked about everything, and I received tremendous blows that I never expected. My only haven now is to study. I will cling to it as my only refuge. Faced with social denial, the fictitious daughter, I will seek intellectual validation, the true daughter of self-worth. I'll be a doctor, Consuelito, in every field that I set out to master. My diplomas will be a tremendous blow to those who eternally persecute me. I will collect these degrees using my own innate powers. They will prove to be more noble and worthy than empty inheritances.

Burgos believed that education would not only improve her social standing and gain her respect but also provide her with greater opportunities and more financial stability. Jimenes Grullón short-circuited her plan less than two months later when he informed her that she would be returning to New York City—alone. On 22 June, Burgos wrote to her sister,

> El viernes a las 12:00 llegó Juan del interior de Cuba con el dulce regalo de un pasaje para el avión de las 4:00 pm. No tenía nada arreglado, y a esa hora tuve que comenzar a separarlo todo y a llevarme los 55 libros que solo pude cargar por avión. Fue horrible todo, hasta esta triste llegada, sin nadie que me esperara en la estación, con 48 horas de sueño y tenerme que lanzar a buscar un cuarto y con solo cinco míseros pesos para alquilarlo y comenzar a comer. Juan no me dejó ni siquiera esperar tu carta. Encontró una oportunidad para lavarse las manos como Pilatos, y heme aquí, profundamente sola, desecha y asombrada, mucho peor que cuando me encontró. Con sueño y hambre me tiré a la calle a buscar amigos antiguos, pero todos se han ido.

> On Friday at 12:00, Juan returned from the interior region of Cuba with the sweet gift of a plane ticket for the 4:00 pm flight. I was not given time to prepare for this trip. At that moment, I began sorting through my things and selected 55 books, which is all that I was allowed to carry on the plane. It was horrible. I arrived alone with no one to greet me at the station not having slept in 48 hours. At that hour, I had to look for a boarding room and I only had five miserable dollars with which to rent it and find something to eat. Juan did not even let me wait for your letter. He washed his hands of me like Pilate, and here I am, deeply alone, dejected and stunned. I am worse off than when he found me. I was tired and hungry, so I set out to the street in search of old friends, but they are all gone.

Burgos had again been exiled.

As she found her bearings in New York, she sought to focus on her goals and dreams and to deal with her pain. On 12 July 1942, she wrote to her sister,

> Él rebajó con rencores pequeños y desbordada y brutal pasión, aquello tan enorme. El profundo dolor se ha convertido en indignación. No con él, sino con el hombre mismo. Para mí no existe él, sino la humanidad. ¡Y qué pobre es!
>
> Le escribí un profundo, desgarrador, pero inaplazable adiós. Y por veinte días, ya libre, volví a ser yo. . . . Y aquí estoy, llorando no de dolor, sino de decepción.

> He debased everything that we shared with small-mindedness and petty resentments. The deep pain I felt has become indignation. Not with him, but with all of humanity. For me, he does not exist, it is mankind. And how poor it is!
>
> I wrote a deep, wrenching, but urgent good-bye. And free of him for twenty days now, I became myself. . . . And here I am crying not because of pain, but because of disappointment.

Energy and vitality renewed, Burgos integrated herself into New York's Puerto Rican community, lending her voice to the struggle for social justice for Latino/as, Latin Americans, and African Americans in Gotham.

The Sea and Death as Escape
Routes in *El mar y tú*

El mar y tú marks the climax of Burgos's nomadic subject. Images of water figure prominently in these poems, creating avenues for escape from the rigid social norms that attempted to contain her and again demonstrating that the female speaker in her work cannot be restricted. *Poema en veinte surcos* highlights imagery of walking, as the nomadic subject creates new paths and avenues. In *Canción de la verdad sencilla*, the nomadic subject moves throughout the cosmos in flights that often culminate in exuberant union with the lover or nature. In Burgos's final book, the sea becomes the open space without borders where the speaker is freed from all restrictions. In addition, the sea imagery mixes with death, offering a final escape. Many of the poems follow a pattern of loss and abjection followed by renewal and transformation. According to Mercedes López-Baralt, *El mar y tú* is intensely aligned with *vanguardia* currents and is surrealist, with strong echoes of Neruda.[48] The *vanguardias* connection is felt strongly in the quest for "new levels of consciousness, through the desired primary experience of created languages."[49] The *vanguardias* sought to reinvigorate language by returning to linguistic beginnings: "These diverse imaginings of unmediated verbal worlds posit a universe with no language at all as the site for linguistic creation. Verbal activity in these mute worlds ranges from a preverbal chaos of expression without form to absolute silence. In any case, language appears to emerge from nothingness, but the closer to the original void, the greater the language's power."[50] The sea is a primeval chaos, offering the possibility of emergence out of the void.

The paths and waterways that Burgos created in her work diverge from ordinary routes and roads. They have a nomadic quality to them. Gilles Deleuze and Félix Guattari distinguish between customary paths and nomadic trajectories. Customary roads and trails assign people to closed spaces—in other words, they follow routes that take travelers to "sedentary space" that is "striated, by walls, enclosures, and roads between enclosures." The nomadic trajectory, conversely, distributes people into open spaces that are indefinite, smooth, "marked only by 'traits' that are effaced and displaced with the trajectory."[51] Furthermore, nomads transform the open spaces they visit and inhabit.

In *El mar y tú*, the nomadic subject's paths lead to the sea, a creative and dynamic open space. In "Naufragio" (Lost at Sea), the nomad asks, "¿Que mi camino es mío? / ¡Sí todos los caminos son míos, / todos los que comienzan en el pecho de Dios! [Is my route my own? / Yes, all routes are mine, all those that emerge from God's bosom!]."[52] In "Víctima de luz" (Victim of Light), the nomadic subject urges others to leave behind all paths: "Tienes que olvidar sendas / y disponerte a manejar el viento [You must abandon the road / and ride the wind]" (29). The wind, like the sea, is open space that cannot be contained. In the final stanza of "Mi senda es el espacio" (My Path Is the Cosmos), the nomadic subject transforms the road through which it moves: "Recorrerme es huirse de todos los senderos . . . / Soy el desequilibrio danzante de los astros [To map my body is to forsake all roads . . . / I am erratic dancing stars]" (34). The dialogic structure of the poems leads the reader to ask who the nomadic subject's interlocutor is.

As in much of Burgos's poetry, she is often speaking to the self. Critics have typically read the poems collected in *El mar y tú* as giving insight into her mental state during and after the dissolution of her relationship with Jimenes Grullón. However, Luz María Umpierre reads the open space of the sea in this book as a site of creativity, imagination, and renewal. The sea is the "poetic *locus*" of these poems, but neither the "tú" nor the sea should be read as a symbol of the beloved man; rather, they are "the pleasure of a no less erotic act, that of writing."[53] In these poems, the woman poet sets out to protect her ability to create. The quest is an ontological search that ultimately ends in a desire for death when the poet loses her ability to write and create.

The nomad inhabits and occupies smooth spaces. In "Letanía del mar" (Litany of the Sea), the subject metaphorically identifies with the sea: "Mar mío / mar profundo que comienzas en mí [My sea / deep well that begins in me]" (64). In this poem, the trajectory begins with an identification between the speaker and the sea that then expands into the universe. The sea is a volatile and tumultuous space where eroticism and death, though opposites, merge. In this text as in others by Burgos, the sea is the space of amplitude, a direct contrast to Antonio S. Pedreira's *Insularismo*, which describes the sea as separating and isolating Puerto Rico from the rest of the world: "El cinturón de mar que nos crea y nos oprime va cerrando cada vez más el espectáculo universal y opera en nosotros un angostamiento de la visión estimativa [The sea surrounds us like a belt, oppressively closing in on us, shutting out the universal spectacle and narrowing our vision]."[54] Yet for Burgos, these open spaces are sites of creativity, places where poems are born. In contrast to Pedreira's image of the sea, "Poema con la tonada última" (Poem with the Last Tune), depicts becoming one with the sea as a way to escape the roots that bind the speaker "a deshacerme en olas más altas que los pájaros / a quitarme caminos que ya andaban en mí como raíces [undo myself in waves that soar higher than birds / release myself from paths that moved within me like roots]" (65). Metaphorically becoming one with the sea engenders transformations and reincarnations.

The multiple incarnations of the body in both *Canción de la verdad sencilla* and *El mar y tú* are manifestations of the nomad. Braidotti notes that the nomadic body is "multifunctional and complex, as a transformer of flows and

energies, affects, desires, and imaginings. . . . [I]t is a threshold of transforma-
tions."[55] The ultimate transformation in *El mar y tú* is from life to death, as
illustrated by the final poem, "Poema para mi muerte" (Poem for My Death),
in which death is a welcome escape from societal demands and expectations,
embodying the final expression of freedom.

> Que nadie me profane la muerte con sollozos,
> ni me arropen por siempre con inocente tierra;
> que en el libre momento me dejen libremente
> disponer de la única libertad del planeta.
>
> ¡Con qué fiera alegría comenzarán mis huesos
> a buscar ventanitas por la carne morena
> y yo, dándome, dándome, feroz y libremente
> a la intemperie y sola rompiéndome cadenas! (91)

> Let none profane my dying with their weeping,
> nor dress me forever in the plain, good earth;
> in that unfettered moment let me freely
> use the planet's only freedom.
>
> With what ferocious joy will my bones start
> to look for air holes in the russet flesh
> while I, yielding, ferally and freely
> to the elements break, all alone, my chains![56]

Subsequent stanzas describe how, in death, she returns to the earth and fer-
tilizes the soil, from which a flower may grow, highlighting the life cycle and
reincarnation.

> ¿Quién podrá detenerme con ensueños inútiles
> cuando mi alma comience a cumplir su tarea,
> haciendo de mis sueños un amasijo fértil
> para el frágil gusano que tocará a mi puerta?
>
> Cada vez más pequeña mi pequeñez rendida,
> cada instante más grande y más simple la entrega;
> mi pecho quizás ruede a iniciar un capullo,
> acaso irán mis labios a nutrir azucenas.
>
> ¿Cómo habré de llamarme cuando sólo me quede
> recordarme, en la roca de una isla desierta?
> Un clavel interpuesto entre el viento y mi sombra,
> hijo mío y de la muerte, me llamarán poeta. (91–92)

Who will detain me with futile fantasies
Once my soul begins on fulfilling its task,
making of all my dreams a savory dough
for the frail worm will come knocking at my door?

My weary smallness growing smaller still,
greater by the second and simpler my surrender;
perhaps, turning, my chest will start budding a flower,
my lips possibly become a nourishment for lilies.

What shall I be called when all remains of me
is a memory, upon a rock of a deserted isle?
A carnation wedged between the wind and my own shadow,
death's child and my own, I will be known as poet.

The final line captures Burgos's greatest ambition. Becoming a world-renowned poet was her guiding beacon, keeping her going through her most difficult moments.

Burgos's second and third volumes of poetry and letters to her sister reveal her conflicted relationship to Puerto Rico as well as notions of home that allow us to read her as a figure of sexile. Despite her patriotism, home and nation became limiting, restrictive, and repressive spaces. She anticipated the subsequent theorization of home as a conflicted space for women of color by feminist theorists such as Cherríe Moraga, Gloria Anzaldúa, bell hooks, and Chandra Mohanty. Women of color exist outside of the national imaginary and frequently live at odds with prescribed notions of womanhood that leave them little room to assert themselves as women, writers, and intellectuals. In this vein, Burgos attempted to create a home and a life for herself beyond the boundaries of the nation. Martínez-San Miguel argues that literary figures of sexile engender diasporic identities that are queer and exist in excess of the national imaginary in the insular Caribbean.[57] She notes that in Pedro Juan Soto's *Spiks*, sexile becomes a point of departure for representation of life in the metropolis, complicating official conceptualizations of massive migration to the United States as a result of the island's modernization. The remainder of this book focuses on the development of Burgos's nomadic subject in her writing from New York and how her nomadic and queer subject exceeds the boundaries of her work, influencing diasporic writers and artists such as Manuel Ramos Otero, Luz María Umpierre, Chiqui Vicioso, and Mariposa and engendering diasporic identities that exist in excess of the insular nation.

3

MÁS ALLÁ DEL MAR

Journalism as Puerto Rican Cultural and Political Transnational Practice

Julia de Burgos is part of the cultural fabric of Puerto Ricans both on the island and in New York. She is recognized primarily for her poetry and for what her short life has come to symbolize for so many people. Yet her writing for the Spanish-language newspaper *Pueblos Hispanos* in New York during the 1940s has received little critical attention. Burgos participated actively in the cultural, political, and social life of the Puerto Rican *colonia* in New York City, where she lived mostly in East Harlem's El Barrio. This chapter contributes to the understanding of how New York's early Puerto Rican community used journalism and newspapers as a form of cultural and political transnational practice.

Puerto Ricans have been migrating to the United States in increasing numbers since 1898. By the 1940s and 1950s, many people left the island in search of work and higher pay in the expanding U.S. economy. Travel was facilitated not only by developments in transportation but also by Puerto Rican government support for emigration as a solution to the island's unemployment and overpopulation problems.[1] In 1947, the Migration Office of Puerto Rico (changed in 1951 to the Migration Division of Puerto Rico's Department of Labor), was created. The agency facilitated work agreements between migrants and farming associations along the eastern seaboard of the United States.

New York was a favored destination for these migrants, and the Puerto Rican *colonia* there developed dense social ties that helped ideas, people, money, and goods circulate between the island and the city. Acknowledging the island's ambiguous political relationship with the United States, Jorge Duany uses the term *transnational colonial migration* to describe the Puerto Rican diaspora in the United States. This approach allows for an understanding of Puerto Rico as "a nation, an imagined community with its own territory, history, language, and culture," yet acknowledges that the island "lacks a sovereign state" and an independent government that "represents the population of that territory."[2] As colonial migrants, Puerto Ricans used the press to demand recognition as full U.S. citizens and to remain involved in politics on the island.

As early as the nineteenth century, editors and publishers of the Spanish-language press in New York acted as arbiters of culture between Latin America and the United States. As cultural mediators, they bridged linguistic and cultural gaps between Anglo and Hispanic cultures, defended Spanish speakers, trained their readers in "high culture," and shaped as well as reflected readers' tastes. These cultural mediators fostered a cosmopolitan identity among global Spanish speakers. Kirsten Silva Gruesz and Rodrigo Lazo highlight the significance of trans-American writing and the multilingual press in the United States, written mostly by the light-skinned Creole elites of the nineteenth century. Gruesz describes the earlier generations of editors and writers as "ambassadors."[3] With few exceptions, these statesmen and politicians did not see the dangers of imitating and extending U.S. racial hierarchies across Latin America. José Martí and his generation would be the first to take a pro-independence, anti-annexation, and antiracist stand against U.S. imperial modernity and bourgeois Anglo norms. In Laura Lomas's view, Martí's readings move beyond the goal of equal rights within U.S. boundaries and fall within the tradition of economic migrants and noncitizen workers who are American (broadly defined). She uses the nomadic and unsettling term *migrant* to refer to residents who come to the United States to protect their interests in the South and to seek protections and rights in the place where they live and work.[4]

The Spanish-language press that developed in the 1880s, beginning with Martí and those following in this tradition, opposed the pressures to assimilate to bourgeois Anglo cultural norms. This opposition took several forms, among them ideologies of Hispanism, a project of Hispanization through imposed language, customs, and beliefs beginning with the imperial expansion into the so-called New World. It operated as a political, representational, and epistemological paradigm throughout the development of Spanish America's and Spain's cultural histories from the colonial period to the consolidation of nation-states and in the context of globalization.[5] The development of Hispanism reached one of its most productive stages during the 1930s and 1940s, when the Spanish Civil War drove many scholars and intellectuals into exile in Latin America and metropolitan centers such as New York. As a concept, Hispanism was fraught with ideological tensions, some of them linked to fascism and others concerned with the cultural and spiritual mission of spreading Hispanic culture to North and Latin America as a way to counter U.S. imperial modernity. Rooted in the Spanish language, Hispanism has an assimilationist impulse, as it homogenizes Latin American countries and silences their linguistic, cultural, and racial diversity. It also reinforces cultural and linguistic ties between postcolonial Latin American countries and Spain. As Sebastiaan Faber notes, Hispanism "ends up repressing or erasing most forms of internal otherness" as it attempts to vindicate cultural differences relative to the Anglo cultural norms of the North; it encodes an "erasure of difference in the name of difference." Faber concludes that Hispanism "should be rejected precisely because it *assimilates* a reality whose main characteristic is its heterogeneity."[6]

New York City's numerous Spanish-language newspapers used Hispanism as a bulwark against the pressures to assimilate.[7] These publications represented various political and social interests, demanded rights and protections for Spanish speakers in the United States, and attempted to influence and defend the interests of writers and editors in their home countries. *Gráfico* (1927–31), for example, promoted unity among Spanish-speaking New Yorkers as well as transnational connections with Latin America, as the mission statement published in its 27 February 1927 issue indicates:

> El constante aumento de la colonia española e iberoamericana nos ha impelido a editar este semanario que viene a cooperar a la defensa de todos los que forman la gran familia hispana. Haremos una labor tendente a buscar la mayor compenetración y bienestar de los que ausentes de la patria amada debemos en suelo extraño agruparnos bajo una sola bandera: la de la fraternidad.

> The constant growth of the Spanish and Spanish American colony has led us to publish this weekly that comes to participate in the defense of all those who make up the grand Hispanic family. We shall make an effort to further the greatest advancement and well being of us, who far from our beloved homelands, must join together on foreign soil under only one banner: that of brotherhood.[8]

The paper's mission statement clearly promotes Hispanism, and the defense of both the Spanish and South American communities in New York, whose interests were quite different. With a focus on brotherhood, the paper also ignores gender difference. However, the paper published work by Afro–Puerto Rican Jesús Colón and feminist Clotilde Betances Jaeger that challenged this orientation.[9] Other articles and columns demonstrated an incisive critique of the racialization that Latin Americans and Spanish speakers from the Caribbean experienced as they migrated north. *Gráfico*'s first editor was an Afro-Cuban, Alberto O'Farrill, who also served as the paper's chief cartoonist. He developed a mulatto immigrant character, Ofa, and used him as a first-person narrator whose main preoccupation was finding work and keeping it in the big city. Colón began his career as a writer and political activist as a *cronista* (editorial columnist) for *Gráfico* before moving on to write for *Pueblos Hispanos* and the *Daily Worker*. He authored insightful critiques of U.S. and Puerto Rican racism, writing in English by the mid-1950s. His articles and those of other contributors to *Gráfico* do not have an investment in whiteness, as the term *Hispanism* suggests.[10]

Figure 5. Jesús Colón, ca. 1973. Jesús Colón Papers, Archives of the Puerto Rican Diaspora, Center for Puerto Rican Studies, Hunter College, City University of New York.

In addition to promoting Hispanism as a way to unite the *colonia* in New York, writers and editors used the Hispanophone press to demand their rights and challenge the notions of "foreignness" that shrouded migrants from Latin America and other parts of the global South as well as their children. When mainstream newspapers depicted the members of the Puerto Rican *colonia* as criminals, as lazy, and as incapable of self-determination, the Spanish-language press defended the community. This sense of foreignness was a part of the racialization process Latino/as experienced based on race, language, and culture. The editors of *Gráfico* published an English-language editorial on 7 August 1927 in which they pointed out that their critics "forget that the citizens residing in the Harlem vicinity enjoy the prerogatives and privileges that American citizenship brings. We are almost all originally from Puerto Rico and the rest of us are naturalized citizens." By publishing the piece in English, the editor indicated that the audience was the larger surrounding community. Yet the editorial takes an assimilationist tone, arguing that the Italian and Irish immigrants who had previously arrived in Harlem were "no better than [the Puerto Rican migrants] before learning the customs and ways of this country." This wording suggests that assimilation is desirable and that after Puerto Ricans become Americanized, they will also become part of the melting pot. The editors did not conceptualize the growing members of the Puerto Rican *colonia* as racialized, minoritized, and marginalized because of their colonial migrant status.[11] In 1927, the editors of *Gráfico* did not see—or chose not to see—the differences between Puerto Ricans as colonial migrants and their Italian and Irish neighbors. A decade and a half later, the editors of *Pueblos Hispanos* had a different understanding of their position in the U.S. cultural and political landscape.

In addition to concerns about race and citizenship rights, Spanish-language newspapers discussed ideas about Hispanic women's gender roles and feminism. Viewing women as the heart of the family and the community and as preservers of the home culture and language, the predominantly male *cronistas*, writers, and editors used their influence to tighten the reins on Hispanic women. They were concerned about the influence American flappers, often characterized as having loose morals, might have on Hispanic women.[12]

Puerto Rican women contributed to the Spanish-language press nearly a decade before Burgos's arrival in New York. In 1933, Josefina (Pepina) Silva de Cintrón founded *Artes y Letras* in association with the Grupo Cultural Cervantes, made up mostly of Puerto Rican actors and writers. The monthly cultural magazine catered to the middle-class Hispanic bourgeoisie, cultivating women readers who were involved in philanthropic and cultural undertakings, and was distributed throughout Latin America and the Caribbean. Among the women who published essays, short stories, and poems in *Artes y Letras* were Alfonsina Storni, Gabriela Mistral, Carmen Alicia Cadilla, Martha Lomar, Concha Meléndez, and Isabel Cuchí Coll. Virginia Sánchez Korrol notes that the educated Puerto Rican women who migrated to New York prior to 1930 chose to "civilize rather than liberate their working class sisters." They clung to their domestic roles, which, Sánchez Korrol argues, "inhibited the spread of anything other than the most basic feminist consciousness." The transnational ties these women maintained perpetuated the ideas of patriarchy in the new environment as they concentrated on "influencing the transfer of a bourgeois Puerto Rican family model to the new environment."[13]

Other papers took much more mainstream positions. *La Prensa*, for example, was founded in 1913 by José Campubrí to serve Manhattan's Spanish and Cuban immigrant communities; it adapted to the subsequent waves of Latin American and Caribbean arrivals to the city. Because *La Prensa* was conceived as a business enterprise, it was less radical than other publications: rather than favoring Puerto Rican independence, the paper backed Luis Muñoz Marín and commonwealth status for the island. The paper's politically moderate views and ability to adapt to the communities arriving in the city may help account for its longevity (it was published until 1962, when it merged with *El Diario de Nueva York*).[14]

Pueblos Hispanos (1943–44) forged another alternative.[15] Like other Hispano-phone papers of the time, it sought to build a sense of solidarity with the broader imagined community of Spanish speakers in both New York and Latin America. Through its director, Juan Antonio Corretjer, the paper was affiliated with both the Puerto Rican Nationalist Party and the Communist Party of America (at the time the only U.S. party that supported the island's independence). The idea for the paper was birthed in the Atlanta Federal Penitentiary, where Pedro Albizu

Campos, Corretjer, and other leaders of the Puerto Rican Nationalist Party were imprisoned for sedition and conspiring to overthrow the U.S. government in Puerto Rico.[16] While in prison, Albizu Campos and Corretjer met Earl Browder, the Communist Party's candidate in the 1940 presidential election, who had been imprisoned after being found guilty of passport irregularities. The paper adopted the Communist Party's antiwar position, continued the struggle for Puerto Rican independence, and supported liberation movements across Latin America as part of an agreement among Albizu Campos, Browder, and Vito Marcantonio, a left-wing congressman from New York. Given the multiple and at times seemingly conflicting agendas of those involved, getting the paper off the ground appeared to be an insurmountable challenge until Corretjer was released from prison and met Consuelo Lee Tapia in 1942 in New York.[17]

On the surface, Lee Tapia appeared to be an unlikely participant in the paper's development. The granddaughter of an important literary figure, Alejandro Tapia y Rivera, she was born into a prominent Puerto Rican capitalist family. She was moved by the island's poverty during the 1930s, the trial and conviction of Puerto Rican nationalist leaders, and the Ponce Massacre, influencing her decision to join the Puerto Rican Communist Party in 1937. In New York, she sought out the Communist Party's offices and began volunteering there. Initially treated with distrust because of her social class, she soon became an integral element of the party, working with Spanish-speaking communities abroad. That work led her to anti-Franco and antifascist groups. Working alongside Corretjer, whom she married in 1945, Lee Tapia was instrumental in getting the paper started. Corretjer assumed the position of director, while she served as the paper's administrator. Her political activities subsequently turned away from the international Spanish-speaking communities to the Puerto Rican *colonia* in New York and Puerto Rico. *Pueblos Hispanos* appeared weekly for twenty months before ceasing publication. The couple then departed for Cuba.[18]

Julia de Burgos knew Corretjer through her involvement in the Puerto Rican nationalist movement between 1936 and 1939, and she joined the staff of the paper at its inception, serving as the art and culture editor and a regular contributor. In *Pueblos Hispanos*, Burgos published poetry and essays supporting socialist causes. Her writings also critiqued the United States for failing to live up to its democratic ideals, supported Puerto Rican independence, and kept New York's Spanish-speaking community tied to Latin America by publishing news from that region. Her essays promoted the integration of Latin Americans, Caribbean immigrants, and African Americans into New York City. In contrast to the women writing for *Artes y Letras*, Burgos had already rejected Puerto Rican notions of bourgeois domesticity before leaving the island. Developing transnational connections with her home island through the paper allowed her the space to create more flexible and fluid notions of Puerto Rican identity.

Pueblos Hispanos: News from Latin America

Pueblos Hispanos promoted pan-Hispanism, the integration of Latin American countries, and socialist causes throughout the world, with a focus on Latin American countries such as Peru, Ecuador, Brazil, and Mexico. The paper offered detailed coverage of the politics of Puerto Rico and the Puerto Rican *colonia* while encouraging solidarity in the struggle for freedom and justice in countries across Latin America. In sharing news from Latin America and specifically Puerto Rico, the paper kept Spanish-speaking residents of New York City informed, establishing transnational connections as they tried to influence local politics.

The paper's socialist mission and communist affiliations provided it with an international framework that facilitated the development of transnational ties. The ninth point of the paper's mission, published on the first page of every issue, was "la unidad sindical en las Américas [labor union unity throughout the Americas]." The paper's association with the International Labour Organization and similar groups facilitated the publication and circulation of news from Latin America. For example, on 6 June 1944 (coincidentally, D-Day), the *Pueblos Hispanos* offices welcomed Salvador Ocampo and Alberto Durán, the Chilean and Colombian delegates, respectively, to the International Labour Conference, which had been held in Philadelphia in April and May. Burgos's account of the visit, which appeared in *Pueblos Hispanos* on 17 June, highlighted not only the paper's guests but also the day's other notable world event: "Habíamos previsto que íbamos a tener un gran día en P.H. con la dicha y el privilegio de recibir

EL PORQUE DE PUEBLOS HISPANOS

Porque la VICTORIA necesita:

1 . . . la unificacion de todas las colonias hispanas en Estados Unidos para la derrota del Nazi-fascismo, en unidad con todas las fuerzas democraticas.

2 . . . que se defiendan todos los derechos de las minorias hispanas en Estados Unidos—puertorriquenos, filipinos, mexicanos, etc.

3 . . . la inmediata independencia de la nacion puertorriquena.

4 . . . combatir el prejuicio contra los hispanos por su raza, color o credo, y la difusion de prejuicios contra otras minorias.

5 . . . la lucha tenaz contra la enemiga Falange Espanola como parte integrante de la Quinta Columna del Eje operando en las Americas, y ayudar e impulsar la unidad de todos los espanoles por las libertades democraticas en Espana.

6 . . . la liberacion de todo preso politico en el mundo.

7 . . . mejores relaciones entre las Americas mediante la difusion de las culturas hispanicas.

8 . . . la inmediata liberacion de Filipinas, ganada en el heroismo de Bataan.

9 . . . la unidad sindical en las Americas.

Figure 6. *Pueblos Hispanos* mission statement, 1943–44. Pre-1960s Publications Collection, Archives of the Puerto Rican Diaspora, Center for Puerto Rican Studies, Hunter College, City University of New York.

en nuestra casa a dos grandes líderes de América Latina. Pero no habíamos previsto que nos íbamos a reunir en el día de la apertura del Segundo Frente [We had anticipated that we would have a great day here at P.H. with the joy and privilege of receiving in our offices two great Latin American leaders. But we did not foresee that we would meet on the day of the opening of the Second Front]."

As part of an international movement, the paper was a vehicle for disseminating news supporting international labor movements and freedom from oppressive governments in Latin America and the Caribbean. With its words, it fought fascism, colonialism, and dictatorship. Also present at the meeting were an opponent of Rafael Trujillo's government and Max Audicourt, the general secretary of the Haitian Democratic Party, a vocal critic of his country's current administration. According to Burgos's article, Audicourt "señaló la esclavitud en que por muchos años ha vivido el pueblo haitiano, que también forman parte de América y parte de la lucha por la redención de las masas sufridas del mundo. Prometió seguir luchando por la liberación de Haití, y por la victoria de las naciones que luchan por esa misma libertad, dondequiera se encuentre usurpada [noted that the Haitian people, who also form part of America and the struggle for redemption of the suffering masses of the world, have lived in slavery for many years. He promised to continue fighting for the liberation of Haiti, and the victory of nations struggling for that very freedom, wherever it has been usurped]."

Pueblos Hispanos also printed creative works by Burgos that supported the paper's mission of social justice and liberation. An original poem, "Canción a los Pueblos Hispanos de América y del mundo" (Song to the Hispanic Peoples of America and the World), appeared in the paper on 11 March 1944, commemorating its first anniversary. She highlighted the mission of freedom and justice for which the editors and writers of the *Pueblos Hispanos* collective struggled. The poem suggests that the countries of América (with an accent) remain "tímidas patrias" having yet to fulfill their potential, which can be realized only through liberation from tyranny, education of the masses, and political independence: "Pero tu voz camina herida en cada brisa / y en cada suelo manso te reciben las lágrimas, / todavía reza un trueno de tiranos y dólares / sobre el vuelo tendido de tus tímidas patrias [But your voice wanders wounded in the wind / throughout the meek earth, you are welcomed with tears / still a thunderous reign of tyrants and dollars / hovers over your timid nations]." In Burgos's view, Latin America's stunted development resulted from the uneven relationship between the United States and economically dependent nations whose elites cooperated in various economic and political endeavors that strengthened the dollar and the elites' position but harmed the people. The editors of *Pueblos Hispanos* struggled to realize a vision that represented an expansion of Martí's project of self-determination for Latin American nations.

The imperial United States that aggressively pursued greater political and economic influence in Latin America and the one against which José Martí cautioned in his writings from New York had reared its monstrous head. Burgos saw Puerto Rican independence as part of the continuation of Martí's legacy. In her poem, "Canto a Martí" (Song to Martí), which appeared in *Pueblos Hispanos* on 20 May 1944, Burgos criticized the United States for betraying its democratic ideals of self-determination and freedom:

> Con una voz apenas comenzada,
> apenas recogida, apenas hecha;
> con una voz flotando entre horizontes
> de ansiada libertad, sin poseerla,
> de uniformes robustos, y de estrellas,
> con voz herida que se arrastra
> bajo el grito de América incompleta,
> con una voz de angustia desoída
> por donde pueda el alma de mi tierra;
> con una voz de suelo exasperado,
> vengo a decirte, santo, que despiertes . . .

> In a voice barely beginning;
> faintly collected, faintly formed;
> in a voice that hangs over horizons
> eager for freedom, desiring it
> robust, uniform, stars;
> a wounded voice lingers
> under the cry of the promise of America
> a voice of unheard anguish
> where the soul of my homeland
> in the voice of this exasperated soil
> I say to you, apostle, arise.

Just as Martí cautioned against U.S. annexation of Cuba in the 1880s, Burgos viewed with great suspicion the idea of Puerto Rico as a free associated state in a permanent relationship with the United States. Her desire to see Puerto Rico become one of the free and independent nations of America would remain Burgos's lifelong mission.

The 1940s saw the rise of the Partido Popular Democrático (Popular Democratic Party), founded in 1938 and led by Luis Muñoz Marín. The party's motto was "Pan, Tierra, y Libertad [Bread, Land, and Liberty]," and most of its constituents were workers, farmers, and members of the middle class. An early supporter of independence, Muñoz Marín turned away from the status question and focused on immediate social reforms. According to César Ayala and Rafael Bernabe, Muñoz Marín gradually realized that political independence was economically unviable and by 1946 began to embrace U.S. capital as a way to industrialize the island.[19] In response to the Puerto Rican political situation, Burgos wrote "Ser o no ser es la divisa" (To Be or Not to Be Is the Motto), published in 1945 in *Semanario Hispano*, a short-lived Spanish-language paper. The essay garnered her the Instituto de Literatura Puertorriqueña's Premio de Periodismo (Journalism Prize) the following year. Juan Antonio Rodríguez Pagán rightly notes that in this essay, Burgos "esboza su ideología político-social en relación con Puerto Rico y la América Latina [elaborates her sociopolitical ideology on Puerto Rico and Latin America]." He draws a parallel between her concerns in this essay and those expressed in a June 1945 letter to her sister in which she articulated an "auténtica preocupación por el futuro de la Humanidad [authentic preoccupation with the future of Humanity]."[20]

Figure 7. Flyer for a public discussion of "Estadidad o Independencia?" (Statehood or Independence?), 4 November [1945]. Jesús Colón Papers, Archives of the Puerto Rican Diaspora, Center for Puerto Rican Studies, Hunter College, City University of New York.

Burgos's essay went beyond simply expressing her concern for humanity. She framed the debate regarding Puerto Rican independence in the language of human rights—the right of a people to govern themselves rather than to be merely pawns in capitalist and imperialist designs. She connected the question of Puerto Rico's status to the global struggles of World War II as well as the despotic governments in power in the Dominican Republic, Nicaragua, and Honduras.

> A esta hora de encrucijada a que ha llegado la humanidad, podemos llamar la era de las definiciones. No de las definiciones de carácter lingüístico, sino de las definiciones de carácter humano que tienen su tronco en el hombre, y se esparcen sobre las colectividades en una dinámica social que rige el destino de los pueblos por el bien o por el mal. Estamos en la era de la definición del hombre.

> Today, humanity finds itself at a crossroads. We might call this the era of the definitions. Not definitions of a linguistic character, but definitions of human character, with its roots found in man, and it spread to collectivities in a social dynamic that governs the fate of the people for good or bad. This is the age of the definition of man.

Burgos argues that people have the right to develop and define themselves free from coercion and intimidation present in the colonial and imperial relationships in Puerto Rico and Latin American nations. Burgos's insight anticipates Albert Memmi's understanding of colonialism: "Revolt is the only way out of the colonial situation," and the colonial condition is "absolute and cries for an absolute solution; a break and not a compromise."[21] Burgos argued that the colonial situation could be escaped only through a complete break with the United States—through independence: "En Puerto Rico hay sólo dos caminos. O exigir el reconocimiento incondicional de nuestra independencia, o ser traidores a la libertad, en cualquiera otra forma de solución a nuestro problema que se nos ofrezca [In Puerto Rico there are only two paths. Either we demand the unconditional recognition of our independence, or we become traitors to freedom by accepting any other solution to our problem that is offered]."

U.S. culture promoted amnesia about home cultures and criminalized Puerto Ricans and Hispanics. One of the goals of the early Hispanophone papers was to keep migrants in New York informed of newsworthy events in Latin America that did not make the mainstream U.S. papers. In so doing, the Spanish-language papers offered alternative images of Latin American peoples and countries deemed unable to self-govern. Memmi argues that "the colonized's liberation must be carried out through a recovery of self and autonomous dignity."[22] To counter the negative images of the global South, Burgos highlighted Latin American icons such as Juan Bosch, José de Diego, Carmen Alicia Cadilla, and Marigloria Palma. Burgos's writing for the paper offered an opportunity for self-study and self-knowledge. Recounting the history of resistance in Latin America offered powerful counternarratives to those found in the mainstream media. In "Triunfa Juan Bosch en Concurso Periodista" (Juan Bosch Wins Journalism Prize), published in *Pueblos Hispanos* on 26 March 1944, she reported that the Dominican intellectual and statesman had won the prestigious Cuban Hatuey prize, named for a Taíno cacique who waged a legendary fight against Spanish colonizers in the early sixteenth century. Burgos drew international lines of allegiance connecting supporters of freedom from materialism, colonialism, and imperialism.

Bosch received the prize as part of a celebration of the centenary of Dominican independence. Burgos pointed out the irony of celebrating independence when the country had been ruled for fourteen years by Trujillo, "uno de los más sangrientos déspotas hispánoamericanos, traidor a las esencias que hicieron posible el acto [one of the most bloodthirsty despots of Hispanic America, a traitor to the ideals that made this act possible]." Just two weeks earlier, on 11 March 1944, Burgos had published "Himno de sangre a Trujillo" (Blood Song for Trujillo) in *Pueblos Hispanos*. The poem is haunting, as Burgos curses Trujillo for having the blood of innocents on his hands. She foretold that his legacy would be shame, death, and blood: "General Rafael, Trujillo General, / que tu nombre sea un eco eterno de cadáveres / rodando entre ti mismo, sin piedad, persiguiéndote [General Rafael, Trujillo General, / Your name will echo eternally among the corpses / wandering through you, no pity, in pursuit]." She predicted that his legacy would be a specter that would haunt the history of the Dominican Republic: "Sombra para tu nombre, General. / Sombra para tu crimen, General. / Sombra para tu sombra [Shadow of your name, General. / Shadow of your crime, / Shadow of your shadow]."

In two short essays in *Pueblos Hispanos*, Burgos brought news from Puerto Rico and Latin America to the *colonia* in New York while highlighting the literary, cultural, and political contributions of two Puerto Rican women writers who, like Burgos, had migrated among Puerto Rico, Cuba, and New York. In "Presentación de Marigloria Palma" (Introducing Marigloria Palma), published on 8 July 1944, Burgos noted that Palma had won the Premio de Literatura Puertorriqueña in 1941, becoming only the second woman to win this prize, after Burgos. Now in New York, Palma went on to become a regular contributor to *Pueblos Hispanos*.

The second essay, "Carmen Alicia Cadilla," was published two weeks after the first and brought readers the news that Cadilla had recently received a scholarship to study journalism in Cuba and would soon be taking up residence there. Burgos praised Cadilla's ability to separate sugarcane from its association with U.S. exploitation of Puerto Rican workers: "Se pegó Carmen Alicia a la tierra épicamente. Se pegó a su tierra puertorriqueña. Y vio en la zafra su mayor tragedia, su más amarga cruz. Destruyó la villana bandera de la caña dentro y fuera de Puerto Rico como pabellón de explotación, y ofreció la caña limpia de pecado, redimida, a la flora natural del mundo [Carmen Alicia praised the land epically. She is committed to her homeland Puerto Rico. She noted in the sugarcane plantations the island's greatest tragedy and a bitter cross. She destroyed the association of sugarcane with exploitation both inside and outside of Puerto Rico, and in her writing sugar emerged redeemed, free of sin, as part of the natural world.]" In her writing, Cadilla restored Puerto Rican symbols to the island without the negative connotations in which they had been shrouded. Her contributions are important to Puerto Ricans' efforts to free themselves from oppression, since, according to Memmi, the "colonizer's rejection is the indispensable prelude to self-discovery. That accusing and annihilating image must be shaken off."[23]

In these essays, Burgos questions the idea that culture emanates from the center to the periphery and suggests that traditions from the peripheries and the provinces can challenge ideas of objectivity and reason. Burgos praised Palma as "completamente subjetivo [completely subjective]." This subjectivity comes through self-knowledge. Palma's work, much like Burgos's poetry, frequently examines the writer's interiority and autobiography, leading to a sense of social justice that comes from within and thus, in Burgos's words, "rehuye formas objetivas de rebelión [rejecting objective forms of rebellion]." Burgos also explored this idea in her poetry published in *Pueblos Hispanos*. In "Campo," which appeared on 3 July 1943, she praises the provinces as the place from which ideas, traditions, and hope spring: "¡La tradición está ardiendo en el campó! / ¡La esperanza está ardiendo en el campó! / ¡El hombre está ardiendo en el campó! [Tradition is burning in the country! / Hope is burning in the country! / Man is burning in the country!]." By contrast, when writing about Palma, she described New York, the great metropolis, as "la ciudad del ruido y del cansancio [the city of noise and lassitude]." This description suggests that the center produces ideas that lack originality and are unintelligible—nothing but noise.

New York's Spanish-language newspapers often led campaigns for community action or to raise funds for particular crises.[24] In 1944, when Luis Lloréns Torres was seriously ill, he came to the United States for surgery and medical care. After visiting the poet in the hospital, Burgos penned a piece published in the 10 June issue of *Pueblos Hispanos* in which she identified herself as a New York Puerto Rican and appealed to the solidarity between Puerto Ricans on the island and in New York: "La crisis de su vida lo ha tomado lejos del más hondo motivo de su existencia: Puerto Rico. Somos los puertorriqueños de Nueva York los que tenemos el deber de cuidar de esa vida preciosa. Unámonos todos, alrededor de PUEBLOS HISPANOS para homenaje de su vida [This life crisis has taken him far away from his reason for living: Puerto Rico. We Puerto Ricans from New York have a duty to take care of this precious life. Let us stand in solidarity with PUEBLOS HISPANOS to honor his life]." Burgos saw Puerto Ricans on the island and in New York not as two separate groups but rather as one people divided by U.S. intervention and harsh economic conditions that led to the massive migration of Puerto Ricans. Creating this transnational political and cultural relationship allowed Burgos to express a more fluid and flexible sense of Puerto Rican identity, a continuation of the process she had begun with her creation of a nomadic subject in her earlier poetry. In her New York prose, the migratory subject moves along the cityscape and urban geography.[25]

Sharing news from Latin America with the migrant community in New York was an important step in the development of transnational relationships. News stories allowed migrants to influence politics in their home countries. In the

Figure 8. Cover of *Pueblos Hispanos*, 3 July 1943. Pre-1960s Publications Collection, Archives of the Puerto Rican Diaspora, Center for Puerto Rican Studies, Hunter College, City University of New York.

case of Puerto Rico, for example, the community pressed for resolution of the status question by raising awareness of U.S. colonialism on the island. They elected Marcantonio, the only lawmaker of this era who referred to Puerto Rico as a colony and a supporter of independence.[26] The cultural news émigrés read in the paper allowed them to remain connected to a sense of cultural identity from the home country while adding their experiences in their new home to generate new knowledge and self-awareness.

Promoting Hispanic Culture in New York

In one of the most interesting articles that Burgos wrote for *Pueblos Hispanos*, "Cultura en Función Social" (The Social Function of Culture), which appeared on 1 April 1944, she laid out the objectives of the newspaper and of the art and culture section, for which she was the editor. This essay demonstrates that the paper had been created in defense of the community and sought to facilitate the development of Hispanic-serving institutions. Burgos looked forward to working with Corretjer again because of their shared political beliefs: "Es por coincidencia de principios y de posiciones frente a la batalla general entre las fuerzas reaccionarias y la justicia humana, y frente a la lucha específica que sostienen los pueblos hispanos en Nueva York por su supervivencia y superación [Because of our shared principles and political beliefs in the overall struggle between reactionary forces and human justice. We stand united in the struggle that the Hispanic people of New York face for survival and human dignity]." The editors understood themselves as part of a minoritarian identity within the United States, and as such, they understood they did not enjoy full citizenship rights. They framed their demands for justice in the language of human rights. This idea differs from the sense of identity Puerto Ricans described approximately fifteen years earlier in *Gráfico*.[27]

United in vision and purpose, Burgos and Corretjer endeavored to confront the challenges, prejudice, and discrimination faced by Puerto Ricans and Latinos in the United States by defining, preserving, and promoting the cultures of Hispanic America. Hispanism was thriving in New York during the 1930s and 1940s. Whereas Faber criticizes the Hispanism of the 1930s for its assimilationism and for denying Latin America's heterogeneity, Burgos promotes "culturas hispánicas" while acknowledging heterogeneity and diversity as among the region's greatest assets. Rather than praising Hispanismo, she strives for solidarity among Latin Americans—"hispanoamericanos"—and the diffusion of "cultura hispanoamericana." She focuses on what she perceives as authentically "Americano," distinct from Spain: "Por razones de colonización la cultura, refrescada y enriquecida en la virginidad americana, aportó elementos determinantes en la estructuración de nuevas formas de cultura [Because of colonialism, our culture, renewed and enriched by the pristine virginity of America, provided determining elements in the structure of new forms of culture]." Burgos had a sophisticated understanding of culture, which she defined as "una proyección o manifestación directa del espíritu de una colectividad [a projection or direct manifestation of a collective spirit]." In her view, Latin American heterogeneity, or "el mestizaje," "ha sido la fuente máxima de nuestra expresión autóctona [has been the greatest source of autochthonous expression]."[28] Burgos saw the cultural identities of the home countries as offering strength and resistance against the assimilationist culture of the United States. Her sense of Hispanismo clearly focused on the Americas and acknowledged the cultural diversity and heterogeneity of Latin America as a source of power.

Burgos believed that for *nuestra América* (our America, the title of Martí's best-known essay) to free itself from the U.S. imperial grip, it would have to turn inward. The path to freedom, according to Burgos in this essay, could be found in critical self-study:

> Antes que nada, afrontar, con mente abierta y espíritu crítico, todos nuestros problemas; analizarlos, sin olvidarnos del marco limitado donde se presentan, con mente universal; someterlos desnudos al pueblo para concienzudo estudio, y fijarle causas auténticas y soluciones permanentes. . . . Ha sido una mano leal al pueblo que ha presentado abiertamente, en toda su tragedia y en todas sus posibilidades, los problemas mayores de nuestra América.

> First of all, we want to confront all of our problems with an open mind and critical spirit; analyzing with a universal mind without forgetting the limited framework that surrounds our challenges; revealing them with all transparency to the people for judicious study; and finding authentic causes and permanent solutions. . . . With a fair hand we should openly present to the people the greatest problems of our America, with all of its tragedy and all of its possibilities.

Burgos saw sustained, critical study as the key to finding permanent solutions to local problems. Latin American countries could then reject the solutions offered to them by a U.S. imperial project.

One of the manifestations of this idea of self-study was an effort to educate Puerto Ricans and Latin American migrants in New York, who were disconnected from their home countries and from Latin American peoples' history of resistance. Writing for the newspaper, Burgos shared stories of important historical and political figures. "El hombre transmutado" (The Transmuted Man), a short article printed on 15 April 1944, provided an account of the legacy of Puerto Rican poet José de Diego, who fought for the island's independence from Spain in the late nineteenth century. The essay educated the community about the idea and history of Puerto Rican independence, lifting morale and encouraging solidarity while providing a positive Puerto Rican role model. Burgos also used this article to denounce U.S. intervention in Puerto Rican politics, as she did in most of these short essays.

As a cultural mediator, Burgos educated her readers about cultural institutions, art exhibits, and other important local events. In several pieces that appeared in *Pueblos Hispanos* in 1944, she featured two characters, Paloma and Iris, and their experiences while exploring New York City. Paloma was a young woman of Iberian descent whose family had fled to Mexico during the Spanish Civil War and been taken in by Iris's family. In the vignette that appeared on 1 June, the two women met by chance at New York's Museo de Arte Hispánico. Burgos enticed her readers to visit the museum with descriptions of some of the best paintings of the Hispanic world that were housed there, including works by Goya and El Greco. She drew attention to the museum's sculpture, ceramics, and pottery collections as well as its samples of old lace, brocades, fabrics, and tapestries that echoed back to the "hispano-moriscos" (Spanish Moors), again affirming the heterogeneity of the Hispanic world. She told readers about the museum's beautiful tiles, mosaics, and furniture from previous centuries as well as its first edition copy of Miguel Cervantes's *Don Quijote*, which caused Paloma to exclaim in surprise, "¡Quién me diría que en tu América, iba yo a ver la primera edición del Quijote! [Who would have thought that in your America I would come across a first edition of Quixote!]." This tactic enabled Burgos to familiarize readers with the impressive history, arts, accomplishments, and traditions of the Spanish-speaking world, including Latin America, and to point out the museum's early editions of books by Rubén Darío, Heredia, and Sor Juana. In addition, by highlighting the fact that some of the greatest treasures of Latin America and Spain were now housed in New York City, Burgos bolstered the concept that important ideas and culture move from the periphery to the center and reflected the late nineteenth-century shift of power in the Americas from Spain to the United States.

As art and culture editor, Burgos served as mediator and promoter of Hispanic American culture. She used the paper to educate the Latin American migrant community in New York and established transnational connections between the metropolis and the home countries. Although she promoted Hispanic American culture as a way to fend off the assimilationist push coming from U.S. culture, her writings focused on what she saw as uniquely "Americano"—the indigenous people of South America and the African cultures brought to this part of the world. In this way, Burgos avoided the assimilationist drive within Hispanismo and celebrated the heterogeneity of Latin America as a source of strength.

Early Diaspora Identities and Transnational Cultural Forms in the United States.

In addition to promoting Hispanic American culture in New York, Burgos began to use her work to articulate diaspora identities and transnational cultural forms. While interviewing artists of Latin American origin, she often reflected on art and culture in the diaspora, exploring how migration and nostalgia for their homelands informed the artists' work. The paper informed the Puerto Rican community in New York and the larger Latino/a readership of upcoming events, educated and encouraged the community to support the artists by attending, and helped unite the community. As part of her quest to find allies and create broader political and social connections for members of the Puerto Rican and Latino community, she also wrote about important events involving Harlem's African American community, among them a Paul Robeson concert and the 1944 Negro Freedom Rally.

Burgos highlighted the fluidity and complexity regarding national identity that is not bound to geography. In the dominant migration story in the United States, immigrants are depicted as leaving their home countries to start a new and better life in the United States. Accordingly, immigrants should shift their focus away from their origins in favor of their lives here in their new country. However, Burgos's narratives and interviews for *Pueblos Hispanos* disrupt this account of migration as unidirectional and unilateral, suggesting instead that Latinos who migrate retain connections to their countries of origin while establishing new relationships in the United States, thereby creating transnational social ties. In particular, Puerto Ricans on the island and in the States share a strong cultural nationalism that resists the politics of assimilation. Juan Flores notes that the main thrust of this cultural expression is "toward self-affirmation and association with other cultures caught up in comparable processes of historical recovery and strategic resistance."[29]

In her interview "Con Narciso Figueroa, pianista puertorriqueño" (With Narciso Figueroa, Puerto Rican Pianist), published in *Pueblos Hispanos* on 13 May 1944, she revealed migrants' transnational bonds to their homeland. Figueroa was a classically trained pianist who had studied first in Puerto Rico and then later in a conservatory in Spain before moving to New York City as an adult. Burgos beautifully described the artist's enduring familial ties to his homeland, and the two shared a visceral attachment to the sea:

> NF: Me encantaba el monte, y especialmente el mar. Tenía ambiciones de ser marinero. Aún hoy día el bote de vela me subyuga.
>
> JB: Le comprendo, Narciso. No puede sentirse de otro modo un artista nacido en una isla atajada por doquiera de mares azules y eternos.

NF: I loved the mountains, and especially the sea. I had ambitions of becoming a sailor. Still today, the sailboat inspires me.

JB: I sympathize, Narciso. An artist born on an island cannot feel any other way surrounded by eternal blue seas.

However, as artists, it was important for them to leave their small island and explore the world. Many Caribbean artists have expressed this dilemma, which Burgos encapsulated in her discussion of Figueroa: "En este punto me semeja el mismo una tierna y ponderosa vela del mar antillano que se ha alejado de sus islas, sin soltarse nunca de ellas, para dar al mundo la altiva presencia musical de Puerto Rico, en lo más selecto, en lo más grandioso, y perfecto del maravilloso arte [At this moment he resembles to me a tender and powerful sailboat on the Caribbean Sea that has distanced himself from the shore without ever letting go, to offer to the world the pride of Puerto Rico, its music. His music is a grand and perfect expression of this wonderful art]." The sailboat metaphor highlights the strong, lingering ties to the homeland.

Although the conversation with Figueroa showed that Puerto Ricans who migrated as adults maintained close familial and emotional ties to the homeland, Burgos's "Plática con Esteban Soriano" (Chat with Esteban Soriano), which appeared in *Pueblos Hispanos* on 22 April 1944, is even more compelling. Born in Puerto Rico, Soriano moved to New York at the age of sixteen. Almost three decades later, his work continued to be influenced by nostalgia for Puerto Rico. Burgos opens the article with a poetic description of New York City that contrasts the descriptions of the unruffled landscape of Puerto Rico portrayed in Soriano's paintings. Her feelings of longing for the island are revealed in the contrast:

La tarde, terca como toda tarde neoyorkina avisada ya de la llegada de la primavera, no quiere subirse a las lejanas azoteas a desaparecer, humilde, sobre su destino. Quiere ser compañera de un encuentro de artes, fijado en apacible rincón humano de esta ciudad, tenebrosamente silenciosa a veces, otras veces demoniacamente a gritos. La amplia tarde, intrigada, nos lleva, sin saberlo, a un bello rinconcito de Puerto Rico, animado por la encendida mano de uno de sus más grandes artistas, Esteban Soriano.

The late afternoon hangs on stubbornly like all New York sunsets that hint at the coming of spring, refusing to climb over the rooftops to recede, to accept humbly its fate. It lingers and longs to be part of this artistic encounter, set in a quiet corner of this city, eerily quiet at times, while at other times it rages in demonic screams. The expansive afternoon, intrigued, leads unwittingly to a beautiful corner of Puerto Rico, animated by the fiery hand of one of its greatest artists, Esteban Soriano.

The city is anthropomorphized in this beautiful description. Burgos recognized the city's intrigue and its ability to be quiet and times and bustling at others, but always with the excitement of the unexpected. Soriano's paintings of Puerto Rico's still landscape appear as an oasis of serenity.

Burgos was surprised by the island's continued influence on Soriano's work, and, she wrote, "La curiosidad o la picardía de saber cómo le ha impresionado, en su arte, el lugar donde salió a la vida [Curiosity or mischief lead me to ask what role his native land has played in the development of his art]." She revealed to readers, "Casi con rubor de haber avanzado demasiado, me dejo conducir hasta la dulce visión de otra acuarela cuyo título corresponde a la pregunta: MI CIUDAD NATAL. Allí está San Juan como lo dejó Esteban Soriano hace veinticinco años, tranquilo y simple. Es una pintura cubista sin complicaciones [Blushing for having gone almost too far, I allow my eyes to rest on the title of the sweet watercolor that responds to my question: MY HOMETOWN. There is San Juan, just as Esteban Soriano left it twenty-five years ago, quiet and simple]." The peaceful and simple image of Puerto Rico clashes with the vibrant description of New York City that opens the article. His work reveals his strong affinities and the ways the homeland still figures prominently in his art and inspires him.

Burgos applauded Soriano's promotion of Puerto Rican culture in the United States: "Es Soriano exponente reconocido e indiscutible de nuestra vida nacional, viva para siempre en sus cuadros [Soriano is a recognized and indisputable proponent of our national life, which lives forever in his paintings]."

Burgos again explored the complexities of identity in migrant families in her interview "Con Josephine Premice: Y su arte folklórico haitiano" (With Josephine Premice: And her Haitian Folklore Art), which appeared on 24 June 1944. Premice later became a famous American television and Broadway actress, performing with stars such as Lena Horne and Diahann Carroll.[30] The story of Premice, a high school student of Haitian descent who studied Vodun dance traditions, challenged dominant notions of migration and emphasized the cultural alliances between Puerto Ricans and other minority groups of Caribbean descent as well as African Americans in New York. All of these groups are caught in the process of migration from the periphery to the metropole and cohabitate in New York's inner-city neighborhoods. The interview demonstrates the Caribbeanization of New York through the cultural alliances among ethnic minority groups.[31]

The conversation with Premice demonstrated the way Haitians, much like Puerto Ricans and other minority groups, struggled for self-affirmation. Premice had come to the United States when she was only eighteen months old, and early in the interview, her American accent led Burgos to ask about her background:

JB—Al notar el perfecto acento de su inglés, inquirimos el tiempo de su estadía aquí. Para nuestro asombro, contesta:

JP—Apenas conozco a mi patria natal. Casi no la recuerdo. Nací en Port Au Prince. Cuando contaba año y medio mis padres se trasladaron a Nueva York. Volví a Haití a los cuatro años, pero por breve tiempo. De manera que casi toda mi vida la he pasado aquí.

JB—Pero, ¿Cómo es posible que exprese ud. una parte de la cultura haitiana tan admirablemente, cuando no ha tenido contacto con el origen de esa cultura?

JP—Eso se lo debo a mi familia. Mi casa, dentro de esta misma ciudad cosmopólita, es haitiana. Aunque vivimos normalmente la vida norteamericana, rendimos culto a las más bellas y altas tradiciones nuestras, seguimos muy de cerca los aconteci-mientos políticos y sociales de nuestra patria y somos, antes que nada, y para ser más universales, haitianos.

JB—Noticing her perfect unaccented English, we inquired about the time of her stay here. To our surprise, she responded:

JP—I barely know my homeland. I hardly remember it. I was born in Port-au-Prince. When I was a year and a half old my parents moved to New York. I returned to Haiti four years later for a brief visit. So I have spent most of my life here.

JB—But how can you convey Haitian culture so admirably when you have had little contact with its source?

JP—I owe that to my family. My home, in the midst of this very cosmopolitan city, is Haitian. Although we live a normal American life, we worship the most beauti-ful and highest traditions of our culture, we closely follow the political and social developments of our country, and we are universally and above all else Haitian.

Premice was thus consciously bicultural. She was raised with traditional Haitian values and customs. She went on to explain,

Cada pueblo tiene su expresión rudimentaria y su expresión más culta de una tradición o de un culto. A unos parece salvaje lo que para otros es completamente normal. En la interpretación de otras culturas se llega hasta la exageración. Mi misión será aclarar la verdad de la cultura haitiana.

Every society has its rudimentary expressions and its most learned and cultivated traditions. What appears to be savage to some is completely ordinary and normal to others. At times, cultures that seem exotic are represented through gross exag-gerations. My mission will be to clarify and reveal the truth about Haitian culture.

New York City provided artists, writers, musicians, and actors the opportunity to cross-pollinate and form bonds and coalitions that over time led to new forms of cultural expression. Burgos anticipated the questions regarding art and identity in the diaspora that intensified with the increased movement of people from the Caribbean to New York City. These artists were creating diaspora identities before the large Caribbean migration to New York in the middle of the century and the establishment of large ethnic enclaves.

The essay "Perfiles Mexicanos—Voces de México en Baltimore" (Mexican Profiles—Mexican Voices in Baltimore), published on 6 May 1944, describes an encounter between Burgos and a group of Mexicans who were in the United States as temporary workers to help alleviate the wartime labor shortage. Burgos opened the article with a poetic description of Penn Station that highlighted U.S. racism and the way it is reflected in the country's economic structure:

"Rostros negros. Rostros negros de hermosas mujeres que barren el camino de los blancos. Rostros agitados de prisa y de cansancio en un vaivén de vueltas que choca por su uniformidad [Black faces. Black faces of beautiful women who sweep the paths of white passers-by. Faces of hectic hurry and fatigue, revealing their exhaustion in the sway of the crowd that is shocking in its uniformity]." She demonstrated how the monotonous repetition of the train station dehumanized the scene. She was drawn toward a group of people who she suspected were Latin American. An attraction to the familiar and the recognizable stood out in this homogenized crowd. The description expressed a desire to fit in with and humanize a crowd that appeared estranged and unfamiliar.

> De pronto, una mancha distinta del tono blanco y negro atrae mis ojos. Es una mancha India, sola y quieta, que en un rincón disuelve la monotonía de la estación de Pennsylvania. Sin poder explicar por qué, mis pies avanzan con dirección definida.—Parecen hispanos—me digo, para mí vista, cae sobre un grupo de piel morena tostada por el sol, de rostros suaves y expresivos, de ademanes pausados que contrastan notablemente con el marco convulso de hombre y trenes que los circunda.

> Suddenly, my eyes are drawn to a tanned patch that disrupts the black and white faces of the crowd. Their skin carries a red, indigenous tone. Alone and quiet, they stand in a corner and their presence interrupts the monotony of Pennsylvania Station. Unable to explain why, my feet move decidedly toward them. "They appear to be Hispanic"—I say to myself as my sight falls upon a group with dark skin bronzed by the sun, their faces are soft and expressive, their gestures deliberate, a notable contrast to the mechanical movements of the crowd and the trains that surround us.

As she approached the group, a member asked if she was Mexican. She expressed her pleasure in the mutual and immediate sense of familiarity and connectedness they felt: "En mis oídos la pregunta suena a música, en mi corazón se alegra de contenido humano y en mi mente se contesta con un saludo y un cariño hondo para aquellos hermanos hispanoamericanos [The question is music to my ears, my heart swells with joy and human compassion, and in my mind I respond with a warm greeting and a deep affection for my brothers from Hispanic America]." This article conveys the sense of loneliness and isolation that Latino/as felt in the absence of established communities.

This article highlights the importance of the newspapers for early communities as they provided emotional support and a sense of solidarity when more advanced technology, such as telephones, television, and transportation, were a luxury. In so doing, newspapers helped create what Benedict Anderson has described as "imagined communities." The Mexican workers Burgos encountered elaborated, "No hemos visto ninguna cara hispana, ni un periódico, ni

nada. Por eso le hemos hablado. Perdone usted; es que todos los pueblos his-
panos nos atraemos, sobre todo en estos sitios tan desolados de un alma que
nos comprenda o nos quiera [We have not seen a single Hispanic face, or
newspaper, or anything. So this is why we have approached you. Excuse us,
it's just that Hispanic people are drawn to each other, especially in these parts
so destitute of souls who can understand and love us]." New York's Hispanic
community was largely Puerto Rican at the time, but it also included people
from other countries of origin and was segregated from the rest of the city.
In her words, "Estoy un tanto sorprendida de encontrar en semejante sitio un
grupo completo de mexicanos, ya que en Nueva York las colonias hispanas se
mezclan unas con las otras y es difícil encontrar un conglomerado exclusiva-
mente de mexicanos, de puertorriqueños o de cubanos. Pienso enseguida en la
inmigración [I'm a little surprised to come across a group of Mexicans. In New
York the Hispanic colonies are quite mixed and diverse and it is unusual to find
a cluster exclusively of Mexicans, Puerto Ricans or Cubans. My thoughts turn
quickly to the experience of immigration]." Migration thus created alliances
that would otherwise have been unlikely.

Printed on 12 August 1944, the final article featuring Burgos's two fictional
immigrant characters was "Iris y Paloma caminan por Harlem" (Iris and Paloma
Walk through Harlem). In it, Burgos stressed precisely this transnationalism
within the city's Latino/a community and the importance of solidarity. She
opened the article illustrating this point: "Solamente guardaron la localización
de sus espíritus en la cosa latina, especialmente en lo latinoamericano, que en
Nueva York forma una sola familia sin fronteras, que es necesario unir más
cada día [They kept their spirits focused on Latino things, which in New York
continues to expand as a single family without borders. We must become more
united every day]." Paralleling the struggles of different groups and accentuat-
ing their similarities, she further stressed the need for members to unite. Iris
goes on to note, "Quiero vivir de cerca y detenerme hoy en la vida que es casi
toda dolor, del pueblo puertorriqueño en esta famosa barriada. Quiero sentir,
a pleno corazón, con el pueblo hermano que hace tiempo quiero y vigilo [I
long to live near and intimately get to know Puerto Rican people's life, today
almost all pain, in this famous neighborhood. I want to feel with an open heart
a fraternal bond with these people whom I have loved and watched over]."

This article explores the problems faced by Hispanics who are natives of the
United States, underscoring the injustices, prejudice, inequality, and discrimina-
tion that the community faces. A narrator conveys what Iris and Paloma see as
they walk through Harlem: "Ven las viviendas casi inhabitables, sin ventilación,
sin calor, sin seguridad, sin higiene, del pueblo puertorriqueño de Harlem
[They observe the homes that are almost inhabitable. The dwelling places of

the Puerto Rican people in Harlem lack proper ventilation, heat, security, and hygiene]."

For Puerto Ricans, Harlem was not the land of opportunity they had expected:

Porque en el negro de Estados Unidos la persecución está centralizada en el color del pellejo, lo que implica naturalmente, la negación a todo su desenvolvimiento. Para el puertorriqueño, en cambio, el azote no tiene ni siquiera enfoque directo; es un azote mitad político y mitad bárbaro-pasión y cálculo mezclado para la liquidación de un pedazo del mundo completamente hecho en sus propias raíces, pero violado en su crecimiento natural.

In the United States, the persecution of blacks is centralized in the color of their skin, which of course means denying all of their development as a people. In contrast, for Puerto Ricans, the blow has no clear focus; it is a blow that is partially political and partially a barbaric passion and is calculated to totally annihilate a part of the world completely made of its own roots but violated and not allowed to develop naturally.

The vignette ends abruptly with a note that the women cannot understand the community in a single afternoon and that they therefore will return to learn more.

The problems associated with poverty—malnutrition, disease, poor hygiene, lack of education, and unemployment—continue to plague Puerto Ricans both on the island and on the U.S. mainland. The central difference is setting and environment. In the 1940s, Puerto Rico was primarily rural, so for migrants, those challenges were complicated by the urban setting, crime, discrimination, and prejudice. The solution Burgos proposed in New York was similar to the one that she proposed on the island—solidarity, mutual support, and organizing around a cause. In El Barrio, Iris and Paloma also witnessed

la humanidad, que contra la corriente destructora quiere unirse en fraternal abrazo, casi siempre proletario, organizándose para la verdad mientras traicioneramente es azotado por ráfagas y demagogos de sus causas. Ven en el lado positivo, inspiradores grupos como los Clubs de Marcantonio, el Club de Hostos, el Club Obrero, La Mutualista Obrera, *Pueblos Hispanos*, que son y serán la vanguardia de la defensa de las clases explotadas y sufridas, especialmente la puertorriqueña.

Humanity fights an uphill battle to stand united in a fraternal embrace against destructive forces. It is almost always the proletariat who are organizing around the truth while it is treacherously whipped by demagogues and their causes. They see, on the positive side, inspiring groups such as Marcantonio's Club, Hostos's Club, the Workers Club, the Mutual Workers Club, and *Pueblos Hispanos*, who are and will be at the vanguard of the defense of the exploited classes, especially Puerto Ricans.

As in the previous article, Burgos concluded this essay with information vital to the community, naming social organizations and resources that were available to those in need. Burgos had great insight regarding the challenges members of the community faced and was committed to improving their living conditions.

The reasons for *Pueblos Hispanos*'s abrupt demise remain unclear, but the climate had unquestionably changed. McCarthyism offered a different political landscape for communists, nationalists, and *independentistas* both in New York and in Puerto Rico. In a climate in which anticommunism was a matter of national security, the communist menace extended beyond official party members to include almost any group that challenged the established economic, social, or racial order. FBI director J. Edgar Hoover targeted foreigners, radicals, and striking workers and considered "non-conformity to be as dangerous as communism"[32] In an attempt to gather support for the anticommunist movement, the U.S. government presented communism as fundamentally un-American.[33]

One of the goals of *Pueblos Hispanos'* founders had been creating a publisher and bookstore to promote books that revealed a sense of "Americanidad," but that ambition was never realized. Nevertheless, *Pueblos Hispanos* and New York's other Spanish-language newspapers made other significant contributions. The press assisted in the development of transnational ties between the island and the growing migrant community in the metropolis. It allowed migrants to remain connected to Puerto Rico while integrating their experiences in New York into their understanding of themselves. This chapter shows the importance of Burgos's contributions to the Spanish-language press in New York during the 1940s. Burgos conveyed feelings of bonding and connection to "la cosa latina" in the United States. Political and cultural relationships cultivated at the paper allowed her to imagine more expansive and inclusive ways to be Puerto Rican, a process she had begun in her poetry written on the island and in Cuba. She embraced a heterogeneous sense of identity in which racial and gender differences encouraged hemispheric bonds of solidarity with migrants from across Latin America and the Caribbean. This more fluid sense of national identity drew later generations of writers to her work, particularly Puerto Rican women writers and artists, and sexual minorities in the diaspora.

4

Multiple Legacies

Julia de Burgos and Caribbean Latino Diaspora Writers

Just a decade after Julia de Burgos's death in 1953, New York City was a very different place. In 1954, the U.S. Supreme Court ruled in *Brown v. Board of Education* that separate facilities are inherently unequal, putting an end to de jure racial segregation in the United States. In 1963, 250,000 people participated in the March on Washington for Freedom and Jobs, demanding the passage of meaningful civil rights legislation outlawing discrimination on the basis of color, race, or national origin. A year later, the Civil Rights Act was signed into law. Members of the Young Lords Party, which advocated on behalf of Puerto Rican independence, civil rights, and improved living conditions in New York, fought gentrification and unfair living conditions, efforts that ultimately became a political movement in the 1970s.[1] The Nuyorican arts and intellectual movement spread, and in 1973, Miguel Algarín opened the Nuyorican Poets Cafe, where poets, writers, and artists came to express themselves and the reality of their neighborhoods. Puerto Rican women such as Lorrain Sutton and Sandra María Esteves emerged on the New York poetry scene.

Powered by the social movements of the era, queer and feminist writers, most of them from Puerto Rico but also some from the Dominican Republic and Cuba, reclaimed Burgos as a symbol for their cause. Today, Puerto Rican writers and artists on the island and in New York keep her spirit alive in their work. Burgos became a cultural icon in New York for three central reasons. First, these writers identify with Burgos's fight for self-determination and recognition as expressed in her life and in her writing. Second, her intensely personal and autobiographical style of writing lends itself to developing these themes and resonates with a shift in poetry conventions away from the impersonal modernist style and in favor of the art of authenticity and presence. These changes led to the mid-twentieth-century performance poetry of the Beats and several decades later to slam and spoken-word poetry embraced by the Nuyorican poets and the Black Arts movement, among others.[2] Finally, Burgos's politics as well as her life story lend themselves as symbols for coalition building among marginalized groups. This chapter explores the way that feminist, queer, and diaspora writers—all of whom had been excluded from the Puerto Rican and American literary canons—deploy the writing and the figure of Julia de Burgos to critique and challenge patriarchy, suggest alternative family models, affirm their blackness and their sexuality, expand the borders of the island nation to include the diaspora, and broaden traditional notions of American literature.[3]

The Puerto Rican literary canon of the 1930s remained uncontested until the 1970s, when the previously silenced voices of women, blacks, migrants, and members of the lesbian, gay, bisexual, transgender, and queer (LGBTQ) community burst onto the literary scene.[4] Burgos was one of the most significant voices challenging the canon's patriarchy, classism, racism, and geographical borders. During the consolidation of the canon, the writers of the Generación del Treinta had revitalized the concept of *la gran familia* (the great family) as a strategy to resist American colonial power on the island.[5] The myth of *la gran familia* "was instrumental in delineating the contours of the canon because it was used to legitimize its 'silences' through three main tenets: social harmony and racial democracy, the glorification of the past, and the cult of patriarchy."[6] Many queer and feminist Puerto Rican diaspora writers developed countercanonical literature that took eroticism as a point of departure in the same way that Burgos did.

This chapter looks at Burgos's significance as a figure of sexile in the work of Manuel Ramos Otero and Luz María Umpierre as well as her influence on Caribbean diaspora writers in New York such as Rosario Ferré, Chiqui Vicioso, and Sonia Rivera-Valdés. It then examines Burgos's legacy among Nuyorican writers Esteves and Mariposa (María Teresa Fernández) and others.[7] Trends in performance poetry intersected with Burgos's legacy to magnify her importance among writers in the diaspora. Her legacy among queer, feminist, and diaspora writers highlights the challenge to the Puerto Rican literary canon, the cult of patriarchy, and the foundational myth of *la gran familia* in Puerto Rican literature, which began to decline in the 1970s.[8] For groups traditionally omitted from the national imaginary, claiming Burgos offered a way to tap into the island's nationalistic impulses, shared history, and social memory. Moreover, in a cosmopolitan city such as New York, Burgos became a transnational Latina/o cultural icon. Reinventing, reimagining, and riffing off Burgos becomes a way for artists to voice their struggles for recognition and self-determination in New York, echoing the themes developed in her writing.

Autobiographical writing and intensely personal lyric poetry developed among Puerto Rican writers in the United States throughout the twentieth century.

According to Juan Flores, Puerto Rican literature in the United States can be divided into three stages. The "pioneer" stage (1916–45) was primarily autobiographical and journalistic and was exemplified by Jesús Colón and Bernardo Vega. The midcentury stage (1945–65) coincides with the Great Migration of Puerto Ricans to New York, with established authors such as Pedro Juan Soto and René Marqués writing about the New York Puerto Rican community without really being a part of it. They offered an outside view. The third stage, Nuyorican literature, arose in the 1960s and 1970s with no direct reference to or apparent awareness of the earlier literature created by Puerto Ricans in New York. Flores notes that despite this seeming lack of connection, Nuyorican literature draws on the autobiographical stance of the pioneer stage as well as on the imaginative literature of the midcentury stage. Consequently, with the "Nuyoricans, the Puerto Rican community in the United States has arrived at a modality of literary expression corresponding to its position as a non-assimilating colonial minority."[9] The most distinctive quality emanating from this new literature is the shift in language from Spanish to English and bilingual writing, which is a sign of being here although not necessarily of belonging.

Firsthand autobiographical and testimonial accounts also emanated from a rise in conventions regarding "poetry performance as a spectacle of personality."[10] In the late nineteenth and early twentieth centuries, poetry recitation played an important role in American education, enhancing patriotism, encouraging assimilation, and commemorating community celebrations. Twentieth-century advances in technology led to new forms of entertainment and may have promoted the contemporary poetry reading, in which poets recite their own work.[11] Some of the most skilled oral performers reached the public via the mass media, while opportunities to hear and see poets personally became rarer. Lesley Wheeler notes that "as its audience shrank, poetry became even more intensely an art of authenticity, representing the opposite of the polished, distant televised world."[12]

Algarín, a poet and professor as well as the founder of the Nuyorican Poets Cafe, offers a poignant example. In his essay defining Nuyorican literature, he writes, "Languages are struggling to possess us; English wants to own us completely; Spanish wants to own us completely. We, in fact, have mixed both." The choice to mix both languages constitutes a rejection not only of the Hispanism of the island but also of the assimilation pressures of Anglo-American culture. The experience of migration has left generations "stripped of all historical consciousness."[13] Like earlier generations of writers, Algarín argues for political recognition, consciousness-raising, coalition building, and expression of the self. Giving voice to the self is both a political and a self-defining action. He privileges oral expression and notes that the "expression of the self" and the "transformations before the public eye are a very important way of psychic cure" for those who have experienced cultural alienation, racism, poverty, and marginality.[14] Algarín and Miguel Piñero edited *Nuyorican Poetry: An Anthology of Words and Feelings* (1975), the first collection of such works. The 1994 publication of *Aloud: Voices from the Nuyorican Poets Cafe*, edited by Algarín and Bob Holman, included extensive works by poets of many different nationalities who used the café as a place for oral self-expression and transformation before the public eye. Both titles and collections stress poetry's importance for expressing personal voices, emotions, and self-definition.

As multiethnic and inter-Latino spaces flourished in New York, Burgos became an icon of New York Latino culture. Demographic shifts since the 1990s have created urban spaces in which Latino/as of various nationalities interact with each other. Today, nearly all Latin American and Caribbean countries are represented in New York, meaning that the city's Latino community is now only half Puerto Rican, with numerous other nationalities represented—Dominicans, Mexicans, Colombians, and Ecuadoreans, among others.[15] Claiming Burgos enables more recent Latino migrants to establish a connection to a place and space while acknowledging the Puerto Rican legacy of El Barrio. In Frances Aparicio's words, "The social mosaic leads to new forms of interaction, affinities, and power dynamics between and among Latinas/os from various national groups," creating new cultural objects and practices from multiple national influences. Further, while the "media and journalism seem to zero in on the ensuing cultural conflicts and national tensions that have arisen from these new social spaces," the different forms of affiliations, solidarity, identifications, and desires among Latino/as enjoy less visibility.[16] Collectively remembering Burgos as a part of the mythology of El Barrio acts as a site of solidarity, identification, and association among Latino/as. Yolanda Martínez—San Miguel has used the term *contact zone* to reflect on the postcolonial and neocolonial cultural exchanges among migrants from the insular Spanish-speaking Caribbean.[17] Their apparent similarities mask the great difference in social and political power. Marisel Moreno extends the idea to reflect on the "literary contact zones" that address the continuities that can be observed between the works of Puerto Rican women writers on the island and those in the diaspora.[18] These new inter-Latino cultural objects offer opportunities to reimagine *Latinidad* as a site of resistance.

The term *Latino* first came into circulation to recognize the heterogeneity of Latin America and acknowledge the African and indigenous legacies in South American cultures.[19] Yet the consumer version of Latino ethnicity tends to racialize Latinos toward whiteness, reflecting the racist ideologies found in the U.S. media and building on the racism of Caribbean and Latin American home cultures.[20] The North American media today highlight only a few spectacular success stories of Latino/as, masking the ongoing reality of racism, economic misery, and political disenfranchisement most Latinos face as a consequence of persistent regional and global inequalities. Discrimination in the educational and criminal justice systems and the desire to confront it continues to unite Latinos. Similarly, the media have defined *Latinidad* as a hegemonic concept that homogenizes Latino/as. However, Aparicio argues for reclaiming *Latinindad* as an idea that can be useful for exploring "(post)colonial historical experiences and for finding affinities and similarities that may empower us rather than fragment us."[21] New York–based Latino/as affirm their blackness in the image of Burgos, confronting the ideas of Puerto Rican and Caribbean social harmony and racial democracy that form part of the national narratives of the Caribbean and Latin America.[22] For writers such as Vicioso, Esteves, and Mariposa, claiming Burgos is a way to affirm their blackness and resist racialization toward whiteness.[23] Remembering Burgos offers contemporary writers a way to claim *Latinidad*, resist assimilation, struggle against consumerism and gentrification, and reimagine new futures for themselves and their communities.

Diaspora writers have invoked Burgos simultaneously to express cultural difference and to summon the transnational connections to home through which diaspora communities recognize each other. Brent Hayes Edwards explains that diaspora involves a real or imagined relationship to a homeland mediated through the dynamics of collective memory and the politics of return: "As a frame for knowledge production, diaspora inaugurates an ambitious and radically decentered analysis of transnational circuits of culture and politics that are resistant or exorbitant to the frames of nations and continents." The African diaspora, according to Edwards, is "formulated expressly through an attempt to come to terms with diverse and cross-fertilized black traditions of resistance and anticolonialism."[24] James Clifford observes that while diaspora discourses are defined and constrained by the structures of the nation-state and global capitalism, "they also exceed and criticize them, offering resources for emergent post-colonialisms." He argues that "there are no postcolonial cultures or places: only moments, tactics, discourses. . . . Yet 'postcolonial' does describe real, if incomplete, ruptures with past structures of domination, sites of current struggle and imagined futures."[25] Thus, identifications that mediate relationships to cultural traditions and ruptured, shifting, and displaced histories emerge from diasporic literature. Diasporic expressions are never purely nationalist but rather, as Clifford notes, "are deployed in transnational networks built from multiple attachments, and they encode practices of accommodation with, as well as resistance to, host countries and their norms."[26] When diasporic writers reference, remember, and riff off Burgos, they resist U.S. assimilation and Puerto Rican Hispanismo while identifying with island-based traditions and affirming their place in U.S. society.

Sexile

Economic and political conditions are widely recognized motivations for migrating from the Caribbean. More recent studies, however, have looked at such social motivations for migrating as persecution, ostracism, and feelings of rejection as a consequence of sexual orientation.[27] In *Queer Ricans: Cultures and Sexualities in the Diaspora*, Lawrence La Fountain-Stokes argues for the centrality of sexuality in the experience of Puerto Rican migration to the United States. Just as women's sexuality and eroticism challenge the foundational myth of *la gran familia puertorriqueña*, LGBTQ sexuality is seen as a menace to the nation and patriarchy. Homosexuality has been viewed as a "threat to the national character" and nonnormative sexual orientation as "a form of deviant behavior against which the national population needs protection."[28] Migration from Puerto Rico may not be forced in the way writer Reinaldo Arenas describes in *Before Night Falls,* his memoir of homosexual persecution in Cuba, but social intolerance, harassment, discrimination, and persecution nevertheless inform people's decisions to leave. In Puerto Rico, sexuality as a factor in migration was discussed openly for the first time when cultural workers began to document and explore experiences of sexile (forced migration from the home nation because of sexual orientation) in the 1970s and 1980s. Scholars have subsequently begun to recognize the importance of migration as both a regulatory measure and a liberatory strategy for nonnormative sexuality. Burgos became an icon for gay and lesbian writers who migrate to the United States as part of a liberatory strategy.[29]

Writer Manuel Ramos Otero's autobiographical and personal writing echoes Burgos's work and resists the notions of the Puerto Rican family and the insular nation. In "El cuento de la mujer del mar" (The Story of the Woman of the Sea), Ramos Otero creates a fictionalized Julia de Burgos in the peripatetic Palmira Parés.[30] As Burgos does, Ramos Otero takes up images of water, fluidity, and movement. Similarly, transformation through submersion and abjection are central to poetry by queer Puerto Rican Luz María Umpierre. Their sexuality as well as the topics they explore challenge the patriarchal canon by confronting the paternalistic family and the hacienda metaphors. In claiming Burgos as part of their legacy, they attempt to establish an alternative literary canon. If the nation, the canon, and the Puerto Rican family supposedly work against dispersion and insubordination, it is no surprise that these writers both transgress the boundaries of the national imaginary in their writing and migrate permanently to the United States. Theorist Cathy Cohen sees the concept of "queer" as offering the possibility of "construct[ing] a new political identity that is truly liberating, transformative, and inclusive of all those who stand on the outside of the dominant constructed norm of state-sanctioned white middle- and upper-class heterosexuality."[31] Gay and lesbian Latino writers queer Burgos in their work and develop the metaphor of her as an early figure of sexile, highlighting the possibilities of coalitions and shared resistance among all marginal communities.

Ramos Otero left Puerto Rico in 1968 because of persecution and ostracism he experienced as an openly gay man. He died of AIDS-related illnesses in 1990 in New York. According to La Fountain-Stokes, Ramos Otero was "looked upon with suspicion everywhere because of his openly militant gay liberationist and feminist politics."[32] Like other Puerto Rican writers, Ramos Otero's work has been overlooked in Latin America because of Puerto Rico's peripheral status there. Furthermore, he was marginalized in the United States because of his racialized, colonial status and because he wrote in Spanish. In the Caribbean, his work has been ignored because of his homosexuality and his decision to move north. Burgos's legacy in Ramos Otero's work is crystallized in "El cuento de la mujer del mar," in which the main character's queerness as a historical figure is dramatized. In the story, she appears as a poet who has a lesbian affair and then leaves Puerto Rico when the relationship is severed. "El cuento de la mujer del mar" is set on New York City's Christopher Street, the heart of the gay area of Greenwich Village. In this short story, the central character, Palmira, forms part of a mythology of the Village (as opposed to the mythology of El Barrio). Christopher Street is the site of the Stonewall Inn, where a series of 1969 riots strengthened and consolidated a much longer tradition of struggle for basic gay rights in the face of police harassment and social vilification. The larger story turns on the relationship between a nameless and unemployed gay writer (el cuentero, "the storyteller") and Angelo, his Italian American boyfriend. Their relationship is sustained by their retelling of competing versions of the tale of the woman of the sea. The protagonist of that story is the dark-skinned Puerto Rican poet Palmira Parés. In Angelo's retelling, the woman of the sea represents his Italian grandmother, Vicenza Vitale, suggesting the experiences shared by immigrants who arrive in New York. In Ramos Otero's version, Parés's blackness is evoked in her lesbian love affair with Filimelé, who also appears as the subject and muse of Luis Palés Matos's poetry, highlighting the two women's affinity in the author's mind. Parés leaves the island in 1939 after she ends her affair with Filimelé. A metacritical essay on the exclusionary and hypocritical quality of Puerto Rican literary and cultural institutions on the island and in New York weaves through the story.[33] Literary critic Betsy Sandlin argues that Ramos Otero queers his literary precursor, Burgos, to critique homophobic notions of Puerto Rican literary history.[34]

Using both fictional characters and the names of historical Puerto Rican literary figures in "El cuento de la mujer del mar," Ramos Otero assesses the same exclusive Puerto Rican institutions that Burgos criticized. He quotes from fictitious publications that capture the rumors and gossip that surrounded Parés's life, mirroring Burgos's history. El cuentero intimates that it was only a matter of time before Parés's tragic moments would evolve into a melodramatic story. In the end, he argues that critics brush off Parés as a morbid poet whom no one will ever really understand.[35] Twenty-five years after her death, el cuentero notes, criticism of her work remains anecdotal, personal, and dismissive. He contends that she is ignored partly because of her complexity and partly because she "escandalizó el orden de su época [scandalized the established order]" (102). The narrator suggests that rather than attempting to understand her, critics relegate her complexity to the realm of madness. Despite superficial critical praise, el cuentero believes that Parés really "es el poeta puertorriqueño más ignorado de su tiempo (el cielo y el infierno habitan en su poesía) [is the most ignored Puerto Rican poet of her time (heaven and hell live in her poetry)]" (108). He highlights the universal appeal of her work: the isolation and solitude reflected in her poems speak to all travelers and migrants. Ultimately, he finds himself in her story.

As travelers from disparate places bond over Parés's story, el cuentero remembers the Czechoslovakian woman who first revealed it to him:

> Contándome del viaje, de la llegada a la ciudad, del poemario póstumo de Palmira Parés, *El mar*, de los ojos inolvidablemente negros de Filimelé, de la voluntad para el suicidio lento, heroína en su abrazo y su poesía, de su muerte en Nueva York en el 1954. Nublada y llorosa por el humo (el tiempo había cincelado el acento) me dijo, "You must tell the story of Palmira." Pero uno sabe que hay cosas que no deberían contarse. (112)

> She told me of her journey, of her arrival to the city, of Palmira Parés's posthumous poetry collection, *The Sea*, of Filimelé's unforgettable black eyes, of her slow, voluntary suicide, heroine in her embrace and her poetry, of her death in New York in 1954. Hazy and tearful because of the smoke (time had chiseled away her accent) she said, "You must tell Palmira's story." But I know that there are stories that should not be told.

Parés's story (like Burgos's and Otero's) is the story that must not be told. They are shrouded in secrecy and gossip. The official versions are whitewashed and sanitized, with omissions, elisions, and ellipses. At times, stories circulate among those communities that identify with her story, exaggerating the more sensational aspects. Puerto Rican literary journals published scathing critiques of Ramos Otero's work, accusing him, like Burgos, of writing literature that was personal, solipsistic, and thinly veiled autobiography.[36] Similarly, Burgos and many other women of her era were faulted for writing nothing but love poetry, a style of literature that was too personal to be generalizable and was thus inaccessible to readers. The twentieth century saw a shift toward more autobiographical writing in both prose and poetry, with poets' personalities, authenticity, and presence highlighted as a way to rebel against modernist impersonality.[37] La Fountain-Stokes notes that autobiographical writing allows for self-reflexivity. It is grounded in experiential reality and communal history and offers a space for imaginative flights and creative expression.[38] Like Burgos's, Ramos Otero's life was surrounded by relentless gossip that ultimately led him to migrate. As he recalled, "I couldn't stand the repressive atmosphere of Puerto Rico. I had realized that New York was a city where I could live without feeling persecuted all the time. In Puerto Rico, I felt too much persecution because of the openness of my sexuality."[39]

Ramos Otero's short stories, poems, and essays chart his migratory experience. His self-reflexive texts are personal mythmaking and theorize exile as an emancipatory position.[40] At the core of "El cuento de la mujer del mar" lie Ramos Otero's obsessions with loneliness and death (often associated with the experience of exile for both him and Burgos). Burgos's and Ramos Otero's lives are similarly shrouded in secrecy and isolation. In the story, exile constitutes a displacement not only from communal belonging but also from the place where love, intimacy, and writing live. Ramos Otero's metaphysical use of exile echoes that of Burgos, who uses exile as a metaphor for love in *Canción de la verdad sencilla* (Song of the Simple Truth) and as a site of writing and death in *El mar y tú* (The Sea and You). By identifying himself with Burgos, Ramos Otero rejects the island's patriarchal canon, choosing instead to align himself with someone who was doubly marginalized as a poet and a woman, just as he was doubly marginalized as a writer and as a gay man.[41]

Umpierre has much in common with Ramos Otero and other first-generation queer diasporic writers of the 1970s and 1980s. Both Umpierre and Ramos Otero explore the experience of encountering traditional Puerto Rican cultural norms on the island and in the diaspora, and both closely identify with Burgos's life and work.[42] In Umpierre's words, "Julia de Burgos is part of the cultural consciousness of Puerto Rico. You cannot grow up in Puerto Rico and not know of Julia de Burgos."[43] Born in Santurce, Umpierre was head of the Spanish Department at the Academia María Reina, a private Catholic middle and high school for girls in San Juan, when gossip about her sexuality led to pressure on the school board to fire her. In 1974, acting on the advice of friends and colleagues, she decided to leave the island to pursue a doctorate at Bryn Mawr College in Pennsylvania.[44] After forty years in the United States, Umpierre considers herself both a Puerto Rican and a Nuyorican. She has described in interviews the sexuality-based discrimination she has experienced in Latino/a communities in the United States as well as from Puerto Ricans on the island.[45]

Umpierre has published five poetry collections, of which *The Margarita Poems* (1987) is considered the most important. It has been called a lesbian manifesto, and it is controversial because it was the first time she wrote openly as a lesbian.[46] The book begins with three essays by Julia Alvarez, Carlos Rodríguez Matos, and Roger Platizky—strategic choices as a Latina writer, a Puerto Rican critic writing in Spanish, and a mainstream male poet, respectively. *The Margarita Poems* was published in the wake of Cherríe Moraga and Gloria Anzaldúa's groundbreaking 1981 anthology, *This Bridge Called My Back: Writings by Radical Women of Color*, and clearly situates Umpierre as a critical writer in the development of Latina feminism, although her importance frequently goes unacknowledged.[47]

The Margarita Poems, which bears the dedication "For Margaret and Julia," consists of nine poems and a powerful introduction, "In Cycle," where Umpierre asserts the driving force behind the collection:

> I needed to say, to speak, "lo que nunca pasó por mis labios," that which I had not uttered, and which was being used as a tool in my oppression by others, murmured behind closed doors, brought up as an issue to deny me my rights by those enemies who read my poetry too well. What I needed to verbalize is the fact that I am, among many other things, a Lesbian.[48]

Umpierre goes on to express her desire to communicate with a love object who had come to represent all women. This love object is both Margarita and Julia, Umpierre's two muses, who fuse into the same person and ultimately into the self. Umpierre writes, "And as you read these you may ask yourself: Who is Julia? Julia is our greatest woman poet in Puerto Rico, Julia is a teacher, Julia is an idol, Julia is a friend. But Julia is, most of all, Margarita. We are all Margaritas and have a Julia within."[49] Two poems exemplify this treatment of Burgos as a muse: the opening poem of the collection, "Immanence," and the closing one, "The Mar/Garita Poem."[50]

Burgos's influence is felt most strongly in "Immanence," where she appears as a lesbian, evoking her image as a figure of sexile and reinforcing the possibility for alliances among marginalized communities. Queering Burgos highlights "struggles against sexual normalization as central to the politics of all marginal communities."[51] The poem opens with the speaker literally crossing Ohio's Mad River, a crossing that suggests other kinds of border crossings. The speaker is crossing into madness, a state effectively conjured in the poem's frenzied tone: it consists of short lines—sometimes only one word—that visually suggest the poem's intensity and quick pace. The speaker crosses into the other, the love object, as the lovers become one in the sexual act. The speaker calls forth Julia as a woman poet who can set aside social conventions and reach within, descending into madness and abjection to call forth the creative, writing woman.

I am crossing
the MAD river in Ohio,
looking for Julia
who is carrying me away
in this desire.[52]

Umpierre brings madness and creativity into relationship and connects these traits with creative women such as Julia de Burgos, Virginia Woolf, Sylvia Plath, and Frida Kahlo, positioning herself in dialogue with them. In the poem, Umpierre refers to Plath's famous "Lady Lazarus," where the poet writes of her spectacular ability to die and be resurrected. In this autobiographical/confessional poem, Plath alludes to the three times she had experienced death and to how death transformed her: first, at the age of ten, when her father died; second, when she attempted suicide while in college; and finally, when her husband left her. In the final lines of the poem, Plath's speaker has transformed herself into a powerful inhuman force: "out of the ash / I rise with my red hair / and I eat men like air."[53] Much like the ending of "Lady Lazarus," the speaker in "Immanence" closes the poem empowered. The tone of sexual frenzy is indistinguishable from madness. Julia is the inner woman who lives in a liminal space on the border of madness and defies all social conventions. In queer theorizing, "the sexual subject is understood to be constructed and contained by multiple practices of categorization and regulation that systematically marginalize and oppress those subjects thereby defined as deviant and 'other.'"[54] The Julia called forth in Umpierre's poem is the triumphant Julia of Burgos's "A Julia de Burgos" (To Julia de Burgos). She is the inner poet who defies the bourgeois society of her husband and kills off the submissive woman. This inner Julia then allows herself to enjoy sex with another woman.

The speaker becomes Julia in the final stanzas of "Immanence." She has learned to love herself, as signaled by the act of masturbation. The final stanza evokes the childhood game played with flower petals. Alternatively expressing self-love and self-hatred, the speaker utters to herself, "I touch my petals: / 'I love me. / I love me not.'" According to Umpierre, while Burgos looked outside herself for love, in this poem she finally learns to love herself.[55] The ending also shows the speaker learning to love herself despite the gossip, ostracism, name calling, and rejection she has experienced because of her sexuality. The ability to achieve lesbian love and self-pleasure (autoeroticism) threatens the myth of *la gran familia* because a woman who experiences pleasure without a man calls into question masculinity, procreation, and the family unit.

Readers of *The Margarita Poems* witness a search that is complex and multiple; as literary critic Elena Martínez notes, it is the "search for a lost lover, the search for a cultural and sexual identity, or the quest for a literary expression united to a political search."[56] The final poem of the collection, "The Mar/Garita Poem," culminates the collection's movement. The opening lines, which repeat throughout the poem, are onomatopoeic and suggest the sound of someone/ something drowning—"Glu, glu, glu, glu" (33). The drowning calls to mind the sea of Burgos's poetry as well as her death by alcohol. The poem also evokes Woolf's suicide by drowning: "buried alive, / disconnected from self the Muse / The sea" (34). Separation from the self plus the stagnated impulse to create equal death for the writer. The speaker/poet struggles to develop a language for advancing the creative project of the mother/poets who preceded her. Healing begins through this creative project. The poem moves from silence to English to Spanish. It is a return to the mother tongue, the source, the place of birth— Puerto Rico. In the poem, Umpierre explores two metaphors for the island: the *mar* (sea) and the *garita* (garret), a reference to the lookout post in El Morro, the fort erected in San Juan by the island's colonizers. The sea symbolizes the creative muse, while the *garita* is the vigilante editor, constantly watching. The poet must separate herself from these external influences and voices. This personal reading of the poem is also layered with political significance. The poem is simultaneously a call for Puerto Rican independence and freedom from colonialism. Both the sea and the land can be observed from the garret.

> Los dos símbolos isleños:
> el mar, mi mar, verdoso, azul
> y la garita, el puente de vigia, del colonizador. (35)

> The two island symbols:
> The sea, my sea, greenish blue
> and the garret, the outpost of the colonizer.

The movement from drowning sounds to English and finally to Spanish suggests the search for language and expression. As with other feminist writers of the 1960s and 1970s, Umpierre's search for a poetic voice "merges with voice in the political sense: having the right and the ability to speak, and especially to dissent."[57]

> to dismember the patriarch,
> to destroy the colonizers
> to crush the merchants of her pain,
> undressing herself from dogmatic lies
> and religious guilts. (34)

Martínez has noted the poet's awareness here of the challenge women writers face in discovering their own language, distinct from the language of male domination.[58] Through the creation of a new language, the poetic voice finds liberation. Readers of the collection experience the "process of catharsis and freedom that the poetic voice has proclaimed throughout the entire collection," culminating in the poem that closes the book.[59] This voice is not just a feminist voice but also a voice that speaks in English and in Spanish, highlighting the poet's marginalization as a woman and a Puerto Rican. For feminist studies and for Umpierre, who draws inspiration from feminist writers who came before her, voice "signifies both rhetorical and political power."[60] Many young Latinas and African American women have existed outside the white middle-class norms of heterosexuality. These women "fit into society's categories of marginal, deviant, and 'queer,'" as Cohen has noted, and "at the intersection of oppression and resistance lies the radical potential of queerness to challenge and bring together all those deemed marginal and all those committed to liberatory politics."[61] Ramos Otero and Umpierre use their work to honor Burgos's legacy by highlighting her commitment to freedom from oppression as they explore the possibilities of queer politics and the potential for coalitions with women and all marginalized communities.

Latinidad Feminista

In the 1970s and 1980s, women of color were in the process of defining themselves, asserting their agency, and building their own intellectual traditions. The publication of Moraga and Anzaldúa's *This Bridge Called My Back* and Gloria Hull, Patricia Bell Scott, and Barbara Smith's *All the Women Are White, All the Blacks Are Men, but Some of Us Are Brave* (1982) set out to expand the definition of *feminist* for women of color in the United States. According to Edna Acosta-Belén and Christine Bose,

> Out of the subordination of Latinas and their initial exclusion from both a male-dominated ethnic studies movement and a white-dominated women's movement, Chicanas, puertorriqueñas, and women from other disenfranchised U.S. ethnoracial minorities began to forge and articulate a feminist consciousness and a collective sense of struggle based on their experiences as members of diverse individual nationalities, as well as on their collective panethnic and cross-border identities as Latinas and women of color.[62]

Writing by Latinas surged in the 1980s. Anthologies such as Alma Gómez, Cherríe Moraga, and Mariana Romo-Carmona's *Cuentos: Stories by Latinas* (1983) and Juanita Ramos's *Compañeras: Latina Lesbians* (1987) as well as a book of criticism, *Breaking Boundaries: Latina Writing and Critical Readings* (1989), edited by Asuncíon Horno-Delgado, Eliana Ortega, Nina M. Scott, and Nancy Saporta Sternbach, signal the emergence of literary voices that transcend a single national identification and are told from a hemispheric perspective. Latina writers are conscious of writing for and about their communities, which are defined as both individual national groups and interethnic, extending solidarity to all women writers. Acosta-Belén notes that "while these groups challenge the cultural and socioeconomic hegemony that promotes an unfulfilled American dream, they affirm a distinctive collective identity which preserves, rejects, modifies or transforms elements taken from the culture of origin, from the surrounding world of the oppressor, and from their interaction with other subordinate groups with whom they share cultural and racial affinities or a similar structural position."[63] Women writers who participated in these movements grappled with Burgos's memory and intellectual legacy as part of a search for their history and the creation of new identities. In the process of remembering Burgos, they preserved, rejected, and modified parts of her story as they develop a politicized awareness of their structural position as women.

Women writers struggled against prescribed gender roles. In search of self-definition, they imagined new ways, paths, and roles for themselves as creative women. Umpierre's "No Hatchet Job," published in *The Margarita Poems*, explores the challenges particular to women writers. While the poem is dedicated to Marge Piercy, it tells the story of creative women and explores their structural position in society as women. The poem suggests that society attempts to subdue women writers whose lives are not easily contained within established notions of gender. When Umpierre writes, "We have domesticated this unruly woman" (21), she evokes Burgos's "A Julia de Burgos," where the speaker lashes out against gendered codes of domesticity. Subsequent stanzas of "No Hatchet Job" suggest that society enjoys seeing women broken down, vulnerable, and descending into illness because it keeps patriarchal hierarchy in place: "We have finally reduced this superior woman" (21). In the process, society dismisses the woman genius, cuts her down to size, and diminishes her until she is dead. Only then can society grapple with the creative woman through praise and hagiography. This poem suggests that in death, her genius can be contained, the meaning of her life controlled in the lifeless statues erected in her name.[64] While there is a push to praise her in death and create monuments in her honor, her life and humanity reject these stale narratives of sainthood as well.

> But headstrong she is unleashed,
> intractable she nourishes her mind,
> defiantly she lives on in unity,
> obstinately she refused the limelight, the pomp and the glory.
> Eternally she breathes

one line after next,
unrestrained, unshielded
   willfully
   WRITER
   WOMAN (22)

Umpierre challenges the tragic victim narrative that has cloaked the memory of
Burgos, Plath, Woolf, Kahlo, and Ana Mendieta, suggesting that society prefers
to erase their complexities by containing their legacies in tragedy, simultaneously
leading to their invisibility and hypervisibility as victims. In Burgos's "Poema
para mi muerte" (Poem for My Death), the speaker hopes that once she is
gone and others reflect on her life, she will be remembered above all else as a
poet.[65] In "No Hatchet Job," Umpierre affirms the identities of women artists
who came before her as well as Umpierre's own life as a creative woman. And
in "Manifesto: Whose Taboos?: Theirs, Yours, or Ours?," Umpierre points out
that she has been criticized for speaking her mind, referred to as mentally
unstable, and denied her status as a poet because her identity as a woman, a
lesbian, and a writer grates against the taboos that remain intact in North and
South America's patriarchal societies.

   Short story writer, essayist, and literary critic Sonia Rivera-Valdés was born in
Cuba and first lived in New York City in 1966. The following year, she moved to
Puerto Rico, where she remained until she returned to New York in 1977. Her
first book, *Las historias prohibidas de Marta Venerada* (The Forbidden Stories of
Marta Veneranda), a collection of short stories about the intimate lives of Latino
immigrants in New York, won the Casa de las Americas literary prize in 1997,
making Rivera-Valdés only the second person to win that prestigious Cuban prize
while living abroad. Her second book, *Historias de mujeres grandes y chiquitas*
(Stories of Little Women and Grown-Up Girls), deals with the complex nature
of human sexuality and how it affects all aspects of our lives. Rivera-Valdés first
learned about Burgos through intellectual and literary circles while living in Puerto
Rico. Among Burgos's works that made a lasting impression on Rivera-Valdés were
her feminist, personal poems, "A Julia de Burgos" and "Yo misma fui mi ruta" (I
Make My Own Path), because of their frankness, fearlessness, and determina-
tion.[66] Rivera-Valdés considers herself part of the generation of feminist women
of color writers published in *This Bridge Called My Back*, although she was not
a contributor. Anzaldúa and Mendieta, whose *Body Tracks* (1974) appears on the
cover of *This Bridge*, are part of this tradition, and what most impressed Rivera-
Valdés was that there was "una libertad en ellas tan grande [such a great freedom
in them]."[67] She renders homage to Mendieta in "Ana en cuatro tiempos" (Ana
in Four Times), included in *Historias de mujeres grandes y chiquitas*.[68] Mend-

ieta died in 1985 after falling thirty-four stories from her Manhattan apartment: her husband was tried for her murder and was acquitted. The circumstances surrounding her death and her focus on the female body deeply moved Rivera-Valdés, who had known Mendieta personally.[69] In the short story (perhaps better described as a novella, since it is seventy pages), Rivera-Valdés imagines the life experiences in Havana and Iowa that led the young Ana first to discover her vocation as an artist and later to her death in Manhattan. Rivera-Valdés provides insight into the intensity and drive of women artists such as Burgos, Kahlo, and Mendieta: "Lacking a shape to contain the pain, her suffering had no limits to its intensity. In life, her body would have responded to an upheaval of the soul like this with a headache, stomach ulcers, or high blood pressure. In life, desolation had organs where it could lodge itself." As Ana's spirit considers her own death, she feels confident that in her new state there "would exist only one memory, and that it surely wouldn't be that of her burial." Her spirit escapes in flight, and Rivera-Valdés suggests that her memory will dwell "in the intensity that resides only in the eternal."[70]

Rosario Ferré, a Puerto Rican writer who has lived both on the island and abroad, published a collection of essays, *Sitio a eros* (Eros's Site, 1977), that she described as a tribute to women she considers "saints"—Woolf, Plath, and Burgos—because "supieron, a pesar de sus muertes trágicas, trascender la mortalidad de sus cuerpos gracias a la pasión de su imaginación [they knew, despite their tragic deaths, how to transcend corporeal mortality through the passion of the imagination]."[71] These "cuentos" (stories), as Ferré refers to them, offer advice to young women readers who will face challenges in the world as women. In "Carta a Julia de Burgos" (Letter to Julia de Burgos), Ferré provides a short biographical summary of the poet's life, contrasting it with her work and underscoring those contradictions. As she wrestles with Burgos's legacy, Ferré reprimands the poet for what Ferré sees as poor and unwise choices in love—that is, loving men who were weak and unworthy of her. Ferré judges Burgos for failing to live up to the standards she set for herself in poems such as "A Julia de Burgos" and "Yo misma fui mi ruta," instead playing a submissive role before Juan Isidro Jimenes Grullón and other men: Ferré asks whether Burgos's life was truly the "expresión de una mujer que luchó por sus derechos [portrait of a life of a woman who fought for her own rights]."[72]

Finally, Ferré reconciles the discrepancies and contradictions she sees in Burgos's life and work by looking at the era when Burgos lived, concluding that it is important to avoid judging Burgos in hindsight, since at the time she lived, her life could not have been any other way. Ferré closes her letter to Burgos by noting that if her choices facilitated the development of her craft as an artist, then she made the right decisions.

Lejos de recriminarte tu servidumbre ante el amor, Julia, si te sirvió para crear, tengo que admirarte por ello; lejos de recriminarte tu sometimiento a seres incomparablemente inferiores a ti y de quienes tú forjabas una imagen totalmente irreal y enloquecida, si te sirvió para crear, tengo que admirarte por ello. Porque tú lograste superar la situación opresiva de la mujer, su humillación de siglos. Y al ver que no podías cambiarla, utilizaste esa situación, la empleaste, a pesar de que se te desgarraban las entretelas del alma, para ser lo que en verdad fuiste: ni mujer ni hombre, sino simple y sencillamente, poeta.

Far from reproaching your servitude to love, Julia, if it helped you create, I have to admire you for it; far from reproaching your submissiveness in love to those who were incomparably beneath you and for whom you forged a totally unrealistic and crazy image, if it helped you to create, I have to admire you for it. Because you managed to overcome woman's oppressive situation and centuries of her humiliation. Seeing that you could not change it, you used it, you worked with it, even though it tore your soul to pieces, to be what you really are, neither woman nor man, but quite simply, a poet.[73]

In this letter, Ferré remembers Burgos, contends with her influence, comes to peace with her perceived shortcomings, and envisions a more hopeful future not only for Ferré but for all women writers who follow. Burgos becomes an important literary foremother and helps establish a genealogy of Puerto Rican intellectual women.

Ferré takes up the theme of women who choose a writing life in her novel, *House on the Lagoon* (1996). Isabel, a wealthy housewife in Puerto Rico, finds power in writing a novel that records her experiences. As Isabel becomes more confident and self-assured, her marriage deteriorates. Her newfound strength gives her the courage to leave her husband, Quintín, and she flees the patriarchal culture of the island in search of freedom abroad.

Feminist analysis has always valued the remembering of women's stories as a corrective measure, but Chandra Mohanty reminds us that making visible, remembering, and rewriting "leads to the formation of politicized consciousness and self-identity."[74] Esteves, who is often called the *madrina* (godmother) of Nuyorican poetry, notes that the political awakening of Puerto Rican women in New York is directly connected to the influences of two women: Julia de Burgos and Lolita Lebrón.[75] New York Puerto Rican writers remember being introduced to Burgos's work through Ivan Silén and Alfredo Mantilla's anthology, *The Puerto Rican Poets* (1972). This anthology, which draws poems primarily from *Poema en veinte surcos* ("A Julia de Burgos," "Río Grande de Loíza," "Desde el puente de Martín Peña") and *El mar y tú* ("Poema para mi muerte"), made Burgos's work accessible to Nuyorican writers in English. As these New York–based writers sought to understand their history and identity, Burgos became an important influence, exemplifying social, political, and feminist themes. Every year, a group of women writers including Susana Cabañas, Esteves, and Mariposa gathered in a New York café to read Burgos's work and to perform poems, an activity that helped politicize them.[76] According to Pierre Nora, ethnic minorities, families, and groups in the process of interior decolonization have "possessed reserves of memory but little to no historical capital." In the absence of history, individuals must remember to "protect the trappings of identity; when memory is no longer everywhere, it will not be anywhere unless one takes the responsibility to recapture it through individual means."[77] Individuals do so in part by creating sites of memory, and willfully remembering.

Esteves's work explores her bicultural identity and feelings of detachment from her cultural heritage as a woman of Puerto Rican and Dominican descent growing up in New York City. Burgos's ability to weave together political ideals, the land, and love in her poetry influenced Esteves: "Burgos taught me how to pull all of those things together. She helped me to understand that."[78] The speaker in Esteves's "It Is Raining Today" recalls the violent history of the Caribbean and Puerto Rico as she longs for a deeper understanding of her heritage. In the poem, if rain is her history, the speaker's knowledge is nothing more than mist. She longs to reclaim her past: "Give me back my rituals / Give back truth / Return the remnants of my identity / Bathe me in self-discovered knowledge."[79] She understands that knowledge of her history, her past, and her traditions is critical to Puerto Ricans' sense of identity and self-worth. Joseph Roach notes that in the "absence of direct ancestors of sufficient prestige, the general concept of collective memory organized by race has served to establish a sense of heritage, however fabricated and illusory."[80]

> La lluvia contains our history
> In the space of each tear Cacique valleys and hills
> Taíno, Arawak, Carib, Ife, Congo, Angola, Mesa
> Mandinko, Dahome, Amer, African priests tribes
> Of the past
> Murdered ancestors
> Today, voices in the mist.
>
> Where is our history?[81]

According to Nora, in the absence of history, there is memory that takes root "in the concrete, in spaces, gestures, images, and objects."[82] Esteves remembers being moved the first time she heard about Burgos's life and death, feeling that Burgos's experience of migration echoed the stories of Esteves's mother and many other migrants. Burgos's struggle to survive and find work in the face of

humiliation inspired Esteves. Esteves's "A Julia y a Mí" (To Julia and to Me),
published in *Yerba Buena* (1980), is dedicated to Burgos, although Esteves
notes that she was also thinking of her Titi Julia (Auntie Julia) while writing the
poem. As in Ferré's work, the speaker in Esteves's poem seems to be engaged
in a dialogue with Burgos, wrestling and ultimately rejecting parts of this legacy.
Esteves questions Burgos for giving into the sorrow, despair, and isolation she
felt in New York City: "You let the dragon slay you / You let life cut your sor-
row from wrinkles young / You let the wine mellow your hatred." The speaker
notes that young Latino/as need positive role models to help them overcome
the challenges of the metropolis. Remembering Burgos enables the speaker to
preserve the story of her ancestors, rejecting parts of it, while reinventing and
imagining a more hopeful future. Whereas "Julia" anesthetized her pain with
alcohol, the speaker found alternative ways to confront the pain of life:

> A ti Julia, ya será tarde
> pero a mí no
> ¡yo vivo!
> y grito si me duele la vida
> y canto con la gente
> y bailo con mis hijas
> no soy lágrimas de ser
> soy el río
> la mariposa y culebra
> my fist is my soul
> it cuts into the blood of dragons
> and marks time with the beat
> of an afrocuban drum.[83]

In this poem, she reaches back to her African roots and traditions to sustain her.
She is life, nature, the river, the delicate butterfly, and the snake. The speaker
suggests alternatives to the path of despair and addiction, finding comfort and
joy in family, culture, and community—traditions that will sustain her through
life's challenges. This poem exemplifies the way diaspora discourses and the
experience of displacement involve recovering "non-Western, or not-only-
Western, models for cosmopolitan life, nonaligned transnationalities struggling
within and against nation-states, global technologies, and market resources for
a fraught coexistence."[84]

While sites of memory can be concrete, such as monuments and anniver-
saries, they can also be intellectually elaborate notions such as generations,
lineage, and local memories. Esteves's "Who I Am" is a poem of self-definition,
where the author defines her political position by establishing an intellectual

genealogy. This identity text opens with the speaker claiming to be a "child of Lolita [Lebrón], Julia and Clemente [Soto Vélez]" and looks to the future generation of writers such as La Bruja (Caridad De La Luz) and Mariposa to keep alive the lineage. The speaker defines a community of women who give her strength and sustain her: "Adoro mis hermanas luchadoras, / curanderas, maestras, comadres, / cocineras, cosejeras, / amigas fuertes siempre a mi lado [I adore my sisters in the struggle / healers, teachers, godmothers / cooks, advisers / strong friends always by my side]."[85] Esteves references Burgos's most iconic poetry when the speaker claims to "choose the path I travel" while inheriting and extending the legacy of those writers who came before her. Esteves aligns herself politically with Burgos, Soto Vélez, Lebrón, and the Young Lords in the 1970s; she marched to the United Nations for Puerto Rico and to Philadelphia for Mumia Abu Jamal. Through the act of remembering, she affirms her intellectual genealogy and defines her political position.

Preserving the stories of their ancestors allows Puerto Rican diaspora writers to re-create the past and envision a more hopeful future. It allows them to break the historical silence that has characterized their place in society as women while offering the infinite possibilities of self-invention.[86] Writer, artist, and historian Aurora Levins Morales was born in Puerto Rico to a Puerto Rican mother and a Jewish father. She was raised on the island and since 1970 has lived in Berkeley, California, and most recently in Cambridge, Massachusetts. An important figure of Latina and Third World feminism, she is a contributor to *This Bridge Called My Back* and the author of several books, including *Medicine Stories: History, Culture and the Politics of Integrity* (1999) and *Kindling: Writings on the Body* (2013). Levins Morales describes herself as "an activist, a healer, a revolutionary. I tell stories with medicinal powers. Herbalists who collect wild plants to make medicine call it wildcrafting. I wildcraft the details of the world, of history, of people's lives, and concentrate them through art in order to shift consciousness, to change how we think about ourselves, each other and the world."[87] Her *Remedios: Stories of Earth and Iron from the History of Puertorriqueñas* (2001) is a powerful account of Puerto Rican women's history written in an innovative mix of prose and verse, first- and third-person accounts. Drawing on both memory and history, *Remedios* begins in Africa and ends in New York in 1954, the year of the author's birth. Levins Morales draws on the lives of African, indigenous, Spanish, and Jewish women—women who were stolen and sold and the everyday women who kept communities together. The remarkable women in the book include Burgos, Francisca Brignoni, Ida B. Wells, and Lola Rodríguez de Tió. Levins Morales weaves her own story/history into the narrative. Writing about Burgos, Plath, and Sylvia Rexach, Levins Morales reflects on the deadly mid-twentieth-century cult of domesticity:

Literary men will write about these women's sadness and suicide as if it were the greatest poetic achievement of their lives, a glorious celebration of women's inevitable suffering, an accomplishment that merely living women must strive to emulate. They will poke among the lyrics looking for evidence that nothing could have been done to save them.

Their fingerprints are everywhere, but I proclaim that these women did not die by their own hands, that their fingers were in captivity, that death was prepared for them by others. That they fell in a brutal decade, murdered in the gender wars, unable to imagine there was solace to be found in the collective rage of women if they could have only waited five or six years, that they were not alone, that there could have been another ending to the song.[88]

By remembering, writing and revising history, *Remedios* demonstrates that literature is a powerful antidote to historical amnesia. As Nora writes, "Every great historical revision"—including that of Levins Morales—"has sought to enlarge the basis for collective memory."[89]

Award-winning Nuyorican playwright Carmen Rivera was born in the Bronx and joined the Puerto Rican Traveling Theater's professional playwriting unit.[90] Some of her best-known plays are *La Lupe: My Life, My Destiny* and *Celia: The Life and Music of Celia Cruz*, a critically acclaimed off-Broadway musical cowritten with Cándido Tirado that focuses on the lives of iconic Cuban women performers who migrated to New York. Rivera's play *Julia de Burgos: Child of Water/Julia de Burgos, Criatura del Agua* was first produced at the Puerto Rican Traveling Theater on 12 May 1999. The plot loosely follows Burgos's life. A surrealist play, it is structured around Burgos's poem "A Julia de Burgos," where two dueling parts of the self speak to each other. The soul (or the poet self) appears as a separate character who has been abandoned by Burgos. The play suggests that in her search to find love outside of herself, she lost sight of her soul. One of the highlights is a powerful exchange in which Pablo Neruda tells the passionate Julia, "Art should come from love, not hate." When asked what she should do if she is surrounded by anger, Neruda responds, "Feel it, transform it and release it."[91] The struggle between Julia and the Woman/Soul carries the play, as Julia copes with how to be a woman and an artist. Julia tells the Woman/Soul, "It's a curse—this longing to write."[92] Julia is free to reconcile with the Woman/Soul in the final scene after rejecting men who mistreated her. The play suggests that both Burgos and Rivera find themselves through art and writing. In the final scene, Julia awakens disoriented on stage and asks why the audience is there. When told that the play is a tribute to her life and legacy, Julia responds, "Don't remember me!"; the Woman/Soul, now also the playwright, says "Feel free."[93] Through the process of possessing Julia and reliving her story, Rivera becomes a proxy for Julia, who ultimately understands the quest for freedom to be Burgos's most enduring legacy.

Dominican writer Chiqui Vicioso shows how Burgos's influence moved beyond the Puerto Rican community and was a way for women of different national origins to come together to form a shared political consciousness. In April 1967, Vicioso moved to New York, seeking a path to freedom, according to her autobiographical essay, "Discovering Myself: Un Testimonio."[94] In New York, she worked various factory jobs while studying English. She was one of eight Dominican students admitted to Brooklyn College when the City University of New York opened its doors to more students of color. There, "since there were only eight of us, and it was very tough to survive in such a racist atmosphere, we joined up with other minority students, principally Puerto Ricans, Blacks, other people from the Caribbean—we formed a Third World Alliance."[95] Thus, in New York, she discovered her black, Caribbean, and Latin American identity.

Vicioso remembers Burgos as her salvation at a time when she no longer felt the will to live. Indeed, Vicioso's interviews with Juan Bosch and Jimenes Grullón are incredibly valuable contributions to the study of Burgos and her legacy, since they are the only interviews with these men that focus on her and her work. As Vicioso became active in social justice and civil rights causes in New York, she increasingly felt a conflict of loyalties with the white feminist movement. She felt that collaborating with them betrayed the men of her racial and ethnic group. In her home country, she would have been considered a failure: "I would have been frustrated, unhappy in a marriage, or divorced several times over because I would not have understood that within me was a woman who needed to express her own truths, articulate her own words. That, in Santo Domingo, would have been impossible."[96]

Vicioso published a beautiful collectible book, *Julia de Burgos: La nuestra* (1987) with woodcuts by artist Belkis Ramírez, honoring Julia in prose, poetry, and engravings. Vicioso relives the moment when she first learned of Burgos as she walked past that infamous El Barrio street corner with a friend in 1977, a site of memory that Vicioso has memorialized with a poem.[97] She writes explicitly of Burgos's multiple connections to the Dominican Republic and notes that few Dominicans today, at least in literary circles, have not heard of Julia.[98] According to Vicioso, "To pay homage to [Burgos] in the Dominican Republic, the land she so loved but could never visit, and to make known her contributions to the struggle for our own true independence is not only a moral obligation but another way to proffer our love."[99] Vicioso's identification grew as she learned how Burgos's "consciousness of the United States' role in Puerto Rico" broadened as she came into contact with other Antilleans in Puerto Rico, New York, and Cuba, all of them "exiles from the same tyranny."[100] Remembering Julia is a way for Vicioso to explore the various manifestations of U.S. colonialism and occupation as well as the "common destiny as Caribbean countries and the unbreakable bonds" that link the two islands.[101]

Cuban professor turned playwright Oscar Montero has lived in New York City for many years. As professor of Latin American literature and culture, Montero noticed that many of his students, particularly Latinas in search of role models, connected powerfully to Burgos's best-known poems such as "Yo misma fui mi ruta" and "A Julia de Burgos." Teaching Burgos thus became a successful introduction to poetry: her lyrical poems—particularly the verses that explore feminist themes of autonomy and breaking with socially acceptable roles—resonated with Latina and first-generation students. This pedagogical focus was a driving force behind the creation of his unpublished debut play, *Las rutas de Julia de Burgos* (The Paths of Julia de Burgos, 2011), which follows the poet's migratory routes. The play offers a biographical portrait of Burgos in three scenes, drawing from correspondence as well as poetry, placing her poetry in its historical and social context, and making it more accessible for the general public. The play opens with her death, then flashes back to Puerto Rico, where Burgos and her sister talk passionately about the nationalist movement, their mother, and the intellectual circles of which both women were a part. This scene reveals the centrality of this form of relationship—the feminist bond between sisters—for Burgos's development as a writer and intellectual. The subsequent scenes recount her experiences in Havana with Jimenes Grullón and her final years in New York City.

At the end of the play, the characters read in unison Burgos's poem "Yo misma fui mi ruta," suggesting that she was a woman who followed her own path. Montero's Julia de Burgos is an unconventional 1930s Puerto Rican woman and writer. In offering this complex picture, Montero suggests that while Burgos's migration to the United States was not entirely successful, she, like many other Puerto Rican women who migrated to New York, cannot be contained within narratives of tragedy and victimhood.

DiaspoRican Expressions, Redefining Identities

Spoken-word and performance artists take the poetics of presence and authenticity to new levels. Poetry slams and performances "dismantle inherited associations of the lyric with privacy by conceptualizing poetry as a site of conversation," stressing pluralism and dialogism.[102] Oral performances have the power to build community and inspire social change. They are theatrical and populist, characterized by political dissidence and subversiveness; they are antipretentious and anticorporate, rooted in realness, authenticity, and truth telling. While written poetry relies on tropes, diction, syntax, and punctuation to evoke the poet's presence, performance poetry uses gesture, pitch, and timing to "convey grief, rage, and other strong emotions," making the words seem more authentic while playing to a "contemporary understanding of poetry as a deeply personal expression of inner conflict."[103] The themes and subjects of the poems—often race, familial expectations regarding gender, and discrimination—draw attention to the speaking body and often insist on words' embodiment.[104] According to Kathleen Crown, "By focusing on the persona of the poet who takes the stage, spoken word poetry seems at times to exalt the authoritative *presence* of the poet's body and the esoteric *aura* of the poem's voiced body prior to any technology of reproduction."[105] Newer generations of New York–based performance poets invoke Julia de Burgos from the stage as a way to claim their Puerto Ricanness, their blackness, and their presence.

In the United States, blackness/Afro- and *Latinidad*/Latino are often thought of as distinct and mutually exclusive. One is either black or Latino but not both. The term *Afro-Latino* gained currency in the United States in the 1990s to describe those of African descent whose origins are in Latin America and the Spanish-speaking Caribbean. In this formulation, blackness and *Latinidad* are not mutually exclusive concepts, and the Latino concept itself is inadequate to describe this heritage. Juan Flores notes in the introduction to *The Afro-Latin@ Reader* that "in their quest for a full and appropriate sense of social identity, Afro-Latin@s are thus typically pulled in three directions at once." He describes this "three-pronged web of affiliations" as a "triple-consciousness," taking a cue from W. E. B. Du Bois in *The Souls of Black Folk* (1903). The Afro-Latin@ is constantly aware of his/her three-ness—Latin@, black, and American, "three souls, three thoughts, three unreconciled strivings; three warring ideals in one dark body, whose dogged strength alone keeps it from being torn asunder."[106]

The complicated relationships among blackness, *Latinidad*, and gender are exemplified in Mariposa's "Poem for My Grifa-Rican Sistah."[107] Mariposa (María Teresa Fernández) is part of a younger generation of Nuyorican writers. She has acknowledged the importance of Burgos as a literary influence, and that influence is also evident from the multiple references to Burgos in Mariposa's work. The poem's title evokes an Afro-Latina identity as well as refers to Burgos's "Ay ay ay de la grifa negra" (My, Oh My, Oh My, of the Nappy-Haired Negress, 1938). *Grifa* refers to a woman of African descent with coarse hair; *Rican* signals a Puerto Rican identity; and *Sistah*, with its phonetic spelling, educes an African American identity. The poem revolves around the external pressures to suppress blackness through the act of hair straightening, a common ritual among women of African descent with curly hair. In a world where female beauty is associated with long, flowing locks and European features, women of African descent feel pressured to engage in practices that will help them approximate these images of beauty: "Pinches y ribbons / to hold back and tie / oppressing baby naps / Never to be free." The stress to conform to these images appears in the mother's intimate act of fixing her child's hair, suggesting how racism and a colonized mentality are internalized by the oppressed and taught to the next generation: "It hurts to be beautiful, 'ta te quieta. / My mother tells me." In Africa, the ritual of braiding women's hair is a communal bonding activity. In this poem, the bonding practice has been subverted to involve cultural, psychic, and personal alienation. In this case, the mother sends the powerful message that the daughter's hair needs to be fixed.

> Chemical relaxers to melt away the shame
> until new growth reminds us
> that it is time once again
> for the ritual and the fear of
> scalp burns and hair loss
> and the welcoming
> of broken ends
> and broken
> promises.

The final stanza suggests that freedom will come only through self-acceptance—through the affirmation of blackness, not the suppression of it.

Mariposa's signature poem, "Ode to the Diasporican," is commonly referenced to express a New York Puerto Rican identity. Writing in English and Spanish, Mariposa claims the Puerto Rican heritage she learned on the streets of New York. Her free verse features an intense language, passion, and imagination that resembles Burgos's. The poem opens with the speaker's unassimilable physical qualities that mark her difference in American society. She has dark skin, curly hair, and an attachment to another place, Puerto Rico. As Mariposa performs the poem, she often touches her hair and holds out her hands when they are mentioned, commanding audiences' attention to her body and its physical features. Stanzas in Spanish open and close the poem. It contrasts the New York cityscape with the Puerto Rican landscape with a reference to Burgos's "Río Grande de Loíza."

> Some people say that I'm not the real thing
> Boricua, that is
> cause I wasn't born on the enchanted island
> cause I was born on the mainland
> north of Spanish Harlem

cause I was born in the Bronx
some people think that I'm not bonafide
cause my playground was a concrete jungle
cause my Río Grande de Loíza was the Bronx River
cause my Fajardo was City Island
my Luquillo Orchard Beach
and summer nights were filled with city noises
instead of coquis
and Puerto Rico
was just some paradise
that we only saw in pictures.

What does it mean to live in between
What does it take to realize
that being Boricua
is a state of mind
a state of heart
a state of soul.[108]

The third stanza raises the island's ambiguous political status and the bicultural identity of those who live outside of the island. With a play on words, the speaker suggests that Puerto Rico's collective identity is defined by the features of diaspora: a history of dispersal, memories of a homeland, and alienation in the host country. As a stateless nation, Puerto Rico is a state of mind. Although the desire for return often defines diaspora, Mariposa's poem rejects this idea. The connection to that other place, an elsewhere, is clear in her work. But her poem articulates how she has made New York her own, affirming her existence and her right to be there.

The themes of self-determination and rejecting narratives of victimhood abound in the work of Nuyorican writers from the 1970s to the present. Mariposa's "Boricua Butterfly" challenges the migration-as-tragedy narrative by affirming a cultural identity and choosing to live differently.

I am the
Meta-morpho-sized
The reborn
The living phoenix
Rising up out of the ashes
With my conquered people
Not the lost Puerto Rican soul in search of identity
Not the tragic Nuyorican in search of the land of the palm tree

Not fragmented but whole
Not colonized
But free.[109]

Here, Mariposa rejects the migration-as-tragedy narrative by claiming a trans-
formational identity, one that is re-created and metamorphosed like the phoenix
and the butterfly. If Burgos found freedom in a similar confessional tone, Mari-
posa claims liberation through poetry of self-definition. Performance artist La
Bruja's work also remembers Julia as a way to connect to the past and imagine
a better future beyond annihilation and silence. In an untitled and unpublished
poem to Burgos that La Bruja has performed in New York City, she closes with
an exclamation, "Hart Island couldn't keep her spirit silenced / today we scream
her name . . . Julia!"[110] According to Wheeler, slam poems often invite us to
identify with victims because "paradoxically it can be pleasurable to identify with
a victim (as opposed to being a victim)."[111] The poem is often performed with
a small band playing drums in the background. The dancing body of the poet
and performers stand in direct contrast to notions of oppression and tragedy. La
Bruja's poem rejects victimization in the presence of the speaking, screaming,
life-affirming body on stage.

Nuyorican poet and performer Bonafide Rojas protests the gentrification
of El Barrio in his poem "Remember Their Names." He invokes Burgos and
Pedro Pietri as a part of the history and mythology of a neighborhood that is
threatened with erasure.

you can feel it change on 116th st.
la marqueta is staring down its road
and sees the faces bleaching with the gentrification

1st ave is being tidal waved with bullseyes
on the corner children hold signs that say libertad
but you understand it as something that has to be freed
or liberated, so you introduce a slow invasion
instead of self preservation

salsa isn't as loud as it used to be in the streets
the congas are quiet, the bombas have been defused
but there is still a resistance running in the streets

we are looking for pedro pietri to give us our passports
so we can detach ourselves from ourselves
if you don't recognize our birth certificates then we don't
recognize your citizenship

we wander through the streets of our memory
looking for julia de burgos in the concrete of our tongue

where is el barrio?[112]

In a rapid, intense, slam style, the poet goes on to list the names of sixty-two important historical figures who fought in various ways for Puerto Rico's liberation and cultural preservation. The poem seeks to bridge the divide between the island and the diaspora by naming historical figures from both here and there.

Diaspora writers bring legitimacy and attention to a different way of being Puerto Rican and American, a way that is conceived out of the experience of migration, is birthed in urban centers, and creates room for expressions in both English and Spanish. These expressions are visible in the writings of second and third generations that are part of an interethnic Latino background, as in the case of Emanuel Xavier. "Americano," in his 2002 collection by that name, offers a poignant example of a different way of being American. Of Ecuadoran and Puerto Rican heritage, the poem's speaker looks in the mirror, struggling to understand what makes him American. His physical qualities mark his difference. He can see traces of Africa in the orishas he sees reflected in the mirror; when the poem is performed, the audience is his reflection, seeing what he sees. The poem is often performed with a full band. The speaker laments the pressure to assimilate that Latinos experience: "I see my mother trying to be more like Marilyn Monroe than Julia de Burgos / I see myself trying to be more like James Dean than Federico García de Lorca."[113] The push to assimilate leads many Latinos to turn away from their cultural heritage and legacy and instead emulate North American icons of femininity and masculinity. He suggests that Latino culture is intricately woven into the fabric of U.S. culture. But the ideals of democracy have been corrupted by greed. Selfish individualism has distorted the vision of democracy, and the interests of corporations are served over those of the people.

Jose, can you see . . .
I pledge allegiance
To this country 'tis of me
Land of dreams and opportunity
Land of proud detergent names and commercialism
Land of corporations

If I can win gold medals at the Olympics
Sign my life away to die for the United States
No Small-town hick is gonna tell me I ain't an American
Because I can spic in two languages

Coño carajo y fuck you

This is my country too
Where those who do not believe in freedom and diversity
Are the ones who need to get the hell out.[114]

In the current political climate, where Latino/as are seen as foreigners and alien to the body politic, Xavier reverses the script. He contends that those who should leave are those small-minded people who cannot imagine a different America. Those who are threatened by the Latino presence, the Spanish language, and the browning of the United States are destroying the country. Xavier closes by noting that those beliefs are antidemocratic and un-American and need to be excised.

I started this chapter by asking what it means when New York–based Puerto Rican, Caribbean, and Latina writers invoke, remember, and reinvent Julia de Burgos. Queer and feminist writers identify with her as a figure of sexile. As writers seek to establish an intellectual genealogy of women, they come face-to-face with Burgos's legacy, keeping parts of it while rejecting others as they imagine a different life for themselves and their daughters. They find ways to reconcile and come to terms with her legacy through their art. Performance artists connect with Burgos as a poet of presence and authenticity, rejecting the modernist impersonality through oral performance, passion, and rebelliousness. All of these writers deploy Burgos's memory to help them mediate their relationship to history in the process of inventing new identities, new languages, and new ways of thinking.

5

Remembering Julia de Burgos
Cultural Icon, Community, Belonging

Sites of memory—archives, museums, works of art, monuments, anniversaries, rituals—are fundamentally created, Pierre Nora says, "to stop time, to block the work of forgetting, to establish a state of things, to immortalize death, to materialize the immaterial." Without the will to remember, history would soon sweep away these memories. Mass culture and the media toss aside memory in exchange for an endless film of current events. Sites of memory represent an attempt to capture a maximum of meaning in the fewest signs; these sites exist because of their "capacity for metamorphosis, an endless recycling of their meaning and an unpredictable proliferation of their ramifications." Sites of memory help mediate a relationship to the past that is formed of a "subtle play between its intractability and its disappearance." We seek an understanding of what we are in light of what we are no longer.[1] In the act of remembering Julia de Burgos, visual artists are less concerned with finding the "true" Julia; rather, they create sites of memory that are at once collective and individual, mediating our relationship to the past, the present, and the future.

Two distinct historical moments have provided fertile ground for reading Burgos as a historical figure, a writer, and a cultural icon. First, as part of the civil rights movement of the 1960s, women of color sought to correct the elisions and omissions of writers, artists, and intellectuals of color in the historical records and the literary canon, Latina writers reclaimed Burgos and struggled to have her recognized in literary history. Second, during the "Latin explosion" of the 1990s, signaled by the 12 July 1999 issue of *Newsweek* with its cover story "Latino U.S.A.," corporate marketers came to understand Latinos as a consumer category. Simultaneously, anti-immigration sentiment and widespread anxiety about the U.S.-Mexican border swept the United States.

The 1990s witnessed the cultural and commercial iconization of Frida Kahlo and of Eva Duarte Perón, two Latin American women who died tragically at a young age. Selena Quintanilla, a young Latina superstar from Texas, was murdered in 1995 and became lionized across the United States. In her book on Selena, Deborah Paredez notes that in the 1990s, despite the different investments in *Latinidad*, all constituencies, whether cultural or commercial, evoked the symbol of the dead Latina, which was "frequently pressed into service by a range of communities to claim or to contest the political, cultural, or economic force of *Latinidad*."[2] Frida, Evita, Selena, and Julia have been remembered and immortalized in plays, performances, music, biographies, films, murals, paintings, stories, and novels, among other genres. Hollywood made films about the first three icons, no last names required: Madonna played *Evita* (1996), Jennifer Lopez played *Selena* (1997), and Salma Hayek played *Frida* (2002). Burgos, however, has not achieved the same level of mainstream commercial success and visibility. In part, this phenomenon results from the fact that Kahlo, as a visual artist, and Selena, as a pop star, do not rely exclusively on language to communicate their art. Burgos, conversely, was a poet who wrote mostly in Spanish, a medium and language that created obstacles for crossover success. In addition, Puerto Rico's colonial status and continued political and economic dependence obscure the island's cultural production in the United States, while Puerto Rico's affiliation with that cultural juggernaut leads to its omission from discussions of the Caribbean and Latin America.

Icons are remembered and refashioned by each generation. Joseph Roach notes that death offers marginalized communities the opportunity to affirm their "semiautonomous but discreetly submerged existence within or against the obligatory rituals of the better publicized fiction called the dominant culture."[3] As Burgos emerged as an icon specific to New York Latino/a culture, remembering her became one of the memory circuits mapping the migratory routes of New York Latino/a cosmopolitan networks. This chapter charts the course of Burgos's iconography, mapping the migratory trajectories and circulation of her influence from New York to Puerto Rico and the Dominican Republic and consequently offering insight into New York Latino/a cultural production. New York and other cities are affected by neoliberal economic policies that demand that culture be distanced from histories and neighborhoods.[4] The chapter focuses on Burgos's iconography in East Harlem, where she forms part of the neighborhood mythology.

Lorenzo Homar and the Graphic Arts in Puerto Rico

More than any other form of plastic arts, printmaking has shaped the endearing images and icons of that which is recognizably Puerto Rican.[5] The printmaking

movement began in Puerto Rico in 1950 and set the tone for the social realism
that characterizes the prints, though other currents—abstract expressionism,
surrealism, and neodada—are visible from the 1960s onward. In the early stages
of Puerto Rican printmaking, communication and expressiveness were favored
over aesthetic considerations. The nature of the art form gave it privileged
status on the island; prints are easily produced and transported. This art genre
established in unequivocal terms the role of art in depicting a differentiated
image of Puerto Rico.

Lorenzo Homar has been credited with initiating the Puerto Rican tradition
of printmaking. Born in San Juan in 1913 to parents who had migrated from
Mallorca, he was raised in a middle-class household in Santurce and Puerta
de Tierra. His father owned a small film-rental business. In 1928, financial dif-
ficulties caused the family to migrate to New York City; Homar did not return
to San Juan until 1950, when he went to work for the Division of Community
Education. Homar's work is clearly informed by his experiences in both Puerto
Rico and New York. In his work, 1930s and 1940s New York City art, painting,
graphic arts, vaudeville, and jazz are palpable. While living there, he visited movie
houses, museums, and theaters and met artists and architects. Fluent in English,
he conversed comfortably in both languages. He worked at the prestigious Cartier
House designing watches, necklaces, and brooches. After returning from service
in the Pacific theater in World War II, he participated in the city's Arts Student
League and studied at the Brooklyn Museum, where he met Rufiño Tamayo,
Arthur Osver, and Max Beckman. Homar was impressed by the graphic arts and
posters he saw around the city and in the subway, particularly the work of Carl
Binder in the Bauhaus style. The streets of New York were for him a great mu-
seum.[6] His connections with Puerto Rican artists and writers living in New York,
among them René Marqués and José Luis González, eased Homar's transition
into the Puerto Rican art world when he returned to the island.

Homar became reacquainted with life in Puerto Rico by drawing its people,
landscape, cultural geography, and objects. As a consequence of his artistic ex-
perience, he played a key role in the Graphics Art Workshop of the Division of
Community Education, where he worked until 1957. For the next sixteen years,
he contributed to the workshop of the Institute of Puerto Rican Culture. Many
artists, including Homar, felt conflicted about the national cultural institutions
that emerged midcentury. According to Arcadio Díaz Quiñones,

> They desired, on the one hand, a certain amount of autonomy from political
> and economic powers, so as to create an aesthetic vision of the nation. On the
> other hand, they longed to integrate high culture—the theater, museums, bal-
> lets, concerts—with popular culture, coinciding here with the state-run cultural
> projects of the time.[7]

The Division of Community Education launched the Books for the People project in collaboration with the Center for Puerto Rican Art. This was a pedagogical state project created with the working-class population in mind. Graphic artists and writers collaborated on illustrated books for teaching literacy. These inexpensive volumes centered on themes of health, civics, and history. The graphic artists of Puerto Rico found a way to create cultural memory on the island. Homar explores in his prints the polyphonic traditions that influence his work, creating a visual history of Puerto Rico made up of fragments. Perhaps his most famous work is *Portafolio de plenas*, created with Rafael Tufiño in 1954. The prints incorporate popular culture into visual art to celebrate *la plena*, an Afro–Puerto Rican form of music.

Homar has been called the most literary of Puerto Rico's graphic artists.[8] He canonized the words and images of such icons as Pedro Albizu Campos, Luis Palés Matos, René Marqués, and Juan Ramón Jiménez. According to Díaz Quiñones, Homar's work has the ability to "inscribe select quotes and confer upon them an aura that fixed their value and beauty."[9] He illustrated Pedro Juan Soto's *Spiks* as well as works by Luis Lloréns Torres, a tradition Homar passed along to his students. One of those students, José R. Alicea, canonized Burgos's "Río Grande de Loíza."[10]

While working at the Institute of Puerto Rican Culture in 1969, Homar created *Homenaje a Julia de Burgos* (Homage to Julia de Burgos; see plate 1). The image features blue and green tones along with Homar's signature block lettering in bold geometrical shapes. Interestingly, he chose not to use the more feminine ornate calligraphy that appeared in his portrait of Albizu Campos as well as in many of his other works. Inscribed on the print is the second stanza of the Julia de Burgos's poem "Rompeolas" (Seawall), from *El mar y tú* (The Sea and You):

> No quiero que toque el mar
> La orilla acá de mi tierra . . .
> Se me acabaron los sueños,
> Locos de sombra en la arena.[11]

> I do not want the sea to touch
> This other shore of my land . . .
> Dreams? They are all gone,
> Crazed like shadows on the sand.

An image of Burgos's face emerges from behind the letters, partially obscured as hollow eyes peer at the viewer. *Homenaje a Julia de Burgos* has a tombstone quality to it. The words inscribed on the image suggest an epitaph, a genre of

Plate 1. *Homenaje a Julia de Burgos*, by Lorenzo Homar, 1969. Reproduction authorized by Susan Homar Damm and Laura Homar Damm.

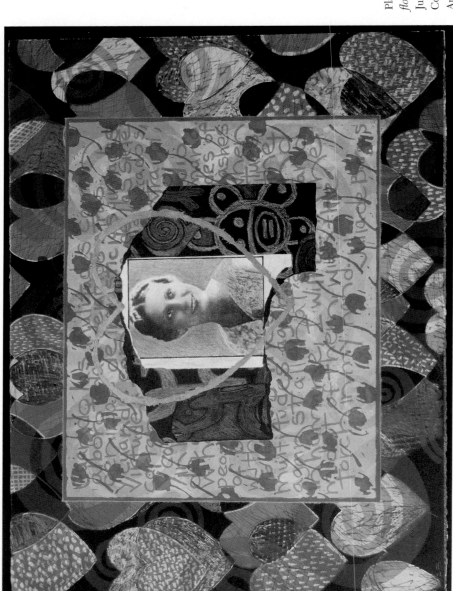

Plate 3. *El pensamiento de Julia*, by
Belkis Ramírez, 1991. Copyright Belkis
Ramírez. Reproduced with permission.

Plate 4. *Despierta*, by Yasmín
Hernández, 2005. *Soul Rebels*
Series. www.yasminhernandez.com.
Reproduced with permission.

Plate 5. *Julia de Burgos*, by Yasmín Hernández, 2006. *Soul Rebels* Series. www.yasmin hernandez.com. Reproduced with permission.

Plate 6. *Carpeta, Julia*, by Yasmín Hernández, 2007. *Archivos subversivos* Series. www.yasmin
hernandez.com. Reproduced with permission.

Plate 7. *A Julia de Burgos*, by Andrea Arroyo, 2009. Copyright Andrea Arroyo 2009.

Plate 8. *Remembering Julia*, by Manny Vega, 2006. Photo by Francisco Molina Reyes II.

Plate 9. *Soldaderas*, by Yasmín Hernández, 2011. Photo by Francisco Molina Reyes II.

lyric poetry that Barbara Johnson describes as having two functions: "to protect the corpse from desecration, and to monumentalize the memory of the deceased."[12] A master of the lyric, William Wordsworth wrote an essay in which he noted that the epitaph genre achieves its function by animating the dead and representing them as speaking from beyond the grave.[13] In the epitaph, rhetorical strategies such as prosopopoeia are employed to animate the dead and blur the lines between life and death. In Homar's visual homage to Burgos, she indeed seems to speak from beyond the grave. Her name and face are inscribed on the lower left side of the painting, visually echoing a signature. The talking grave reverses the progress toward death. However, the image speaks only of death, serving as a reminder of life's brevity.

Wordsworth highlights the connection between epitaphs and the development of writing:

> It needs scarcely to be said, that an epitaph presupposes a Monument, upon which it is to be engraven. Almost all nations have wished that certain external signs should point out the places where their Dead are interred. Among savage Tribes unacquainted with letters, this has mostly been done either with rude stones placed near the graves, or by Mounds of earth raised over them. . . . As soon as Nations learned the use of letters, Epitaphs were inscribed upon these Monuments.[14]

Homenaje a Julia de Burgos functions as a monument to a national poet who was originally buried in an unmarked grave. On a tombstone, as in this image, the proper name of the deceased calls out. In making the dead speak, the epitaph needs to accomplish what all lyric poetry must accomplish: it must give the reader access to the living voice of the poet no matter how long she has been dead. This is the immortality of literature and the written word—a temporality independent of mortality. The privileging of the text in this homage reminds us that the text speaks to us and that through her poetry, Burgos continues to speak to those who are willing to read.

Juan Sánchez: Reconstructing Puerto Rican Identity in the Diaspora

Juan Sánchez was born in Brooklyn in 1954 to Puerto Rican parents. He is a professor of art at Hunter College in New York City and has been a visiting professor at Cornell University. He holds a bachelor of fine arts degree from Cooper Union and a master of fine arts degree from Rutgers University's Mason Gross School for the Arts. Sánchez was inspired by the political and social movements of the 1960s and 1970s, including the Young Lords Party: "My work derived from a deficiency and need within my own community to complement a movement, to raise a level of consciousness, and to foster self-empowerment so that people go out and change the things that are repressing and oppressing them."[15] He also learned from an artist collective, Taller Boricua (Puerto Rican Workshop), and from Hans Haacke and Leon Golub. Sánchez explores political activism and cultural identity in his artwork and the exhibits he curates, taking instruction and politicization as his goals. He combines photographs, found objects, and poetry in his paintings and prints, conjuring the urban milieu and Latin American intimate spaces with portable altars and religious iconography. One of his works, *Rican/Structions*, draws on the language of art to heal the Puerto Rican community and make conscious a history that has long been overlooked.[16]

As a black Puerto Rican born and raised in Brooklyn, Sánchez remembers his first encounters with racism. In the neighborhood, people frequently questioned whether he was Puerto Rican. His experience, shared by many other dark-skinned Puerto Ricans, raises interesting questions about what it means to be Puerto Rican from a racial perspective. After researching the island's history, Sánchez concluded that Puerto Ricans must be able to define themselves if any progress is to be made. He believes that physical borders as well as racial, linguistic, and political splintering prevent Puerto Ricans from coming together. He is searching for a more unified, complex, and rich understanding of who Puerto Ricans are as a people: "We're part of it. We're part of American history. And we're part of Latin American history. We're connected to the African diaspora. We're hooked up to the indigenous struggle and nations. That's how rich we are. That's how powerful we are."[17]

Sánchez believes that polarization within the community leads to fragmentation and that Burgos's legacy is caught in the web of these polarized positions. Her story has not been told in its full complexity. Her political self, her involvement with the Nationalist Party and the independence movement, her Communist Party of America affiliation through *Pueblos Hispanos*, and her decision to leave the island with a Dominican intellectual in many ways defy the insular vision on the island. Her writings complicate and expand traditional notions of American literature. Sánchez's art urges the viewer to see Puerto Rican history and historical figures as an important part of American history. He feels that the stories of Albizu Campos and Burgos need to be woven into the fabric of the United States in tangible ways.

> This colonial ordeal in one form or another has made us part of American history. The moment they invaded the island and imposed citizenship and all that has manifested since then makes us part of that history. So my argument, which is very critical, is that the literature of Julia de Burgos and everybody else before and after her is part of American literature. Punto [Period].[18]

Sánchez describes his encounters with Burgos's work as a love story. Before they married, the woman who is now his wife, Alma, introduced him to Burgos's poetry. Alma was born in Brooklyn to Puerto Rican parents, but unlike Juan Sánchez, she returned to the island at the age of five, was educated there (including earning a bachelor's degree at the University of Puerto Rico), and lived on the island until she was in her early thirties. Sánchez was intrigued when Alma brought Burgos to his attention, and in 1982, he made his first artwork depicting Burgos, *Para Julia de Burgos* (For Julia de Burgos). A mixed-media collage using oil, acrylic, and photo on canvas, the work features a photo of Burgos in the center, with her poetry text surrounding the image. A studio subsequently invited Sánchez to make a limited-edition print of Burgos, *Corazones y flores para Julia* (Hearts and Flowers for Julia, 1994; see plate 2), that comprises lithography, linoleum cut, laser print, and collage. Sánchez finished the print with a gold-leaf heart framing a photo of Burgos. The text surrounding the image is the last stanza of her "A Julia de Burgos" (To Julia de Burgos).

Sánchez's images and their lovely, childlike quality contribute to the iconography of Burgos. "You have to marvel at her," Sánchez says, and this sense of wonder comes through in the images. He describes Burgos as "extremely universal" and having a "progressive mentality." While he finds evidence of this in her poetry, when he looks back at the artwork he created twenty to thirty years ago, he wonders if it stereotypes her. For both collages, the photo of her shows her with her hair neatly pulled back, and she is wearing a floral dress. In the 1982 collage, the photo is framed in pink, while in the 1994 piece, he surrounds the photo with hearts and flowers and places a symbol of Atabex, the Taíno mother of creation and fertility, in the lower left corner of the inner frame. The images surrounding her suggest and celebrate femininity. Sánchez now seems to question whether this image and iconography evokes the socially acceptable Julia de Burgos she harshly criticized in "A Julia de Burgos."[19] Or does the collage portray the strong, inner poet-self who struggled for social justice? Perhaps the images do not summon either Julia. But they highlight the gap between the smiling image of the woman in the photo and her words, inviting us to explore the contradictions that arise there.

Photography, Women Artists, and Julia de Burgos

Studio photographs of Julia de Burgos from the 1930s and 1940s have circulated widely in the public domain, with no indication when they were taken or who took them. The complicated questions of race, gender, and class are implicated in the way that Burgos is remembered in these photos. They highlight her femininity.

The most popular image is a black-and-white studio photograph taken between 1938 and 1940 in which she seems to mimic Rodin's *The Thinker*, with head bowed and chin resting in her hands, a pensive and somewhat submissive look on her face (see fig. 4, p. 57).[20] This image certainly depicts a subdued woman. Some might even say she looks demure, as her eyes never meet the camera. Her hair is neat and pulled back tightly. She wears a high-necked top and no jewelry. Her body is not visible. The photo is simple. Her long fingers fan out delicately and femininely to frame her face. Her dark hair and black top also create the illusion of fairer skin. Cropped to show only her face, the same photo was used for the banner that now marks Julia de Burgos Boulevard, on E. 106th Street near Lexington Avenue.

Although many readers use "Ay ay ay de la grifa negra" as evidence of Burgos's blackness, her racial identity has been the subject of public debate. Representations of her skin tone range from fair, as seen on a 2010 stamp issued by the U.S. Postal Service, to dark, as seen in Manny Vega's 2006 East Harlem mural, *Remembering Julia de Burgos*. The extant black-and-white photos of Burgos make determining her complexion difficult. In a 1967 tribute to her life and work at New York City's Caravan House, her contemporary, Clemente Soto Vélez, described her as "una bella muchacha de rostro acanelado por el sol de Puerto Rico [a beautiful woman who captured Puerto Rico's sun in her cinnamon-colored face]."[21] Photos of Burgos's father show him to be fair with European-looking features, but no images of her mother are known to exist. Some family members in Puerto Rico have described Burgos's mother as *bien trigueña*, a term that has no English equivalent but denotes dark skin, while others in Brooklyn have described her as black, highlighting the difference in racial identification on the island and in the United States. Family members and scholars agree that Julia de Burgos was of African descent.[22]

However, her story has been consistently whitened, sanitized, and depoliticized, most recently on the stamp, which shows a very fair Burgos in front of the Loíza River. The prejudice and racism she experienced as a working-class woman of color have been overlooked in favor of an explanation that attributes many of her problems to a pattern of self-destructive behavior. Women visual artists who have lived in New York or learned of Burgos through the city's cosmopolitan networks have challenged this whitewashing with new and imaginative visual representations that contest the narrative of migration and tragedy. Their work suggests that Burgos, like many other Latina migrants to New York City, is too complex and multifaceted to be contained in the narratives of femininity, tragedy, and victimhood. These artists engage Burgos's image in compelling ways, exemplifying the idea of inter-Latino sites of cultural production, which Frances Aparicio defines as "those sites where two or more Latinos from various national origins encounter, construct, and transculturate each other." *Latinidad* has often been defined as homogenizing toward whiteness while erasing the historical and cultural specificities that make up the panethnic identity. These identifications allow for inter-Latina knowledge that "represents alternative discourses" that challenge the silences that exist about various national origins and home countries in search of analogous decolonizing ideology that is both (post)colonial and antipatriarchal.[23]

Yasmín Hernández's Liberation Art

Yasmín Hernández is a Brooklyn-born artist of Puerto Rican descent who creates works rooted in struggles for personal, spiritual, and political liberation. Hernández attended LaGuardia High School of the Arts in Manhattan and earned a bachelor of fine arts in painting from Cornell University, where she studied with Juan Sánchez. In her senior thesis, she reconfigured American history icons with the icons and heroes of Puerto Rican history who often go unrecognized or are even vilified, such as Pedro Albizu Campos and Lolita Lebrón. For example, she replaced Abraham Lincoln's image on the penny with that of Albizu Campos. She revised Paul Revere's engraving, *The Bloody Massacre in King Street, March 5, 1770*, as *The Ponce Massacre, March 21, 1937*. While in Ithaca, she found her peers to be hostile toward the art she was making and found a sense of validation in working with Sánchez, an established artist and professor who had been reworking American icons for more than a decade. Since her graduation, Hernández has continued to explore themes of art and liberation as an artist and as an educator. She has worked on community education initiatives at the Studio Museum of Harlem and El Museo del Barrio as well as Philadelphia's Taller Puertorriqueño. Her work explores the spiritual, personal, and political dimensions of freedom and their interrelationships. Focused on Boricua imagery, lingering on clandestine histories and marginalized communities, she portrays various important yet often forgotten figures of history as warriors and sacred beings. Her work contains multiple references to the orishas and the deities of the Yoruba tradition, important symbols of resistance to annihilation in the African diaspora, while her use of calligraphy and text acknowledges the influence of the twentieth-century Puerto Rican printmakers such as Homar and Rafael Tufiño.[24]

Hernández's *Soul Rebels* project debuted at El Museo del Barrio in 2005 as a tribute to musicians and poets who were committed to social justice and whose work raised awareness about injustice. The series features images of Nuyorican poets Tato Laviera, Pedro Pietri, and Piri Thomas, among others. Musicians in the series include Andrés Jiménez, Eddie Palmieri, Bob Marley, Ricanstruction, and Public Enemy, a combination that establishes the political and ideological connections among jazz, hip-hop, reggae, and punk. The only woman included in the series (and the only figure to appear in two paintings) is Julia de Burgos. *Despierta* (Awake, 2005; see plate 4) is bright and colorful, while *Julia de Burgos* (2006; see plate 5) is on burlap in earth tones. While the portraits resemble Burgos, viewers might not initially recognize her without close study. These portraits challenge the hyperfeminine, staged photographs from the 1930s and 1940s by portraying her as a warrior and a revolutionary, highlighting her anticolonial and anti-imperial feminist politics.

Inspired by Burgos's liberation poetry, Hernández based *Despierta* on an undated photograph of the poet seated on the bank of an unknown river that evokes Burgos's "Río Grande de Loíza." The river rushes mightily behind the poet, who wears a white dress and sits with her hands gently folded in her lap. This is one of the few photographs in which her hair is down around her shoulders. She sits sideways with her face turned toward the camera. The photo evokes the eternal feminine and the virginal poet who sits in nature with her lover, the river, behind her. The photo hides the violent imagery evoked in the

Figure 9. Julia de Burgos by a river, ca. 1936–39. General Collections, Archives of the Puerto Rican Diaspora, Center for Puerto Rican Studies, Hunter College, City University of New York.

poem and the history of colonization that the poet remembers. This particular image appealed to Hernández because of the water and its significance in Burgos's poetry: "I set out to paint that Julia that she had been criticizing [in her poems], and I really feel that when the painting emerged, I painted the author of 'A Julia de Burgos.'" Frustrated by the fact that the extant visuals of Burgos do not represent the person she imagined her to be, Hernández set out to represent the poet as Hernández imagined that she would want to be represented.[25]

Despierta shows Burgos wearing pants, fists clenched and holding a machete. She is standing at the edge of a river, legs apart and feet in the water and arms at her side, as if prepared for battle. Her stance is robust and resilient. She towers, extending beyond the horizon line, the rising sun behind her. Across her abdomen is a quotation from her poem "23 de septiembre" (23 September): "Vivo en el gran desfile de todos los patriotas / que murieron de ira y de ira despiertan [I live among the great procession of patriots / who died in fury and in fury awake]."[26] The poem's title references the 1868 Revolt of Lares, an uprising against the Spanish colonial government. In addition to "23 de septiembre," the painting references fifteen of Burgos's other poems.[27] Every visual aspect is dictated by one of the sixteen poems. The painting channels her most political, anti-imperial, and socialist poetry. In addition to the water imagery, the bright blues and yellows are Yoruba references to orishas Yemaya and Oshun. Burgos's clenched fists conjure "Somos puños cerrados" (Clench your fists). The machete is a reference to the worker in "Pentacromia" (Pentachrome). Hernández includes images of Filiberto Ojeda, Albizu Campos, Clemente Soto Vélez, and Juan Antonio Corretjer, situating Burgos among some of the most well-known nationalists and fighters for Puerto Rican independence. According to Hernández, "A Julia de Burgos" gives

> the sort of psychotic sense that she has to split into these two people, and then when you see these photos of her, you're seeing that person that she's criticizing over and over, so I just felt if I have to paint her, then why not paint her the way she would like to see herself. I'm not going to paint her as a man because today you don't have to be *un hombre* to be all these things that she had wanted to see herself as.[28]

She painted Burgos as a peasant, with the sugarcane and the land in the background. Hernández believes that in Burgos's poetry, the worker is the ultimate symbol of the liberator. In this painting, Burgos becomes an ancestor.

Hernández's second painting of Burgos was part of an installation featuring Latino/a artists at El Museo de Puerto Rico's biennial celebration. The exhibit featured three U.S.-born artists of Puerto Rican descent but did not identify them as Puerto Rican, yet according to Hernández, "our work was most visibly Puerto Rican."[29] This statement suggests the complicated relationship between the diaspora and the island as well as the desired connection to the legacy of the island that will help repair the historical rupture about which Arcadio Díaz Quiñones writes in *La memoria rota* (Ruptured Memory). Separated from her history, she is compelled to remember. Díaz Quiñones contends that recalling and remembering breaks the silence that surrounds the Puerto Rican working class, Afro–Puerto Ricans, and those living in the diaspora.[30] Hernández's depictions of Burgos as a *jíbara* (peasant working in the cane fields) helps restore the severed relationship between the members of the working class who left the island and the island's history. Hernández, like Burgos, challenges the tendency of island elite who have internalized the colonial mentality to perpetuate the elisions and silences.

The installation consisted of an image of Burgos and Andrés Jiménez in a corner, facing each other. The figures painted on burlap summon images of poverty and the burlap sacks used to collect beans and other products from the land. Palm and plantain leaves, shells, and sand were placed in the corner space between the two images. The leaves were green when the exhibit opened and changed to brown over time as they dried up (just as the land did), taking on the colors of the paintings. The seashells were collected from Carolina, Burgos's hometown. Hernández subverts the *jíbaro* image to comment on the abuse and overdevelopment of Puerto Rico's land. Hernández incorporates ornate calligraphy in the style of Homar and Tufiño, with a stanza from Burgos's "Pentacromia" inscribed across the top of the painting.

> Hoy, quiero ser hombre. Sería un obrero
> picando la caña, sudando el jornal;
> a brazos arriba, los puños en alto,
> quitándole al mundo mi parte de pan.[31]

> Today, I want to be a man. I would be a worker.
> cutting cane, sweating my wages
> arms up, with my fists in the air,
> claiming in this world, my slice of bread.

Creating these modernized images of Burgos allows Hernández to identify with traditional aspects of Puerto Rican culture while constructing a different image of Puerto Rican womanhood.

In 2007, Hernández created a series, *Archivos subversivos* (Subversive Archives), to honor the suppressed history of Puerto Rican radicalism and subversion. The series sheds light on the practice of surveillance by U.S. government bodies such as the FBI that sought to quash the Puerto Rican independence movement and other leftist movements in the United States. Hernández began the project after being invited to show her work by the Center for Puerto Rican Studies at Hunter College. She wanted to showcase the center's archival collection and consequently used its sources as well as documents from her personal library to create the series. The project statement for *Archivos subversivos* includes an excerpt from a 1960 FBI memo:

> In order to appraise the caliber of leadership in the Puerto Rican independence movement, particularly as it pertains to our efforts to disrupt their activities and compromise their effectiveness. We must determine their capabilities of influencing others, capabilities of real leadership, why the intense desire for Puerto Rico's independence, what they expect to gain from independence and the support they have from other leaders and rank-and-file members. We must have information concerning their weaknesses, morals, criminal records, spouses, children, family life, educational qualifications and personal activities other than independence activities.

Archivos subversivos celebrates intellectuals, artists, citizens, and others who work to expose and fight against social injustice and challenge the status quo. The collection's aesthetic quality is derived from the files and archives. Hernández uses yellow, sienna, and sepia tones in paintings shaped like manila folders. Some of the images appear worn, suggesting that the practice of surveillance has a long history. Others are partially burnt or damaged, evoking the idea that attempts have been made to destroy the documents and any records of harassment of innocent people. Hernández used the courier font to conjure up McCarthy-era typewritten documents.

The *Archivos subversivos* collection includes a painting of Burgos and features "Es nuestra la hora" (Ours Is the Hour). The poem, a powerful anti-imperial statement, calls on the working class to take up arms and unite against U.S. imperialism and colonialism in Puerto Rico. Hernández's image, *Carpeta, Julia* (Folder, Julia, 2007; see plate 6), includes a group of workers with clenched fists and machetes. Lines from this and other poems, including "Somos puños cerrados," "23 de septiembre," and "Puerto Rico está en tí" (Puerto Rico Is in You), are interspersed throughout the image. Burgos wrote "Puerto Rico está en tí" in New York, and it references Luis Muñoz Marín's political campaign on behalf of a free associated state status for the island. Burgos argues that Puerto Ricans should continue to struggle for independence and should reject handouts from the United States that will only lead to a "Puerto Rico 'estado associado y ridículo' [Puerto Rico 'ridiculous and associated state']."[32] Hernández's image charts Burgos's political convictions as documented in her political activities and her writing. The work effectively contrasts Burgos's words with popular portrayals that highlight her femininity. The word *subversive* is written across the painting, a reminder of the challenges Burgos faced. Hernández's

Archivos subversivos paintings of Jesús Colón and of Filiberto Ojeda also refer-
ence Burgos, restoring her place among important subversive elements of the
Puerto Rican independence and communist movements on the island as well
as in New York.

El Pensamiento de Julia—*Belkis Ramírez*

Belkis Ramírez is a Dominican-born artist and one of the few women to en-
joy some success in visual arts in that country. Her work consists primarily of
installation art, though she is also a master of graphic arts, printmaking, and
woodcuts. Ramírez, an architect by training, graduated from the Universidad
Autónoma de Santo Domingo, Dominican Republic. Her work explores political
themes, the role of women in Latin America, sex tourism, and environmental
problems such as exploitation and destruction. Her work has been exhibited
in Spain, France, New York, and Miami as well as throughout the Caribbean
and Latin America.

In 1987, Belkis Ramírez illustrated Chiqui Vicioso's book, *Julia de Burgos:
La nuestra* (Julia de Burgos: Ours), which demonstrates Burgos's connection
to the Dominican Republic. According to Vicioso, Dominicans claim Burgos
as *nuestra* because she wrote the strongest anti-Trujillo poetry published to
date. Burgos's legacy traveled through the New York metropolitan center to
the Dominican Republic with Vicioso's interest in Burgos and published inter-
views of Juan Bosch and Juan Jimenes Grullón. After making the illustrations
for Vicioso's book, Ramírez developed an interest in Burgos; in 1991, Ramírez
created a woodcut, *El pensamiento de Julia* (Julia's Thought; see plate 3), that
challenged the popular, demure, and pensive image of her. The image replicates
the reserved face with closed eyes, but the poet's hair flies upward and fills the
frame, strong, commanding, and compelling. It focuses on Julia's thought, de-
picting her as an intellectual and defying the narrowing myths of victimization
and love. In this image, Burgos appears larger than life.

Seeing this woodcut print displayed in Vicioso's home in the Dominican
Republic, writer Julia Alvarez was moved to read more of Burgos's work. The
New York–born Alvarez instantly connected to the image as "an accurate pic-
ture of my own head and imagination." The idea "that we can have so much
in our heads and we're not 'crazy' was so affirming." She purchased the wood
block for Ramírez's print as well as a copy of the print, and the image now ap-
pears on her website's homepage.[33] *El pensamiento de Julia* creates knowledge
about different Caribbean and Latino groups challenging the balkanization
of the islands by way of the diaspora. These connections highlight shared
historical experiences as colonial subjects and new oppositional, liberatory
expressions.

Women's Altar Traditions—Andrea Arroyo

Andrea Arroyo was born in Mexico and moved to New York City in the early 1980s at the age of twenty on a scholarship to study the contemporary dance techniques of Merce Cunningham. She danced professionally in New York for five years before switching to the visual arts. Although she always liked to draw, she did not initially believe that being a visual artist was her calling. As a child, she had watched her mother make ceramics and at times would make small clay objects. In New York, she bought some art supplies and created a dozen small sculptures depicting the people she saw every day—homeless women, break-dancers in Central Park, and people on the subway. Galleries soon began to exhibit her work, and she subsequently moved from sculpture to painting, building a career focusing on women in her artwork. Her *Flor de vida* (Flower of Life) project celebrates the lives of historical and mythological women from various cultural traditions—Aztec, Mayan, Egyptian, Greek, Asian, and Indian. The influence of dance and movement in these works is apparent, as the figures seem to glide and swirl across the canvas. The bright, bold colors remind the viewer of the boldness of the lives of these women and convey a sense of celebration and homage. The images suggest connections between the contributions of the historical figures and the experiences of contemporary women. When talking about what inspires her, Arroyo responds without hesitation,

> Women. That's the first thing. Every woman has a story. We all face challenges. I'm inspired by women from history and mythology and their amazing stories, but contemporary women as well. Immigrant women, mothers and daughters and sisters and artists and women in general. I'm just really inspired by them. I think everyone has something special, and every woman is a warrior; we have to be.[34]

Her most recent project, *Flor de tierra* (Flower of the Land), commemorates lives of the mostly immigrant and indigenous women who travel to the border town of Juárez to find work. In the past twenty years, an estimated four hundred of these women have been murdered, and many more have disappeared. The murdered women have been mutilated, tortured, and raped. The state has continued to turn a blind eye to the violence; no one has been held accountable, and the women are often blamed for their own misfortune. The drawings, simple silhouettes drawn in white on black paper, echo the white chalk outlines of bodies at a murder scene. When Arroyo is finished, each woman will have a drawing reflecting her personality, qualities, and characteristics, emphasizing her humanity rather than her tragic death. Arroyo explains, "My idea is that many of these victims could have been the next Frida Kahlo, Marie Curie, an amazing visionary; their lives were cut short and their circumstances were just not good enough for them to explore. They just didn't live long enough for us to know. Through this parallel, I hope to suggest the ways that every woman's life is equally valuable."[35]

In 2009, El Museo del Barrio commissioned Arroyo to create two altar installations for its annual Day of the Dead cultural celebration, which incorporates films, presentations, and family activities. It comes as no surprise that Arroyo dedicated the two altar installations to women. One altar honored Mercedes Sosa, the great Argentine singer known as the Voice of the Voiceless Ones across Latin America, who died that October. The second altar was dedicated to Burgos and simply titled "A Julia de Burgos" (To Julia de Burgos; see plate 7). Arroyo had learned of Burgos and her poetry through New York Latino cultural networks. In *Beautiful Necessity: The Art and Meaning of Women's Altars*, Kay Turner defines the altar as a "place between divine and human realms, a threshold charged with exchange."[36] Arroyo became fascinated by Burgos's story and the tales of heartbreak and misfortune that surround her. Arroyo continued to research the poet's life and noted the anecdotal nature of the accounts and the focus on difficult aspects of her personal life—her love affair and her alcoholism, for example. Arroyo explains,

> The fact that she died a tragic death in El Barrio is often what people remember of Julia, and I wanted to honor her and make her whole. This is the same thing that happens sometimes with the women of Ciudad Juárez. So I try to make them whole, focusing on the whole person instead of just having that particular tragedy define who she was.[37]

The altar installation is bright and colorful, in the traditional Mexican style. It is adorned with flowers, calaveras, and Burgos's poetry, which hangs on paper across the front of the altar. At the center of the altar is a framed portrait of the poet directly above a Puerto Rican flag. The focus on Puerto Rico in a traditional Mexican altar created for public mourning brings together beautifully and powerfully the shared history of Puerto Rico and parts of Mexico that have been incorporated into the United States. The U.S.-Mexican border and Puerto Rico have become dangerous contact zones and gateways for the trafficking of people and drugs and other criminal activity. This altar educes Arroyo's work on the women of Ciudad Juárez. El Barrio has seen an influx of Mexicans. The neighborhood, which borders the Upper East Side, has also been affected by rapid gentrification. Arroyo's altar installation, moored in the community, connects these two cultures and traditions. It offers viewers the opportunity to collectively mourn Burgos while simultaneously mourning the many Latinas who have not found safe passage into the twenty-first century across the U.S.-Mexican border and beyond. As an example of inter-Latina identification, Arroyo's altar installation creates communities of resistance among Latinas in a common struggle against sexism, racism, and exploitative structures. Arroyo champions the lives of poor women of color who have been written out of history and highlights the intersecting histories of race, colonialism, and capitalism in the border zones.

For Latina artists, remembering Julia de Burgos becomes a tool for self-preservation, recovering history, cultural affirmation, and public mourning. Through their work, they validate the power and resilience of living communities.[38] In the political context, Latina artists deploy Burgos's story, her poetry, and her death as symbolic sites for claiming full American citizenship rights for all Latino/as.

El Barrio, East Harlem's Cultural Corridor

The so-called Latin explosion of the 1990s coincided with the Spanish-American War centennial and one hundred years of U.S. domination in Puerto Rico. When the fascination with dead Latinas such as Evita, Frida, and Selena emerged across the nation, Julia became the icon of Latino New York.[39] As the mainstream media touted Latinos as the "new Americans" and recognized them as comprising a significant commercial market, Puerto Rican artists in East Harlem made art that denounced colonialism, erasure, and displacement.[40] Many saw the 1990s as a symbolic moment. Artists sought a way to challenge gentrification, secure their position in El Barrio, and build community. Murals were painted throughout the neighborhood, advocating Puerto Rican independence and affirming Puerto Rican identity.[41] The artist-run Taller Boricua, especially the collective's executive director, Fernando Salicrup, and cofounder and artistic director Marcos Dimas, were instrumental in establishing the East Harlem Cultural Corridor, imagining the Julia de Burgos Latino Cultural Center at 1680 Lexington Avenue as the corridor's heart. Publicly and collectively remembering Burgos revealed the community's fears and anxieties while allowing members to measure their progress and advocate on behalf of a better future.

Before the establishment of Taller Boricua, many Puerto Rican artists belonged to the Art Workers Coalition, which during the 1960s protested the exclusion of black and Puerto Rican art from downtown galleries and museums. Dimas, one of the founders of Taller Boricua, recalls demonstrating with the coalition in front of the Museum of the City of New York, leading the museum to hire a community liaison to work with local artists. Although Dimas lived in the Bronx, his involvement with the Art Workers Coalition and the new community initiative at the Museum of the City of New York led him to spend more time in East Harlem. A group of artists there soon decided to focus on creating their own cultural institutions. Their attitude, as Dimas recalls, was, "Let's stop trying to open these doors. Let's just create our own organizations and cultural institutions. The last straw is this. The Julia de Burgos Cultural Center."[42]

El Museo del Barrio was one of the first grassroots cultural centers the Art Workers Coalition helped establish in the neighborhood. Raphael Montañez Ortiz, an avant-garde artist, became El Museo's director. Early members of El Museo's advisory committee—Dimas, Adrian García, Armando Soto, and Martín Fluvio—turned their own work into a form of public service. In 1970, they formally organized under the name Taller Boricua and obtained their first working space on Madison Avenue between E. 110th and 111th Streets. The headquarters for the Young Lords Party was directly across the street, making it what Dimas calls a "revolutionary block."[43] Many Taller Boricua members protested alongside the Young Lords Party, seeking improved living and working conditions and better educational opportunities for Puerto Ricans. In the mid-1970s, after moving around, Taller secured space in the Heckscher Building at 1230 Fifth Avenue (now the home of El Museo del Barrio).[44] Anthony Drexel Duke, founder of the Boys Harbor School, approached Taller about moving into the building along with the school and other performing arts programs and community organizations. In the mid-1980s, Taller Boricua moved temporarily into a building not far away on Madison Avenue before purchasing a building at the corner of E. 106th Street and Lexington Avenue, which it currently uses as living space for artists. An abandoned former school across the street then caught Taller members' attention, and they began to explore the possibility of using it. It had been abandoned for more than a decade and had become an eyesore. There was talk that the city might use the building as an HIV/AIDS clinic or a homeless shelter, but Taller Boricua wanted to use it to help rebuild the neighborhood. In March 1998, it became the Julia de Burgos Latino Cultural Center after more than a decade of struggles to secure the use of the building as a cultural center. Today, community members who attend local events remember when they attended school in that building as children in the 1950s and 1960s.[45] These long-standing connections make the building a site of memory.

Salicrup and Dimas, the driving forces behind the creation of the Julia, as neighborhood residents call it, chose to name the center after the poet because of her prominence and because she had lived and died in that neighborhood. In Salicrup's words, "She had been an inspiration to many of the artists. We were inspired by her beliefs and the way she wrote poetry. So we chose Julia as the person to inspire us, considering that she had been a part of this community for a long time."[46] Rallies featuring posters bearing Burgos's image were held in front of the boarded-up building, seeking to raise awareness of the initiative. Burgos's story served as a reminder of the need for solidarity and positive anchors for the community. She became a receptacle for the community's dreams, aspirations, and anxieties, mediating between their past and their future.

The Julia not only has become the home of Taller Boricua but also has provided space for a variety of cultural groups, among them Los Pleneros de la 21 and Míriam Colón and the Puerto Rican Traveling Theater. It has brought dance, theater, visual arts, poetry, and other cultural events to the neighborhood and provides a cultural base, cementing the area's identity. Salicrup believes that the Julia and the East Harlem Cultural Corridor have helped preserve El Barrio's history: "This is our little spot. Like Chinatown, like Little Italy, like Historic Harlem, we exist here in this particular area." The Julia offered a way to "get people to recognize our culture and our cultural abilities so that we could actually settle into housing and settle into a lot of other things that we needed as a community."[47] Finally, as a cultural hub, the Julia would draw in restaurants and other businesses. The idea of the East Harlem Cultural Corridor caught on, and local politicians joined the effort. On 27 October 2006, Manny Vega's mosaic honoring Burgos was unveiled on E. 106th Street near Lexington Avenue. In addition, E. 106th Street between Fifth and First Avenues was renamed Julia de Burgos Boulevard. Burgos's mosaic is in good company: the community includes a great deal of public art, including Hank Prussing and Vega's *The Spirit of East Harlem* mural and Vega and Nitza Tufiño's Lexington Avenue line subway mosaics.

A South Bronx native, Vega draws on various ancient art traditions in his work. He infuses it with elements of contemporary New York, Puerto Rico, and Afro-Brazilian iconography of the Candomblé religion. Vega's work has long been known for preserving the cultural and spiritual traditions of the African diaspora in South America. Vega was mostly self-taught in the arts. In the Bronx, he encountered his first mosaic, a tropical fish scene adorning an art deco building on the Grand Concourse north of 165th Street. In high

Figure 10. Julia de Burgos Boulevard. Photo by Francisco Molina Reyes II.

school, he gravitated toward the arts and spent time making prints and drawing. In 1974, after finishing high school, he walked down E. 104th Street near Lexington Avenue, where Hank Prussing was working on a mural, *The Spirit of East Harlem*. Vega recalls, "I was watching this guy paint this wall. And I just screamed at him one day, I said, 'Yo, white boy! Gimme a job!' And he *did*. He hired me. And I learned from him, with the experience of painting this mural in East Harlem. I learned how to appreciate public art. And my trajectory as a muralist began." In 1998, Vega restored *The Spirit of East Harlem*, spending three months using an approach that resembles fresco painting.[48] The mural presents on a grand scale the generosity and dignity of community residents and has become a space of dialogue, evoking memories and oral histories of the neighborhood. It has been a source of love, hope, and pride.

In the late 1970s, Vega joined Taller Boricua. He believes that the collective's members constitute the East Harlem School of art and that "eventually historians will get it." Among the works he has created in the community is the E. 110th Street subway station mosaic, commissioned by the Metropolitan Transit Authority. Its images of dancers and drummers express Afro-Caribbean religious beliefs, making Vega the first artist to translate the Yoruba divination deity into the mosaic medium. Vega's work preserves the cultural and spiritual traditions of Africa, Brazil, and the Caribbean. On 110th Street, he has also created a series of four mosaic panels inspired by Diego Rivera, David Siqueiros, Pablo Picasso, and Thomas Hart Benton.[49]

Hope Community Inc. initially contacted Vega with the idea of creating a mural of Burgos. He felt that the neighborhood needed something grand, significant, and impressive—a source of pride that would foster a sense of community. He also felt that Burgos deserved something majestic:

> What about Julia? What about her spirit? I mean, based on this tragic life and how she was discovered in the streets and died and then all of a sudden was buried in Potter's Field; years later, people flirt with the idea of doing something for her, and then it just falls through. There'd be days when I was working alone. My soul would see Julia walking by, peeking through, opening the door, saying, "Manny, gracias." Literally. Because somebody was actually honoring her.[50]

Hope Community Inc. lacked the funds to create the wall-sized mosaic that would fulfill Vega's vision, so he set out to raise the money, calling on his friends in the neighborhood to help and using his reputation as an artist to gain publicity. In less than two months, he had succeeded, with donations including ten thousand dollars from JPMorgan Chase, five thousand dollars from Harlem congressman Charles Rangel, and another five thousand dollars in individual donations and contributions. Hope Community Inc. provided a storefront to use as a studio. And Vega designed, created, and installed the mosaic, *Remembering Julia* (2006; see plate 8).

Members of the community watched through the storefront window as the mural evolved. Vega worked seven days a week in the open studio, with passers-by coming in to help lay tiles; others recited poetry or brought flowers and wine. On Friday nights, with the music going, Vega, his helpers, and anyone else who stopped by would jam to the sounds of Brazilian beats, Afro-Cuban rhythms, and Puerto Rican timbales. According to Vega, he "created an art scene all over again. Like a mini-renaissance. And the community loved it."[51] Vega selected excerpts from five poems that he felt represented chapters of Burgos's life and put them up on the studio wall, inviting people to comment on the passages and indicate which one resonated most with them. More than half of those who participated chose a passage from "Mi alma" (My Soul), from *Poema en veinte surcos* (see p. 43 of this book). Though it is not one of Burgos's best-known poems, the words reverberated with a community familiar with exile, migration, and being part of a diaspora.

The image of Burgos that Vega chose for the mural is from a lesser-known photo that Vega interpreted in his own way: "I purposely made her more mulatto, because that's who she was, you know? Beautiful, tall, elegant." He gave the image a strong piercing look and depicted her as "a power woman." The upper-right corner of the image includes a figure of Atabex, the Taíno fertility god, as a reminder of women's power to create. The *pitirre* (a hummingbird that aggressively protects its territory against intruders, including larger birds and mammals) to the left of Burgos is the symbol of the Puerto Rican independence movement. The garden at the bottom of the image suggests the poet's love of nature and all that has blossomed and grown from her memory. The tenement building on the left calls to mind New York City. A snail hidden in the image is a personal reminder to Vega of the methodical and meticulous work involved in creating a mosaic.

Vega involved the area's residents in laying tiles, he says, "so that years later, when people walk past the mural with their friends, children, and neighbors, they can say, 'Mira, these are the tiles that I laid.' . . . I have a whole bunch of people saying that, and that's why it's the most successful public piece that I ever did. Not the largest, but the most successful."[52] The mosaic is indeed an enormous success. People place flowers and candles on the street in front of it; people stop to take pictures. Vega has created much more than a mosaic; he has created a community performance space. A group congregates to read and recite poetry at the mural each year on 17 February, Burgos's birthday, with passers-by joining in to learn about the woman whose face is embedded in the culture of El Barrio. Prominent participants in this commemoration have included Vega as well as Puerto Rican writer and artist Nicolasa Mohr; Melissa Mark Viverito, a member of the city council; and numerous poets, among them Sery Colón and Mariposa.

In 2011, Yasmín Hernández's *Soldaderas* mural was unveiled, memorializing both Julia and Frida (see plate 9). With the support of Art for Change, Hope Community Inc., and El Barrio Arts Cluster, Hernández's vision became a reality. Located in the Modesto Flores Community Garden on Lexington Avenue between E. 104th and 105th Streets, the mural is a site of memory that pays tribute to the shared histories of Mexicans and Puerto Ricans who today share the East Harlem neighborhood. The composition was inspired by Kahlo's *Las dos Fridas* (The Two Fridas, 1939), in which two images of the painter sit next to each other, holding hands. In the mural, Frida and Julia hold hands in front of the flags of Mexico and Puerto Rico. The mural was unveiled on 6 July, the anniversary of both Kahlo's birth and Burgos's death. The mural produces knowledge about other Latino groups and brings them into conversation, exploring moments of convergence and divergence in the formation of Latino, Latina feminist, and (post)colonial subjectivities.

The unveiling was a beautiful event on a hot summer afternoon that lasted well into the evening. The *pleneros*, playing drums and African-based forms of Puerto Rican popular music, got the growing crowd to dance, and a local vendor sold homemade tamales.[53] The event opened with a blessing by the Kalpulli Huehuetlahtolli Aztec dance group, which performed a traditional Aztec dance in front of the mural. The mural and the occasion created a space for traditional rituals that otherwise are uncommon in the modernized world. The dancing was a way for the community to "possess themselves again in the spirit of their ancestors, to possess again their memories, to possess again their communities." They danced to resist their "reduction to the status of commodities" and to restore "a heritage that some people would rather see buried alive."[54] Poets and speakers followed before a candlelit procession made its way from the Modestos Flores garden to the Julia de Burgos Latino Cultural Center and the *Remembering Julia* mosaic, reaching the spot on Fifth Avenue where Burgos collapsed. A vigil was held there, permitting the community to both mourn its past and affirm its renewal.

Nora notes that there are dominant and dominated sites of memory. Dominant sites are spectacular and are generally imposed from above by a national authority or established interest; they "characteristically have the coldness and solemnity of official ceremonies." In contrast, dominated sites of memory are "places of refuge, sanctuaries of spontaneous devotion and silent pilgrimage, where one finds the living heart of memory."[55] We might think of the 2010 Julia stamp as this type of spectacular, dominated gesture, while the cultural

Figure 11. La Bruja
(Caridad De La
Luz) in front of the
Remembering Julia mural
during the procession
for the unveiling of the
Soldaderas mural, 6
July 2011. Photo by the
author.

center, the murals, the community gardens, the dancing, and the streets of El
Barrio are inhabited sites of memory where people find refuge, live, and cre-
ate new memories. Local memories become places for writing local histories
that go ignored by official narratives. The practices of everyday life define and
promote alternatives to the official histories. The social histories of marginal
and otherwise forgotten people depend on a return to these countermemories.
Sixty years after Julia de Burgos was found unconscious on an El Barrio street
corner, she now forms part of the neighborhood's urban landscape and cultural
mythology.

CONCLUSION

Creating *Latinidad*

The epigraph for this book, "The voice of an epoch is in the words of its poets," is taken from Victor Hernández Cruz's "Writing Migrations," which explores the linguistic and cultural dislocations of writers and their work. He argues that while history books might recount a series of events, poets' words capture the experience of living through a personal and public event. Hernández Cruz notes that Latin American poets who are unconventional and feel isolated and out of place in their homelands seek to migrate, perhaps first from the countryside to an urban area before moving on to a metropolitan center in another country. He offers José Martí, Rubén Darío, and César Vallejo as examples. He notes that the wandering of Latin American poets is continued by contemporary Latino/a poets. Readers, he claims, will notice that the "journey of their families is analogous to the movement of poets and their poems," and he believes that "history deposits itself inside a poet."[1] It might be more accurate to say that history deposits itself in all lives, but poets, writers, and visual artists give expression to experience in a way that enables readers to see themselves reflected. These artists have the gift of linking their private passion to their social vision and layering the chronology of their private lives with history.

One of the purposes of this book has been to read Julia de Burgos's life, poetry, prose, and death from a Latino studies perspective, adding to the complexity and contradictions of who she was and how she is remembered. As a master with words, imagery, and metaphor, Burgos gave expression to the most significant political moments of her era and connected them with her life. She challenged the early twentieth-century dehumanization of modernity with a fixation with authenticity and the cult of personality. In this way, she allowed others to identify with her work and to construct themselves through the process of identification and differentiation.

Artists remember, reinvent, and reimagine Burgos in their work to claim her as a part of the Puerto Rican history of resistance, a history often repressed to serve colonial interests. This theme is elaborated by Nuyorican poet Martín Espada in "The Lover of a Subversive Is Also a Subversive." The essay highlights the legacy of resistance to both Spanish and U.S. colonialism on the island: "The collective memory of such events, repressed in the interest of colonial power, must be perpetuated by word of mouth, by song, and by poetry" because outright discussion of these events is quickly suppressed.[2] Writers, artists, poets, and musicians must carry this legacy since it is omitted from all official accounts. During the first half of the twentieth century, even the totalizing genre of the novel was often used to narrate the island's official history. Espada writes, "The poets of Puerto Rico have often articulated the vision of independence, creating an alternative to the official history of the kind propagated by occupiers everywhere"; poets also have "taught the next generation the arts of resistance, so that even poets living in the United States and writing in English continue to clamor for the island's independence."[3] They have helped create a bridge between Puerto Ricans on the island and the Puerto Rican community in the United States. In *Resistance Literature*, Barbara Harlow argues that there are two kinds of writing, that of oppression and that of the struggle for liberation. Resistance literature attempts to transform relationships of power and understands that cultural resistance is just as valuable as armed resistance. Cultural resistance is a "political and politicized activity" that is "immediately and directly involved in a struggle against ascendant or dominant forms of ideological and cultural production."[4] Burgos expresses resistance in her alliance with the most vulnerable and marginalized members of society, letting everyone, not just artists and intellectuals, identify with her.

Espada's poem, "Face on the Envelope," included in *A Republic of Poetry*, best captures the power of her legacy.[5] The book is about the power of poetry and is dedicated to Rubén Darío: poems in it are dedicated to Pablo Neruda, Robert Creeley, and Julia de Burgos. Espada believes that poetry is practical to the extent that it humanizes and helps restore a sense of dignity among society's disenfranchised and invisible. In Espada's words, "Poetry helps them maintain their dignity, helps them maintain their sense of self-respect. They will be better suited to defend themselves in the world."[6] Dedicated to Burgos, "Face on the Envelope" tells the story of a Puerto Rican man who is imprisoned in Hartford, Connecticut. This man reads Burgos's poetry and is moved to draw an image of her on an envelope, which he sends to Espada, who has visited the prison to read from his poetry.[7]

Espada suggests that those who are most disenfranchised can restore dignity to her name. She wrote for them. The poem opens with the gossip that has surrounded Burgos's life and afterlife:

Julia was tall, so tall, the whispers said,
the undertakers amputated her legs at the knee
to squeeze her body into the city coffin
for burial at Potter's Field.

Dying on the street in East Harlem:
She had no discharge papers
from Goldwater Memorial Hospital,
no letters from Puerto Rico, no poems.
Without her name, three words
like three pennies stolen from her purse
while she slept off the last bottle of rum,
Julia's coffin sailed to a harbor
where the dead stand in the rain
patient as forgotten umbrellas.

All her poems flowed river-blue, river-brown, river-red.
Her Río Grande de Loíza was a fallen blue piece of sky;
her river was bloody stripe whenever the torrent
burst and the hills would vomit mud.

A monument rose at the cemetery in her hometown.
There were parks and schools. She was memorized.
Yet only the nameless, names plucked as their faces
turned away in labor or sleep, could return Julia's name to her
with the grace of a beggar offering back a stranger's wallet.

Years later, a nameless man from Puerto Rico,
jailed in a city called Hartford, would read her poem
about the great river of Loíza till the river gushed
through the faucet in his cell and sprayed his neck.
Slowly, every night, as fluorescent light grew weary
and threatened to quit, he would paint Julia's face
on an envelope: her hair of black, her lips red,
her eyelids so delicate they almost trembled. Finally,
meticulous as a thief, he inscribed the words: *Julia de Burgos*.

He could never keep such a treasure under his pillow,
so he slipped a letter into the envelope

and mailed it all away, flying through the dark
to find my astonished hands.[8]

Espada has described poetry as a political tool because it allows the poet to speak "on behalf of those without an opportunity to be heard. Not that they couldn't speak for themselves given the chance. They just don't get the chance."[9] This poem highlights the way Burgos spoke for the unheard and how they now advocate on her behalf and continue her tradition.[10] In mailing the drawing of Burgos to Espada, the imprisoned man not only furthers her legacy from his cell in Hartford but also gestures toward rehabilitation in his effort to communicate with the society outside his prison walls.

The United States is beginning to recognize the cultural legacy of Latinos, the country's largest and fastest-growing minority, as it is simultaneously introducing new forms of criminalizing brown-skinned migrants. This book highlights the role that aesthetic production played in defining social and political belonging in the work of an early twentieth-century Latina migrant. At a time when the mainstream media continues to racialize Latino/as toward whiteness and vacate the concept of *Latinidad* of its political possibilities, poets, writers, activists, musicians, artists, and playwrights call on the memory and legacy of Julia de Burgos to affirm the resilience of communities, connect to place, and imagine new possibilities.

NOTES

INTRODUCTION

1. See *La Prensa*, 2, 7 August 1953; *El Mundo*, 4 August 1953,

2. See Gelpí, "Nomadic Subject"; López Jiménez, "Julia de Burgos: Los textos comunicantes."

3. See Gelpí, "Nomadic Subject"; Gelpí, *Literatura y paternalismo*; Beauchamp, "Literatura de la crisis."

4. See Gelpí, *Literatura y paternalismo*.

5. For an examination of the walking motif in Burgos, see López Jiménez, "Julia de Burgos: Los textos comunicantes"; Montero, *Rutas de Julia de Burgos*. See also Montero, "Prosa neoyorquina."

6. See Findlay, *Imposing Decency*. Findlay notes that middle- and upper-class women entered public life in early twentieth-century Puerto Rico by attempting to regulate and control the popular practices of cohabitation of working-class women, often of African descent, through the more stable social arrangement of marriage. In this way, wealthier women often supported the island's patriarchal structures.

7. Gelpí, "Nomadic Subject."

8. Deleuze and Guattari, *Thousand Plateaus*, 382, 380.

9. Braidotti, *Nomadic Subjects*, 58.

10. Ibid., 27.

11. Said, *Representations*, 43.

12. Rodríguez Pagán, *Julia*, xx-xxi. Unless otherwise noted, all translations are by the author.

13. Ibid., xxi.

14. José Emilio González, "Julia de Burgos: Intensa siempreviva," 24.

15. It is not hard to draw parallels here between Burgos and her contemporary, Frida Kahlo, the Mexican painter who also became a cult figure in the 1990s. Kahlo contributed to her own mythmaking by changing her birth date from 1907 to 1910 to coincide with the beginning of the Mexican Revolution.

16. For more on the different stages of Puerto Rican literature in the United States, see Flores, *Divided Borders*, 142–53. For migration history, see Sánchez Korrol, *From Colonia to Community*; Lorrin Thomas, *Puerto Rican Citizen*.

17. Flores notes that these popular songs were central to the cultural life of the Puerto Rican community in New York and should be recognized "as an integral part of the people's 'literary' production" (*Divided Borders*, 147).

18. Ibid., 169.

19. For more on *La carreta*, see ibid., 168–69.

20. Sandra María Esteves to author, 19 December 2010.

21. Several scholars have mentioned that Burgos's final poetry written in English presages the poetry of the Puerto Rican diaspora written in New York. See Márquez, *Puerto Rican Poetry*, 218–19; Luis, *Dance between Two Cultures*; Barradas, Rodríguez, and Marín, *Herejes y mitificadores*; Gelpí, "Nomadic Subject."

22. See Flores, *Divided Borders*; Gelpí, *Literatura y paternalismo*.

23. Said, *Representations*, 64.

24. Ibid., 63.

25. Roach, *Cities of the Dead*, 4.

26. Ibid., 39.

27. See Aparicio, "Jennifer," 91–92, for a partial genealogy of the usages of *Latinidad*.

28. Rodríguez Pagán, *Julia*, 93–96; Falú, "Raza, género, y clase social"; Rodríguez-Castro, "Silencio," 26. For more on Julia de Burgos's schooling, report cards, and graduation, see Rodríguez Pagán, *Julia*, 35–79; for her work with the Emergency Relief Administration, see 85–159; for more early poems, including some excerpts, see 87–155. See also Matos Rodríguez and Delgado, *Puerto Rican Women's History*. From the time of her marriage until 1938, Burgos was known as Julia Burgos de Rodríguez. At that point, rather than reverting to her maiden name, Julia Constanza Burgos García, she chose to be known as Julia de Burgos. However, for simplicity's sake, I refer to her as Julia de Burgos throughout. The canonical status of "Río Grande de Loíza" on the island results at least in part from the woodcuts José R. Alicea made to illustrate the poem as part of the midcentury literacy campaign.

29. See Roy-Féquière, *Women, Creole Identity, and Intellectual Life*, 57–58.

30. See Julia de Burgos to Consuelo Burgos, 12 February 1940 (from New York), 9 September 1940 (from Havana). Jack Agüeros graciously provided copies of many of Burgos's letters in his possession.

31. She did, however, posthumously receive an honorary doctorate from the Spanish Department at the University of Puerto Rico in 1986.

32. Various sources contend that Burgos also wrote essays while in Havana, although those writings have not been recovered.

33. The educational essays have not been translated into English but have been published in Burgos, *Desde la Escuela del Aire*. Likewise, the 1936 essay and the journal have not been translated into English but appear in their entirety in Rodríguez Pagán, *Julia*, 131–34, 411–24. Much of Burgos's prose has been collected in *Julia de Burgos: Periodista en Nueva York*, but it has received only limited distribution and has not been translated into English.

34. In the absence of marriage and divorce certificates, it is not clear whether Burgos was still married when she began her relationship with Jimenes Grullón. He claimed that she was separated from Rodríguez Beauchamp before beginning her affair with Jimenes Grullón, but other accounts suggest that both he and Burgos were divorced when their relationship began. See Vicioso, "Rival to the Río Grande de Loíza," 685. Jiménez de Báez, "Julia de Burgos," 22, notes that they married in 1934 with a question mark and says they divorced by 1937. Rodríguez Pagán, "Cronología," 163, says that she married in 1934 and divorced in 1937.

35. See Findlay, *Imposing Decency*, 10.

36. Vicioso, "Rival to the Río Grande de Loíza," 685.

37. See letter published in Jiménez de Báez, *Julia*, 45.

38. Rodríguez Pagán, *Julia*, 343–45.

39. Julia de Burgos, FBI file, provided to author by Jack Agüeros.

40. Julia de Burgos, "Diario," in Rodríguez Pagán, *Julia*, 418.

41. Burgos describes her symptoms as chronic upper respiratory congestion, excessive mucus, coughing up blood, and nasal bleeding. She attributed them to a fall in which she hit her nose, but her description seems consistent with a form of pneumonia that affects chronic alcoholics (ibid., 411–24).

42. Ibid., 414.

43. Ibid.

44. Ibid., 415.

45. Sandra María Esteves, interview by author, 19 December 2010; Jack Agüeros, interview by author, 18 July 2004. Esteves also remembers hearing that Julia was sedated and given experimental treatments at the hospital. Rodríguez Pagán, *Julia*, 387, says that she was enrolled in experimental treatment in exchange for food and a hospital bed.

46. For details on Burgos's second marriage, illness, and final years in New York, see Rodríguez Pagán, *Julia*, 368–403; for the symbolic significance of her death, see 343–45. I repeatedly heard these stories as I interviewed writers and artists in New York, though the sources for the information are unclear. In the introduction to his collection of Burgos's poetry, *Song of the Simple Truth*, xxxv, Jack Agüeros reports that he heard from his father that Burgos's legs had to be amputated so that she could fit in a city coffin. Espada, *Republic*, 34, opens a poem dedicated to Burgos with this image. For the criminalization of the Puerto Rican community during the early twentieth century, see Vega, *Memoirs*; Lorrin Thomas, *Puerto Rican Citizen*, chapters 1–4.

CHAPTER 1

1. Braidotti, *Nomadic Subjects*, 26.

2. See Díaz-Quiñones, "Recordando," 16–35; Beauchamp, "Literatura de la crisis," 294–369; Gelpí, *Literatura y paternalismo*, 1–16.

3. See Roy-Féquière, *Women, Creole Identity, and Intellectual Life*; Gelpí, *Literatura y paternalismo*; Beauchamp, "Literatura de la crisis."

4. See Unruh, *Latin American Vanguards*, 1–29; Rodríguez Castro, "Silencio y estridencias."

5. See Unruh, *Latin American Vanguards*, 19; Hernández Aquino, *Nuestra aventura literaria*, 15.

6. Unruh, *Latin American Vanguards*, 7.

7. Ibid., 18–19; Rodríguez Castro, "Silencio y estridencias," 17–40.

8. López Jiménez, "Julia de Burgos: El talante vanguardista," 132–34; Diego Padró, "Luis Palés Matos," 22–23.

9. Wheeler, *Voicing American Poetry*, 18.

10. Ibid., 40.

11. Ibid., 40–48.

12. See Roberto Ramos-Perea, introduction to Burgos, *Desde la Escuela del Aire*, 1–2.

13. Ibid., 4. Ramos-Perea also notes that Burgos's contract most likely was not renewed because of her increased political activity. However, the records that contain this information are sealed (4–5).

14. Rodríguez Pagán, *Julia*, 136–37.

15. Braidotti, *Nomadic Subjects*, 58.

16. Other poets from this generation who also promoted a more progressive view of Puerto Rican identity include Juan Antonio Corretjer and Clemente Soto Vélez, both of whom spent long periods of time abroad, as Burgos did.

17. José Emilio González, "La Poesía de Julia de Burgos: Estudio Preliminar," in Burgos, *Julia de Burgos: Obra poética*, xxxvii. In his introduction to her collected works, González notes that in this poem, "Las palabras dicen justamente lo que Julia siente y piensa. El río es el símbolo del hombre ideal. No es ya solamente el Tú de algo que se contempla o se posee. No es sólo un espectáculo de gran belleza, manantial incansable de vivencias estéticas. Es algo más. Se aúpa a una concepción moral. Es figura de la inocencia del espíritu. La palabra 'pureza' que en el primer verso es tan pura y tan Hermosa, desempeña una función artística de acendramiento esencial de lo bello, pero señala también una intuición ética, normativa. Río humano. Hombre fluminal. Virilmente tierno. Que merece el homenaje de la más decantada femineidad. Ante él se inclina Julia por haber logrado la posesión de su espíritu" (405). González reads the poem as a love poem and a prime example of Burgos's "erotización de lo natural" (405), a style to which she returns in her second book of poetry, *Canción de la verdad sencilla*. According to González, "Uno de los fundamentos de esta erotización es la creencia en la vida como la energía universal engendradora de seres y de formas" (414).

18. For more on the *treintista* writers and their deployment of totalizing genres in reaction to the wound of colonialism, see Gelpí, *Literatura y paternalismo*.

19. Unruh, *Latin American Vanguards*, 216.

20. Burgos, *Poema*, 13. Unless otherwise indicated, all poems in Spanish in this chapter appear in Burgos, *Poema*; subsequent citations appear in the text.

21. Burgos, "Río Grande de Loíza," 667.

22. Ibid., 668.

23. Zaragoza, *St. James in the Streets*, 5–20.

24. Burgos, "Río Grande de Loíza," 667–68.

25. Gelpí, *Literatura y paternalismo*; Gelpí, "Nomadic subject"; José Luis González, *El país*, 9–44; Beauchamp, "Literatura de la crisis."

26. Gelpí, "Nomadic subject," 38.

27. See Gelpí, *Literatura y paternalismo*, 1–16; Kleinig, *Paternalism*, 7; Sommer, *One Master for Another*, 1–49.

28. Braidotti, *Nomadic Subjects*, 42.

29. Dietz, *Economic History*, 139.

30. Ayala and Bernabé, *Puerto Rico*, 95–97.

31. Ibid.

32. Puerto Rico, Emergency Relief Administration, *Tariff Problems*.

33. See Roy-Féquière, *Women, Creole Identity, and Intellectual Life*; Findlay, *Imposing Decency*.

34. López Jiménez, "Julia de Burgos: El talante vanguardista," 133.

35. Burgos, *Song of the Simple Truth*, 404.

36. Ibid.

37. Ibid., 406.

38. Although this study focuses on Burgos, other Generación del Treinta poets championed the cause of the working class. Juan Antonio Corretjer, for example, maintained such a commitment throughout his life. See chapter 3.

39. Gelpí, "Nomadic Subject," 45. For the working-class women's movement in Puerto Rico, see Valle Ferrer, *Luisa Capetillo*. See also Capetillo, *Amor y anarquía*; Capetillo, *Nation of Women*.

40. See Findlay, *Imposing Decency*; Roy-Féquière, *Women, Creole Identity, and Intellectual Life*.

41. Findlay, *Imposing Decency*, 179.

42. Ibid., 191.

43. Licia Fiol-Matta, *Queer Mother*.

44. Roy-Féquière, *Women, Creole Identity, and Intellectual Life*, 54, 52.

45. Albizu Campos, *Pedro Albizu Campos*, 91–93.

46. Roy-Féquière, *Women, Creole Identity, and Intellectual Life*, 57.

47. For more on José Martí as an early figure in American cultural studies and U.S. Latino culture, see Belnap and Fernández, *José Martí's "Our America."*

48. "Canción a los pueblos hispanos de América" and "Himno de sangre a Trujillo" were first published in *Pueblos Hispanos* in 1944. "Ibero-América resurge ante Bolívar," "Saludo en ti a la nueva mujer americana," and "Canto a la ciudad primada de América" are collected in Burgos, *Song of the Simple Truth*, 422–27, 410–11, 496–99.

49. Minutes, Frente Unido Femenino meeting, 15 August 1936, San Juan, in Rodríguez Pagán, *Julia*, 125.

50. Ibid., 125–26.

51. Two years later, however, Burgos's "Ay ay ay de la grifa negra" recognized Puerto Rico's African heritage and the legacy of slavery as important cultural components.

52. Julia de Burgos, "La mujer ante el dolor de la patria," in Rodríguez Pagán, *Julia*, 131–34.

53. See Moreno, *Family Matters*, 133–35; Pérez y González, *Puerto Ricans*, 19.

54. Burgos, "Mujer ante el dolor."

55. Roy-Féquière, *Women, Creole Identity, and Intellectual Life*, 68.

56. For further discussion, see ibid., chapters 1–3.

57. The collection created much debate at the time about the African presence on the island. See Blanco, "Refutación y glosa"; Arce, "Poemas negros," originally published in *El Mundo* in 1934. See also Graciany Miranda Archilla, "La broma de una poesia prieta en Puerto Rico," *Alma Latina*, February 1933.

58. Márquez, *Puerto Rican Poetry*, 223–24.

59. Unruh, *Latin American Vanguards*, 130; more generally, see 125–69.

60. Vázquez Arce, "Tuntún de Pasa y Grifería," 87.

61. The *plena* is an Afro–Puerto Rican form of music that developed on the island and is often seen as symbolizing an authentic Puerto Rican culture.

62. See Roy-Féquière, *Women, Creole Identity, and Intellectual Life*, esp. chapters 4, 5, 7.

63. Márquez, *Puerto Rican Poetry*, 223–24.

64. See Coulthard, *Race and Colour*; Roy-Féquière, *Women, Creole Identity, and Intellectual Life*.

65. Márquez, *Puerto Rican Poetry*, 224.

66. In *Imposing Decency*, chapters 5 and 6, Findlay notes the way racialized sexual norms and practices were central to the construction of social and political orders in Puerto Rico in the early twentieth century.

67. Unruh, *Latin American Vanguards*, 131.

68. Márquez, *Puerto Rican Poetry*, 222–23.

69. Ibid.

70. See Wheeler, *Voicing American Poetry*, 2–15; Bernstein, introduction.

71. Unruh, *Latin American Vanguards*, 207–62.

72. Said, *Representations*, 53.

73. Ibid., 62.

CHAPTER 2

1. For an analysis of the narrative of Puerto Rican migration as tragedy in literature, see Flores, *Divided Borders*, 142–53. See also Duany, *Puerto Rican Nation*.

2. See Gelpí's discussion of gay writer Manuel Ramos Otero and of Burgos's influence on his writing in *Literatura y paternalismo*, 120–54; La Fountain-Stokes, "De sexilio(s) y diaspora(s)"; La Fountain-Stokes, "Entre boleros"; La Fountain-Stokes, "Queer Diasporas." See also La Fountain-Stokes, *Queer Ricans*.

3. Guzmán, "'Pa' la Escuelita," 227. See also Guzmán, *Gay Hegemony*.

4. See La Fountain-Stokes, *Queer Ricans*; Guzmán, *Gay Hegemony*; Guzmán, "'Pa' la Escuelita."

5. See Julio Ramos, introduction to Capetillo, *Amor y anarquía*. The book opens with a picture of Capetillo dressed in a man's suit.

6. Capetillo, *Mi opinión*, 30.

7. Capetillo, *Nation of Women*, x–xii.

8. Sánchez González, *Boricua Literature*, 23.

9. There is a growing body of literature on sexuality and gender as a factor shaping Caribbean migration. For some key works, see Guzmán, *Gay Hegemony*; La Fountain-Stokes, *Queer Ricans*; Martínez-San Miguel, "Female Sexiles?"

10. Martínez-San Miguel, "Female Sexiles?," 814, 815.

11. Emelí Vélez de Vando, interview by Nélida Pérez, Archive of the Puerto Rican Diaspora, Center for Puerto Rican Studies, Hunter College, City University of New York.

12. See Gelpí, "Nomadic Subject."

13. See Gelpí, *Literatura y paternalismo*; Sandlin, "Manuel Ramos Otero's Queer Metafictional Resurrection"; Sandlin, "Julia de Burgos as a Cultural Icon"; La Fountain-Stokes, *Queer Ricans*.

14. Vicioso, "Rival to the Río Grande de Loíza," 685–86.

15. Gelpí, "Nomadic Subject," 37.

16. See Luis Lloréns Torres, "Cinco poetisas de América," *Puerto Rico Ilustrado*, 13 November 1937, 14–15, 62.

17. Burgos, *Canción*, 32. Subsequent citations to Burgos, *Canción*, appear in the text.

18. Octavio Paz further defines eroticism as "sex in action, but, because it either diverts it or denies it, it thwarts the goal of the sexual function. In sexuality, pleasure serves procreation; in erotic rituals, pleasure is an end in itself or has ends other than procreation" (*Double Flame*, 3–4).

19. See Ríos Ávila, "Víctima de luz."

20. Braidotti, *Nomadic Subjects*, 29.

21. Vicioso, "Rival to the Río Grande de Loíza," 685.

22. Rodríguez Pagán, *Julia*, 251; information about Burgos's travel is also available on Ancestry.com.

23. To read more about the Puerto Rican music scene in New York in the 1940s, see Glasser, *My Music Is My Flag*.

24. For the history of Latin American writers and artists in New York, see Remeseira, *Hispanic New York*; *Translation Review* 81 (special Nueva York issue, Spring 2011); Sullivan, *Nueva York*.

25. Rodríguez Castro, "Silencio y estridencias," 37.

26. See Lorrin Thomas, *Puerto Rican Citizen*; Vega, *Memoirs*; Ayala and Bernabe, *Puerto Rico*, 113–16.

27. This letter is published in its entirety in *Revista Mairena* 7.20 (1985): 152–53.

28. Braidotti, *Nomadic Subjects*, 50.

29. While Kahlo and Burgos do not appear to have met, their lives and their work share interesting points of convergence. I am not alone in drawing these connections. Nuyorican artist Yasmín Hernández unveiled a mural in East Harlem on 6 July 2010 that retains the structure of *The Two Fridas* but replaces one of the Fridas with Burgos (see chapter 5).

30. See Rodríguez Pagán, "Cronología," 163–7.

31. Program, Pura Belpré Papers, Archives of the Puerto Rican Diaspora, Center for Puerto Rican Studies, Hunter College, City University of New York.

32. For more on Belpré, see Sánchez González, *Boricua Literature*, 71–101; Belpré, *Stories I Read*.

33. See Sánchez Korrol, *From Colonia to Community*; Sánchez Korrol and Hernández, *Pioneros II*. See also Flores, "Puerto Rican Literature," 142–53.

34. A more detailed study of Puerto Rican and Latino intellectual and cultural networks in New York prior to the 1960s would be an important contribution to the scholarly literature. Documents in the papers of Pura Belpré and Emelí Vélez de Vando in the Archives of the Puerto Rican Diaspora at the Center for Puerto Rican Studies, Hunter College, City University of New York, demonstrate Burgos's participation in community activities. In addition to holding poetry readings, she recited her poetry at various events.

35. This letter is quoted in its entirety in *Revista Mairena* 7.20 (1985): 149–51.

36. García Peña, "Más Que Cenizas," 42; Kury, *Juan Bosch*, 35–45.

37. Bosch, who was exiled from the Dominican Republic from 1938 to 1962, was the founder of two of the country's three dominant political parties, the Pártido de la Revolución Dominicana and the Partido de la Liberación Dominicana. He became the first democratically elected president of the Dominican Republic, serving from February to September 1963 before a coup sent him back into exile, where he remained until 1970.

38. García Peña, "Más Que Cenizas," 40.

39. Vicioso, "Interview," 696–97. Bosch says in this interview that Jimenes Grullón and Burgos lived with him and his wife in his house in Havana: "She was not only an exceptional poet but an exceptional woman, and I can tell you because she lived in the same house I did, and it was not a big house" (685).

40. David Dunlap, "Raul Roa of Cuba Dies at 75; Foreign Minister for 17 Years," *New York Times*, 8 July 1982.

41. Vicioso, "Interview," 697.

42. Ibid.

43. López Jiménez, *Julia de Burgos*, 15–76.

44. *Puerto Rico Ilustrado*, 3 August 1940, 38.

45. Said, "Reflections," 174.

46. La Fountain-Stokes, *Queer Ricans*, xxi.

47. See Rodríguez Pagán, *Julia*.

48. López-Baralt, "Julia de Burgos," 17–23.

49. Unruh, *Latin American Vanguards*, 211.

50. Ibid., 216.

51. Deleuze and Guattari, *Thousand Plateaus*, 380–81.

52. Burgos, *Mar y tú*, 28. Subsequent citations to Burgos, *Mar y tú*, appear in the text.

53. Umpierre, "Metapoetic Code," 88, 89.

54. Pedreira, *Insularismo*, 16.

55. Braidotti, *Nomadic Subjects*, 25.

56. Márquez, *Puerto Rican Poetry*, 225.

57. Ibid., 225–26.

58. Martínez-San Miguel, "Female Sexiles?," 826.

Chapter 3

1. Duany, *Blurred Borders*, 83–93; Lorrin Thomas, *Puerto Rican Citizen*, 133–65.
2. Duany, *Blurred Borders*, 83.
3. Silva, *Ambassadors of Culture*; Lazo, *Writing to Cuba*.
4. Lomas, *Translating Empire*, 35–37.
5. For more on Hispanism, see Moraña, "Introduction."
6. Faber, "'La Hora Ha Llegado,'" 89.
7. In *Ambassadors of Culture*, Gruesz argues that the Spanish-language press in the United States established transnational connections as early as the 1850s. According to Gruesz, Rafael Pombo, a Colombian poet, diplomat, and editor who lived in exile in New York from the 1850s to the early 1870s, was one of the first persons to identify New York as a centralized location where Spanish-speaking exiles could meet and to propose using the city as a space for sharing and transmitting ideas about Latin American countries, news, cultures, concerns, and "race" (163–76).
8. Kanellos and Martell, *Hispanic Periodicals*, 54.
9. See Vera-Rrojas, "Polémicas, Feministas, Puertorriqueñas, y Desconocidas."
10. Gruesz notes that most Hispanophone writers of the nineteenth century shared a "possessive investment in whiteness" and were not attuned to the differences of race, class and gender differences separating them from contemporary Latinos (*Ambassadors of Culture*, 208). José Martí later supplied the missing components of racial consciousness in the form of a critique of economic imperialism in the way that writers and *cronistas* before him had not (192).
11. Lorrin Thomas, *Puerto Rican Citizen*, 92–132, notes that a shift occurred in the way that Puerto Rican community members demanded citizens' rights in the 1920s and that by the 1940s, they framed their demand for rights in the context of human rights.
12. Kanellos and Martell, *Hispanic Periodicals*, 50–57.
13. Sánchez Korrol, "Forgotten Migrant," 175.
14. Kanellos and Martell, *Hispanic Periodicals*, 58–59.
15. *Pueblos Hispanos* can be found on microfilm at the 42nd Street branch of the New York Public Library.
16. Rodríguez-Fraticelli, "Pedro Albizu Campos."
17. For information on the founding of *Pueblos Hispanos*, see ibid. For information on the relationship between Consuelo Lee Tapia and Juan Antonio Corretjer, see Kanellos, Dworkin y Méndez, and Balestra, *Herencia*, 28, 442, 592.
18. For biographical information, see Acosta-Belén, "Consuelo Lee Tapia"; Kanellos, Dworkin y Méndez, and Balestra, *Herencia*, 442. For information on *Pueblos Hispanos*, see Rodríguez-Fraticelli, "Pedro Albizu Campos."
19. Ayala and Bernabe, *Puerto Rico*, 148–53.
20. Burgos, *Julia de Burgos: Periodista en Nueva York*, 21.
21. Memmi, *Colonizer*, 127.
22. Ibid., 128.
23. Ibid.
24. Kanellos, "Recovering and Re-Constructing."
25. See Montero, "Prosa neoyorquina."

26. For more on Marcantonio, see Lorrin Thomas, *Puerto Rican Citizen*, 8–10.

27. Lorrin Thomas notes that politically conscious Puerto Ricans in New York shifted their language from a demand for equal citizenship to a request for human rights because "the languages of recognition and human rights were more elastic and capacious, and more precisely descriptive of the growing connections among worldwide justice movements" (ibid., 14).

28. Burgos uses the problematic concept of *mestizaje* propagated by Mexican intellectual and statesman José Vasconcelos in *La raza cósmica* (1927). Though some observers understood *mestizaje* as affirming Latin America's indigenous and African ancestry, others, including Juan Isidro Jimenes Grullón, promoted racial mixing as a way to whiten the race, particularly in the Caribbean, which has a large population of people of African descent (see Jimenes Grullón, *Luchemos por nuestra América*). In fact, Vasconcelos wrote the preface to Jimenes Grullón's volume.

29. Flores, *Divided Borders*, 184–85.

30. Pogrebin, "Josephine Premice." For a memoir of Premice written by her daughter, see Fales-Hill, *Always Wear Joy*.

31. See Flores, *Divided Borders*, 182–95; Boyce Davies, *Left of Karl Marx*.

32. Schrecker, *Age of McCarthyism*, 11. For more on the McCarthy era, see also Schrecker, *Many Are the Crimes*. For more on the suppression of Puerto Rican nationalism during the 1940s, see Ayala and Bernabe, *Puerto Rico*, 165–71.

33. Burgos's submissions to *Pueblos Hispanos* and collaboration with Corretjer and Colón, known party members, would have been enough to call for her surveillance. The FBI kept close watch on Burgos's activities, with neighbors and U.S. Postal Service workers acting as informants and reporting on the type of mail she received as well as such information as the fact that she and her second husband, Armando Marín, had a book by Karl Marx on their coffee table (Julia de Burgos, FBI file, provided to author by Jack Agüeros).

CHAPTER 4

1. See Morales, *Palante*; Enck-Wanzer, *Young Lords*.

2. For more on shifting poetry conventions, see Wheeler, *Voicing American Poetry*; Bernstein, introduction; Middleton, "Contemporary Poetry Reading." For more on the Black Arts movement, see Lorenzo Thomas, "Neon Griot."

3. Such prominent Puerto Rican scholars as Edna Acosta-Belén, Arcadio Díaz Quiñones, Juan Flores, and Efraín Barradas have argued for expanding the canon and viewing diaspora literature as part of the Puerto Rican literary tradition.

4. See Cruz-Malavé, "Toward an Art," 139.

5. See Quintero Rivera, *Conflictos de clase*; Moreno, *Family Matters*; Torres, "Gran familia puertorriqueña."

6. Moreno, *Family Matters*, 13.

7. Luis, *Dance between Two Cultures*; Márquez, *Puerto Rican Poetry*.

8. Gelpí, *Literatura y paternalismo*; Cruz-Malavé, "Toward an Art"; Moreno, *Family Matters*.

9. Flores, *Divided Borders*, 150–51.

10. Wheeler, *Voicing American Poetry*, 131.

11. For further discussion, see Rubin, *Songs of Ourselves*.

12. Wheeler, *Voicing American Poetry*, 13.

13. Algarín, "Nuyorican Literature," 1352, 1351.

14. Ibid., 1353.

15. See Flores, "Nueva York—Diaspora City," 47.

16. Aparicio, "(Re)constructing Latinidad," 44.

17. Martínez-San Miguel, *Caribe Two-Ways*, 38.

18. Moreno, *Family Matters*, 11.

19. See Oboler, *Ethnic Labels*, 3–6. *Latino* was substituted for *Hispanic* to include persons of Latin American descent whose families have been in the United States for several generations and who do not speak Spanish as well as people of African, indigenous, and Brazilian descent who do not have ties to Spain.

20. See Arlene Dávila, *Latino Spin*.

21. Aparicio, "Jennifer as Selena," 103.

22. See Moreno, *Family Matters*; Torres, "Gran familia puertorriqueña"; Torres and Whitten, *Blackness*; Santiago-Díaz, *Escritura afropuertorriqueña*; Rivero, *Tuning Out Blackness*; Flores, *Diaspora Strikes Back*; Aparicio, *Listening to Salsa*; Duany, *Puerto Rican Nation*.

23. For studies exploring inter-Latino spaces, see Kugel, "Latino Culture Wars"; Negrón-Muntaner, "Jennifer's Butt"; Paredez, "Remembering Selena"; Vargas, "Bidi Bidi Bom Bom"; Rúa, "Colao Subjectivities."

24. Edwards, "Uses of Diaspora," 52–53.

25. Clifford, *Routes*, 244, 277.

26. Ibid., 251.

27. See Guzmán, "'Pa' La Escuelita"; La Fountain-Stokes, "De sexilio(s) y diaspora(s)"; La Fountain-Stokes, "Entre boleros"; La Fountain-Stokes, "Queer Diasporas"; La Fountain-Stokes, *Queer Ricans*; Negrón-Muntaner, *Brincando el Charco*.

28. La Fountain-Stokes, *Queer Ricans*, xvii.

29. See ibid. For a study of Otero and Umpierre, see Sandlin, "Julia de Burgos as a Cultural Icon."

30. See Gelpí, *Literatura y paternalismo*, 148–54.

31. Cohen, "Punks, Bulldaggers, and Welfare Queens," 25.

32. La Fountain-Stokes, *Queer Ricans*, 20.

33. Although not much has been written on New York's Puerto Rican literary and cultural institutions during this era, many of the early institutions were Hispanic-focused and run by members of the Generación del Treinta who migrated to New York in 1940. They continued to promote an elitist and Hispanic agenda.

34. Sandlin, "Manuel Ramos Otero's Queer Metafictional Resurrection," 323.

35. Ramos Otero, *Cuento*, 105. Subsequent citations to Ramos Otero, *Cuento*, appear in the text.

36. See Lladó-Ortega, "Community in Transit."

37. Wheeler, *Voicing American Poetry*, 15.

38. La Fountain-Stokes, *Queer Ricans*, 24.

39. Costa, "Entrevista." 59.

40. La Fountain-Stokes, *Queer Ricans*, 20.

41. Gelpí, *Literatura y paternalismo*, 149.

42. See La Fountain-Stokes, *Queer Ricans*, 19–63, 64–82; Sandlin, "Julia de Burgos as a Cultural Icon."

43. Luz María Umpierre, interview by author, 20 March 2011.

44. Martínez, "Interview."

45. Ibid.; Martínez, "Luz María Umpierre"; Umpierre, "Manifesto."

46. Martínez, *Lesbian Voices*, 168, refers to the collection as a lesbian manifesto; La Fountain-Stokes, *Queer Ricans*, 64–65, 68–75.

47. La Fountain-Stokes, *Queer Ricans*, 64–65.

48. Umpierre, *Margarita Poems*, 1.

49. Ibid., 1–2.

50. For more on *The Margarita Poems*, see La Fountain-Stokes, *Queer Ricans*, 75–92; Martínez, *Lesbian Voices*, 167–96.

51. Cohen, "Punks, Bulldaggers, and Welfare Queens," 28.

52. Umpierre, *Margarita Poems*, 16. Subsequent citations to Umpierre, *Margarita Poems*, appear in the text.

53. Sylvia Plath, "Lady Lazarus," in *Ariel*, 14–17.

54. Cohen, "Punks, Bulldaggers, and Welfare Queens," 23.

55. Luz María Umpierre, interview by author, 20 March 2011.

56. Martínez, "Luz María Umpierre," 7.

57. Wheeler, *Voicing American Poetry*, 27.

58. Martínez, "Luz María Umpierre," 8. On language as tool of male domination, see Spender, *Man Made Language*.

59. Martínez, "Luz María Umpierre," 8.

60. Wheeler, *Voicing American Poetry*, 32.

61. Cohen, "Punks, Bulldaggers, and Welfare Queens," 24.

62. Acosta-Belén and Bose, "U.S. Latina and Latin American Feminisms," 1114.

63. Acosta-Belén, "Beyond Island Boundaries," 986–87.

64. Gabriela Mistral immediately comes to mind. See Licia Fiol-Matta, *Queer Mother*.

65. Burgos, *El mar y tú*, 92.

66. Sonia Rivera-Valdés, interview by author, 10 March 2011.

67. Ibid.

68. Rivera-Valdés, *Historias de mujeres grandes y chiquitas*, 13–84.

69. For Mendieta's life and death, see O'Hagan, "Ana Mendieta"; for Rivera-Valdés's impressions of Mendieta, see Sonia Rivera-Valdés, interview by author, 10 March 2011.

70. Rivera-Valdés, *Stories*, 79, 85, 86.

71. Ferré, *Sitio a eros*, 7.

72. Ibid., 148.

73. Ibid., 151.

74. Mohanty, *Feminism without Borders*, 78.

75. Esteves, "Feminist Viewpoint," 171.

76. Sandra María Esteves, interview by author, 19 December 2010; Susana Cabañas, interview by author, 6 March 2011,

77. Nora, "Between Memory and History," 7, 16.

78. Sandra María Esteves, interview by author, 19 December 2010.

79. Sandra María Esteves, "It Is Raining Today," in *Tropical Rain*, 5.

80. Roach, *Cities of the Dead*, 259.

81. Esteves, "It Is Raining Today," 5.

82. Nora, "Between Memory and History," 9.

83. Esteves, *Yerba Buena*, 50–51.

84. Clifford, *Routes*, 177.

85. Sandra María Esteves, "Who I Am" (http://www.sandraesteves.com/poetrybookslinks/newselectedpoems.html). Revised poem emailed to author 21 August 2014.

86. See Kevane and Heredia, *Latina Self-Portraits*, 1–18.

87. Aurora Levins Morales, "About Me" (http://www.auroralevinsmorales.com/about-me.html).

88. Levins Morales, *Remedios*, 203; on 1950s domesticity more broadly, see 200–203.

89. Nora, "Between Memory and History," 9.

90. See Jason Ramírez, "Carmen Rivera."

91. Carmen Rivera, *Julia de Burgos*, 37, 38.

92. Ibid., 77.

93. Ibid., 69.

94. Several different versions of this essay exist. I quote from the version published in *Afro-Latin@ Reader*, ed. Jiménez Román and Flores, 262–65.

95. Ibid., 263.

96. Ibid., 264.

97. Vicioso, *Julia de Burgos*, [4].

98. Ibid., [6], [20], [26].

99. Vicioso, "Julia de Burgos," 683.

100. Ibid., 678.

101. Ibid., 683.

102. Wheeler, *Voicing American Poetry*, 15.

103. Ibid., 150.

104. Ibid., 151.

105. Crown, "Sonic Revolutionaries," 216.

106. Juan Flores, introduction to *Afro-Latin@ Reader*, ed. Jiménez Román and Flores, 14, 15.

107. Different versions of this poem exist. I quote from the version included in ibid., 280–81.

108. Fernández, "Ode to the Diasporican," 2424.

109. Fernández, "Boricua Butterfly," 2423.

110. Caridad De La Luz to author, 25 October 2013.

111. Wheeler, *Voicing American Poetry*, 159.

112. Bonafide Rojas to author, 20 March 2011.

113. Xavier, *Americano*, 54.

114. Ibid., 54–55.

CHAPTER 5

1. Nora, "Between Memory and History," 19, 17, 18.

2. Paredez, *Selenidad*, 9.

3. Roach, *Cities of the Dead*, 60.

4. See Arlene Dávila, *Culture Works*.

5. See Torres Martinó, "Arte puertorriqueño."

6. See Arcadio Díaz Quiñones, "Imágenes de Lorenzo Homar: Entre Nueva York y San Juan," in *Arte de Bregar*, 124–75.

7. Ibid., 129; translation by author.

8. See ibid.

9. Ibid., 158.

10. See Ortiz Rodríguez, "Memory Ricanstruction."

11. Burgos, *El mar y tú*, 31.

12. Johnson, *Persons and Things*, 11.

13. Wordsworth, *Poetry and Prose*, 601–18.

14. Ibid., 605.

15. "Juan Sanchez," 83–84.

16. Ibid.; Juan Sánchez, interview by author, 17 June 2010.

17. Juan Sánchez, interview by author, 17 June 2010.

18. Ibid.

19. Ibid.

20. The approximate date of the photo is determined by the fact that it shows a copy of her first collection, *Poema en veinte surcos* (1938) and that it was used on a flyer promoting a May 1940 poetry reading.

21. "Tribute to Julia de Burgos at Caravan House," Clemente Soto Vélez Papers, Box 10, Folder 6, Series IV, Archives of the Puerto Rican Diaspora, Center for Puerto Rican Studies, Hunter College, City University of New York.

22. See La Fountain-Stokes, *Queer Ricans*, where he refers to her as mulatta. See also the introduction to Lair, *De la herida a la gloria*.

23. Aparicio, "Jennifer as Selena," 93. See also Pérez, *Decolonial Imaginary*.

24. For more on Hernández's work, see her website (www.yasminhernandez.com).

25. Yasmín Hernández, interview by author, 17 March 2010.

26. Burgos, "Song of the Simple Truth," 400.

27. The poems are "Amaneceres," "Responso de ocho partidos," "A Julia de Burgos," "Oración," "Anunciación," "Hora santa, Ya no es canción," "Domingo de Ramos," "Una

canción a Albizu Campos," "Puerto Rico está en ti," "Despierta," "Somos puños cerrados," "Es nuestra la hora," "Viva la republica," "Abajo los asesinos," and "Río Grande de Loíza."

28. Yasmín Hernández, interview by author, 17 March 2010.

29. Ibid.

30. Díaz Quiñones, *Memoria rota*, 67–86.

31. Burgos, *Poema*, 25.

32. Julia de Burgos, "Puerto Rico está en ti," in *Song of the Simple Truth*, 500 (Spanish version); translation by author.

33. Julia Alvarez to author, 21 March 2011; http://www.juliaalvarez.com.

34. Pérez Rosario, "Solidarity across Borders," 94–95.

35. Ibid., 101.

36. Turner, *Beautiful Necessity*, 29.

37. Pérez Rosario, "Solidarity across Borders," 100.

38. For more on how the art world dismisses Latino/a artists because of their connection to space and living communities, see Arlene Dávila, *Culture Works*.

39. See Paredez, *Selenidad*.

40. See Hernández, "Painting Liberation."

41. See ibid.

42. Marcos Dimas, interview by author, 12 April 2011.

43. Ibid.

44. For more on El Barrio, changing demographics, gentrification, and El Museo del Barrio, see Arlene Dávila, *Barrio Dreams*. For the role of art and community, see Wherry, *Philadelphia Barrio*; Small, *Villa Victoria*.

45. Marcos Dimas, interview by author, 12 April 2011.

46. Fernando Salicrup, interview by author, 21 June 2010.

47. Ibid.

48. Manny Vega, interview by author, 5 March 2010.

49. Ibid.

50. Ibid.

51. Ibid.

52. Ibid.

53. For more on *plena* music and *pleneros*, see http://www.folkways.si.edu/explore_folkways/bomba_plena.aspx. See also Glasser, *My Music Is My Flag*, 169–90; Flores, *From Bomba to Hip Hop*, 67–69.

54. Roach, *Cities of the Dead*, 211.

55. Nora, "Between Memory and History," 23.

CONCLUSION

1. Hernández Cruz, "Panoramas," 123, 125.

2. Espada, "Lover of a Subversive," 14.

3. Ibid., 12.

4. Harlow, *Resistance Literature*, 29.

5. Espada, *Republic of Poetry*, 34–35.

6. Espada, "Bill Moyers Talks with Poet, Martín Espada."

7. Martín Espada, personal communication with author, 21 March 2011.

8. Espada, *Republic of Poetry*, 34–35. Espada revised line 5 of them poem from "Dead" to "Dying." Espada to author, 12 June 2014.

9. Espada, "Bill Moyers Talks with Poet, Martín Espada."

10. See Espada, "Lover of a Subversive."

BIBLIOGRAPHY

Acosta-Belén, Edna. "Beyond Island Boundaries: Ethnicity, Gender, and Cultural Re-vitalization in Nuyorican Literature." *Callaloo* 15.4 (Autumn 1992): 979–98.

———. "Consuelo Lee Tapia." *Latinas in United States History: A Historical Encyclope-dia*. Ed. Vicki L. Ruiz and Virginia Sánchez Korrol. Bloomington: Indiana University Press, 2006. 282–83.

Acosta-Belén, Edna, and Christine Bose. "U.S. Latina and Latin American Feminisms: Hemispheric Encounters." *Signs* 25.4 (Summer 2000): 1113–19.

Albizu Campos, Pedro. *Pedro Albizu Campos: Obras Escogidas, 1923–1936*. Book 1. Ed. J. Benjamin Torres. San Juan, P.R.: Jelofe, 1975.

Alegría-Ortega, Isa, and Palmira Ríos-González, eds. *Contrapuntos de género y raza en Puerto Rico*. San Juan: Universidad de Puerto Rico, 2005.

Algarín, Miguel. "Nuyorican Literature." *The Norton Anthology of Latino Literature*. Ed. Ilan Stavans, Edna Acosta-Belén, et al. New York: Norton, 2011. 1344–53.

Algarín, Miguel, and Bob Holman, eds. *Aloud: Voices from the Nuyorican Poets Cafe*. New York: Holt, 1994.

Algarín, Miguel, and Miguel Piñero, eds. *Nuyorican Poetry: An Anthology of Puerto Rican Words and Feelings*. New York: Morrow, 1975.

Anderson, Benedict. *Imagined Communities: Reflections on the Origin and Spread of Nationalism*. Rev. ed. London: Verso, 2006.

Aparicio, Frances R. "Jennifer as Selena: Rethinking Latinidad in Media and Popular Culture." *Latino Studies* 1.1 (March 2003): 90–105.

———. *Listening to Salsa: Gender, Latin Popular Music, and Puerto Rican Cultures*. Hanover, N.H.: University Press of New England, 1998.

———. "(Re)constructing Latinidad: The Challenge of Latina/o Studies." *A Companion to Latina/o Studies*. Ed. Juan Flores and Renato Rosaldo. Malden, Mass.: Wiley-Blackwell, 2011. 39–48.

———. "Writing Migrations: Transnational Readings of Rosario Ferré and Victor Hernández Cruz." *Latino Studies* 4.1–2 (Spring–Summer 2006): 79–95.

Aparicio, Frances R., and Susana Chávez-Silverman. *Tropicalizations: Transcultural Representations of Latinidad*. Hanover, N.H.: Dartmouth College, University Press of New England, 1997.

Arce, Margo. "Los poemas negros." *Impresiones: Notas Puertorriqueñas*. San Juan, P.R.: Yaurel, 1950.

Arenas, Reinaldo. *Before Night Falls*. New York: Viking, 1993.

Ayala, César, and Rafael Bernabe. *Puerto Rico in the American Century: A History since 1898*. Chapel Hill: University of North Carolina Press, 2007.

Azize, Yamila. *La mujer en la lucha*. Río Piedras, P.R.: Cultural, 1985.

Barradas, Efraín. *Partes de un todo: Ensayos y notas sobre literatura puertorriqueña en los Estados Unidos*. San Juan, P.R.: Editorial de la Universidad de Puerto Rico, 1998.

Barradas, Efraín, Rafael Rodríguez, and Carmen Lilianne Marín. *Herejes y mitificadores: Muestra de poesía puertorriqueña en los Estados Unidos*. Río Piedras, P.R.: Huracán, 1980.

Beauchamp, Juan José. "La literatura de la crisis social y cultural de la identidad nacional puertorriqueña (1925–1949): Un ensayo de apertura (parte I, II)." *22 Conferencias de literatura puertorriqueña*. Ed. Edgar Martínez Masdeu. San Juan, P.R.: Librería Editorial Ateneo, 1994. 294–369.

Belnap, Jeffrey, and Raúl Fernández, eds. *José Martí's "Our America": From National to Hemispheric Cultural Studies*. Durham, N.C.: Duke University Press, 1998.

Belpré, Pura. *The Stories I Read to the Children: The Life and Writing of Pura Belpré, the Legendary Storyteller, Children's Author, and New York Public Librarian*. Ed. and intro. Lisa Sánchez González. New York: Center for Puerto Rican Studies, 2013.

Benítez, Marimar. "The Special Case of Puerto Rico." *The Latin American Spirit: Art and Artists in the United States, 1920–1970*. New York: Bronx Museum and Abrams, 1988. 72–105.

Bernstein, Charles. Introduction to *Close Listening: Poetry and the Performed Word*. Ed. Charles Bernstein. New York: Oxford University Press, 1998. 3–26.

Bhabha, Homi K. "DissemiNation: Time, Narrative, and the Margins of the Nation." *The Location of Culture*. London: Routledge, 1994. 139–70.

Binder, Wolfgang. *Los puertorriqueños en Nueva York*. Erlangen, Germany: University of Erlangen, 1979.

Blanco, Tomás. *Prontuario histórico de Puerto Rico: Obras completes*. San Juan, P.R.: Ediciones Huracán, 1981.

———. "Refutación y glosa." *Ateneo Puertorriqueño* 1.4 (1935): 302–9.

Boyce Davies, Carole. *Black Women, Writing, and Identity: Migrations of the Subject*. New York: Routledge, 1994.

———. *Left of Karl Marx: The Political Life of Black Communist Claudia Jones*. New York: Routledge, 1994.

Braidotti, Rosi. *Nomadic Subjects: Embodiment and Sexual Difference in Contemporary Feminist Theory*. 2nd ed. New York: Columbia University Press, 2011.

Burgos, Julia de. *Canción de la verdad sencilla*. 2nd ed. Río Piedras, P.R.: Huracán, 1982.

————. *Desde la Escuela del Aire: Julia de Burgos: Textos de radio teatro escritos por Julia de Burgos*. Ed. Roberto Ramos-Perea. San Juan, P.R.: Ateneo Puertorriqueño, 1992.

————. *Julia de Burgos: Obra poética*. Ed. Consuelo Burgos and Juan Bautista Pagán. Intro. José Emilio González. San Juan, P.R.: Editorial del Instituto de Cultura Puertorriqueña, 2004.

————. *Julia de Burgos: Periodista en Nueva York*. Ed. Juan Antonio Rodríguez Pagán. San Juan, P.R.: Ateneo Puertorriqueño, 1992.

————. *El mar y tú*. Río Piedras, P.R.: Huracán, 1954.

————. *Poema en veinte surcos*. Río Piedras, P.R.: Huracán, 1938.

————. "Río Grande de Loíza." Trans. Grace Schulman. *Callaloo* 17.3 (Summer 1994): 667–68.

————. *Song of the Simple Truth: Obra Completa Poética: The Complete Poems*. Comp. and trans. Jack Agüeros. Willimantic, Conn.: Curbstone, 1997.

Capetillo, Luisa. *Amor y anarquía: Los escritos de Luisa Capetillo*. Ed. Julio Ramos. San Juan, P.R.: Huracán, 1992.

————. *A Nation of Women: An Early Feminist Speaks Out / Mi opinión sobres las libertades, derechos, y deberes de la mujer*. Ed. and intro. Félix V. Matos Rodríguez. Trans. Alan West-Durán. Houston: Arte Público, 2004.

Caragol-Barreto, Taína. "Aesthetics of Exile: The Construction of Nuyorican Identity in the Art of El Taller Boricua." *Centro Journal* 17.2 (Fall 2005): 7–21.

Carrero Peña, Amarilis, and Carmen Rivera Villegas, eds. *Las Vanguardias en Puerto Rico*. Madrid: Ediciones de la Discreta, 2009.

Carroll, Peter, and James Fernandez, eds. *Facing Fascism: New York and the Spanish Civil War*. New York: New York University Press, 2007.

Clifford, James. *Routes: Travel and Translation in the Late Twentieth Century*. Cambridge: Harvard University Press, 1997.

Cohen, Cathy J. "Punks, Bulldaggers, and Welfare Queens: The Radical Potential of Queer Politics?" *Black Queer Studies: A Critical Anthology*. Ed. E. Patrick Johnson and Mae G. Henderson. Durham, N.C.: Duke University Press, 2005. 21–51.

Costa, Marithelma. "Entrevista: Manuel Ramos Otero." *Hispamérica* 20.59 (August 1991): 59–67.

Coulthard, George Robert. *Race and Colour in Caribbean Literature*. London: Oxford University Press, 1962.

Crown, Kathleen. "'Sonic Revolutionaries': Voice and Experiment in the Spoken Word Poetry of Tracie Morris." *We Who Love to Be Astonished: Experimental Women's Writing and Performance Poetrics*. Ed. Laura Hinton and Cynthia Hogue. Tuscaloosa: University of Alabama Press, 2002. 213–26.

Cruz-Malavé, Arnaldo. "Toward an Art of Transvestism: Colonialism and Homosexuality in Puerto Rican." *Entiendes?: Queer Readings, Hispanic Writings*. Ed. Emilie L. Bergmann and Paul Julian Smith. Durham, N.C.: Duke University Press, 1995. 137–67.

Dash, Michael. *The Other America: Caribbean Literature in a New World Context*. Charlottesville: University Press of Virginia, 1998.

Dávila, Angelamaría. "'Un clavel interpuesto': (Apuntes sobre la imagen de Julia de Burgos)." *Claridad, En Rojo* supplement (24 February–1 March 1984): 15.

Dávila, Arlene. *Barrio Dreams: Puerto Ricans, Latinos, and the Neoliberal City*. Berkeley: University of California Press, 2004.

———. *Culture Works: Space, Value, and Mobility across the Neoliberal Americas*. New York: New York University Press, 2012.

———. *Latino Spin: Public Image and the Whitewashing of Race*. New York: New York University Press, 2008.

———. *Sponsored Identities: Cultural Politics in Puerto Rico*. Philadelphia: Temple University Press, 1997.

Davis, Natalie Zemon, and Randolph Starn. Introduction to special issue, "Memory and Counter-Memory." *Representations* 26 (Spring 1989): 1–6.

Deleuze, Gilles, and Félix Guattari. *A Thousand Plateaus: Capitalism and Schizophrenia*. Minneapolis: University of Minnesota Press, 1987.

Díaz Quiñones, Arcadio. *El arte de bregar: Ensayos*. San Juan, P.R.: Callejón, 2000.

———. *La memoria rota*. San Juan, P.R.: Huracán, 2003.

———. "Recordando el futuro imaginario: La escritura histórica en la década del treinta." *Sin Nombre* 14.3 (April–June 1984): 16–35.

Dick, Bruce Allen. *A Poet's Truth: Conversations with Latino/Latina Poets*. Tucson: University of Arizona Press, 2003.

Diego Padró, José I. de. *Luis Palés Matos y su trasmundo poético*. Río Piedras, P.R.: Ediciones Puerto, 1973.

Dietz, James. *Economic History of Puerto Rico: Institutional Change and Capitalist Development*. Princeton: Princeton University Press, 1986.

Dimas, Marcos. "Artist Statement." *Taller Alma Boricua: Reflecting on Twenty Years of the Puerto Rican Workshop, 1969–1989*. New York: Museo del Barrio, 1990.

Duany, Jorge. *Blurred Borders: Transnational Migration between the Hispanic Caribbean and the United States*. Chapel Hill: University of North Carolina Press, 2011.

———. *The Puerto Rican Nation on the Move: Identities on the Island and in the United States*. Chapel Hill: University North Carolina Press, 2002.

Du Bois, W. E. B. *The Souls of Black Folk*. Chicago: McClurg, 1903.

Edwards, Brent Hayes. "The Uses of Diaspora." *Social Text* 19.1 (Spring 2001): 45–73.

Enck-Wanzer, Darrel, ed. *The Young Lords: A Reader*. New York: New York University Press, 2010.

Espada, Martín. "Bill Moyers Talks with Poet, Martín Espada." http://www.martinespada.net/Bill_Moyers.html.

———. *The Lover of a Subversive Is Also a Subversive: Essays and Commentaries*. Ann Arbor: University of Michigan Press, 2010.

———. *The Republic of Poetry*. New York: Norton, 2006.

Esteves, Sandra María. "Ambivalence or Activism from the Nuyorican Perspective in Poetry." *Images and Identities: The Puerto Rican in Two World Contexts*. Ed. Asela Rodríguez de Laguna. New Brunswick, N.J.: Transaction, 1987. 164–70.

———. *Bluestown Mockingbird Mambo*. Houston: Arte Público, 1990.

———. "The Feminist Viewpoint in the Poetry of Puerto Rican Women in the United States." *Images and Identities: The Puerto Rican in Two World Contexts*. Ed. Asela Rodríguez de Laguna. New Brunswick, N.J.: Transaction, 1987. 171–76.

———. *Tropical Rains: A Bilingual Downpour, Poems*. Bronx, N.Y.: African Caribbean Poetry Theater, 1984.

———. *Yerba Buena*. New York: Greenfield Review, 1980.

Faber, Sebastiaan. "'La Hora Ha Llegado': Hispanism, Pan-Americanism, and the Hope of Spanish/American Glory (1938–1948)." *Ideologies of Hispanism*. Ed. Mabel Moraña. Nashville, Tenn.: Vanderbilt University Press, 2005. 62–104.

Fales-Hill, Susan. *Always Wear Joy: My Mother Bold and Beautiful*. New York: Harper Perennial, 2004.

Falú, Aixa Merino. "Raza, género, y clase social: Los efectos del racismo en las mujeres puertorriqueñas negras (siglo veinte)." Ph.D. diss., Universidad de Puerto Rico, 2002.

Fernández, María Teresa (Mariposa). "Boricua Butterfly." *Norton Anthology of Latino Literature*. Ed. Ilan Stavans, Edna Acosta-Belén, et al. New York: Norton, 2011. 2423.

———. "Ode to the Diasporican." *Norton Anthology of Latino Literature*. Ed. Ilan Stavans, Edna Acosta-Belén, et al. New York: Norton, 2011. 2424.

———. "Poem for My Grifa-Rican Sistah; or, Broken Ends Broken Promises." *The Afro-Latin@ Reader: History and Culture in the United States*. Ed. Miriam Jiménez Román and Juan Flores. Durham, N.C.: Duke University Press, 2010. 280–81.

Fernández Olmos, Margarite, and Lizabeth Paravisini-Gebert, eds. *Pleasure in the Word: Erotic Writings by Latin American Women*. New York: White Pine, 1993.

Ferrao, Luis Angel. *Pedro Albizu Campos y el nacionalismo puertorriqueno*. San Juan, P.R.: Cultural, 1990.

Ferré, Rosario. *House on the Lagoon*. New York: Plume, 1996.

———. *Sitio a eros: Quince ensayos literarios*. Mexico City: Moritz, 1986.

Findlay, Eileen J. Suárez. *Imposing Decency: The Politics of Sexuality and Race in Puerto Rico, 1870–1920*. Durham, N.C.: Duke University Press, 1999.

Fiol-Matta, Licia. *A Queer Mother for the Nation: The State and Gabriela Mistral*. Minneapolis: University of Minnesota Press, 2002.

Fiol-Matta, Liza. "Naming Our World, Writing Our History: The Voices of Hispanic Feminist Poets." *Women's Studies Quarterly* 16.3–4 (Fall–Winter 1988): 68–80.

Flores, Juan. *The Diaspora Strikes Back: Caribeño Tales of Learning and Turning*. New York: Routledge, 2009.

———. *Divided Borders: Essays on Puerto Rican Identity*. Houston: Arte Público, 1993.

———. *From Bomba to Hip Hop*. New York: Columbia University Press, 2000.

———. "Nueva York—Diaspora City: U.S. Latinos between and Beyond." *NACLA Report on the Americas* 35.6 (May–June 2002): 46–49.

Fregoso, Rosa Linda. *MeXicana Encounters: The Making of Social Identities on the Borderlands*. Berkeley: University of California Press, 2003.

García Calderón, Myrna. "Prólogo." *Las Vanguardias en Puerto Rico*. Ed. Amarilis Carrero Peña and Carmen Rivera Villegas. Madrid: Ediciones de la Discreta, 2009. 9–14.

García Peña, Lorgia. "Más Que Cenizas: An Analysis of Juan Bosch's Dissident Narration of *Dominicanidad* (Ausente)." *Hispanic Caribbean Literature of Migration: Narratives of Displacement*. Ed. Vanessa Pérez Rosario. New York: Palgrave, 2010. 39–55.

Gelpí, Juan G. *Literatura y paternalismo en Puerto Rico*. San Juan, P.R.: Editorial de la Universidad de Puerto Rico, 1993.

———. "The Nomadic Subject in Julia de Burgos's Poetry." *The Cultures of the Hispanic Caribbean*. Ed. Conrad James and John Perivolaris. Gainesville: University of Florida Press, 2000. 37–49.

Gilroy, Paul. *The Black Atlantic: Modernity and Double Consciousness*. Cambridge: Harvard University Press, 1993.

Glasser, Ruth. *My Music Is My Flag: Puerto Rican Musicians and Their New York Communities, 1917–1940*. Berkeley: University of California Press, 1995.

Gómez, Alma, Cherríe Moraga, and Mariana Romo-Carmona, eds. *Cuentos: Stories by Latinas*. New York: Kitchen Table, 1983.

González, José Emilio. "Algo más sobre la vida y la poesía de Julia de Burgos." *La Torre* 13.51 (September-December 1965): 151–74.

———. "La individualidad poética de Julia de Burgos." *Río Piedras* 3–4 (September–March 1973–74): 47–59.

———. "Julia de Burgos: Intensa siempreviva." *Asomante* 9.4 (October–December 1953): 23–24.

———. "Julia de Burgos: La mujer y la poesía." *Sin Nombre* 7.3 (October–December 1976): 86–100.

———. *La poesía contemporánea de Puerto Rico*. San Juan, P.R.: Instituto de Cultura Puertorriqueña, 1972.

González, José Luis. *El país de cuatro pisos y otros ensayos*. Río Piedras, P.R.: Ediciones Huracán, 1989.

Grazian, David. *Blue Chicago: The Search for Authenticity in Urban Blues Clubs*. Chicago: University of Chicago Press, 2003.

Griffin, Farah Jasmine. *Harlem Nocturne: Women Artists and Progressive Politics during World War II*. New York: Basic Civitas, 2013.

———. *In Search of Billie Holiday: If You Can't Be Free, Be a Mystery*. New York: Ballantine, 2001.

Gruesz, Kirsten Silva. *Ambassadors of Culture: The Transamerican Origins of Latino Writing*. Princeton: Princeton University Press, 2002.

Guerra, Lillian. *Popular Expression and National Identity in Puerto Rico: The Struggle for Self, Community, and Nation*. Gainesville: University Press of Florida, 1998.

Guzmán, Manolo. *Gay Hegemony/Latino Homosexualities*. New York: Routledge, 2006.

———. "'Pa' la Escuelita con Mucho Cuida'o y por la Orillita': A Journey through the Contested Terrains of the Nation and Sexual Orientation." *Puerto Rican Jam: Essays on Culture and Politics*. Ed. Frances Negrón-Muntaner and Ramón Grosfoguel. Minneapolis: University of Minnesota Press, 1997. 209–28.

Harlow, Barbara. *Resistance Literature*. New York: Methuen, 1987.

Haslip-Viera, Gabriel. "The Evolution of the Latino Community in the New York Metropolitan Area, 1810 to the Present." *Latinos in New York: Communities in Transi-*

tion. Ed. Gabriel Haslip-Viera and Sherrie Baver. Notre Dame, Ind.: Notre Dame University Press, 1996. 3–29.

Heredia, Juanita. *Transnational Latina Narratives in the Twenty-First Century: The Politics of Gender, Race, and Migration*. New York: Palgrave Macmillan, 2009.

Hernández, Yasmín. "Painting Liberation: 1998 and Its Pivotal Role in the Formation of a New Boricua Political Art Movement." *Centro Journal* 17.2 (Fall 2005): 112–33.

Hernández Aquino, Luis. *Nuestra aventura literaria: Los ismos en la poesía puertorriqueña, 1913–1948*. 2nd ed. San Juan, P.R.: Ediciones de la Torre, Universidad de Puerto Rico, 1966.

Hernández Cruz, Victor. *Panoramas*. Saint Paul, Minn.: Coffee House, 1997.

Horno-Delgado, Asunción, Eliana Ortega, Nina M. Scott, and Nancy Saporta Sternbach, eds. *Breaking Boundaries: Latina Writing and Critical Readings*. Amherst: University of Massachusetts Press, 1989.

Hull, Gloria, Patricia Bell Scott, and Barbara Smith, eds. *All the Women Are White, All the Blacks Are Men, but Some of Us Are Brave: Black Women's Studies*. Old Westbury, N.Y.: Feminist, 1982.

Jimenes Grullón, Juan Isidro. *Luchemos por nuestra América: Cuatro ensayos de interpretación y orientación de la realidad ibero-americana*. 2nd ed. Havana, Cuba: Empresa Editora de Publicaciones, 1936.

———. *Una Gestapo en América*. 5th ed. Santo Domingo, D.R.: Montalvo, 1962.

Jiménez de Báez, Yvette. *Julia de Burgos: Vida y poesía*. San Juan, P.R.: Coquí, 1966.

Jiménez-Muñoz, Gladys. "Carmen María Colón Pellot: On 'Womanhood' and 'Race' in Puerto Rico during the Interwar Period." *CR: The New Centennial Review* 3.3 (Fall 2003): 71–91.

———. "'So We Decided to Come and Ask You Ourselves': The 1928 U.S. Congressional Hearings on Women's Suffrage in Puerto Rico." *Puerto Rican Jam: Essays on Culture and Politics*. Ed. Frances Negrón-Muntaner and Ramón Grosfoguel. Minneapolis: University of Minnesota Press, 1997. 140–65.

Jiménez Román, Miriam, and Juan Flores, eds. *The Afro-Latin@ Reader: History and Culture in the United States*. Durham, N.C.: Duke University Press, 2010.

Johnson, Barbara. *Persons and Things*. Cambridge: Harvard University Press, 2008.

"Juan Sanchez [*sic*] interviewed by Susan Canning." *Interventions and Provocations: Conversations on Art, Culture, and Resistance*. Ed. Glen Harper. Albany: State University of New York Press, 1998. 77–84.

Kanellos, Nicolás. "Recovering and Re-Constructing Early Twentieth-Century Hispanic Immigrant Print Culture in the U.S." *American Literary History* 19.2 (Summer 2007): 435–55.

Kanellos, Nicolás, and Helvetia Martell. *Hispanic Periodicals in the United States: Origins to 1960*. Houston: Arte Público, 2000.

Kanellos, Nicolás, Kenya Dworkin y Méndez, and Alejandra Balestra. *Herencia: The Anthology of Hispanic Literature of the United States*. New York: Oxford University Press, 2002.

Kevane, Bridget, and Juanita Heredia, eds. *Latina Self-Portraits: Interviews with Contemporary Women Writers*. Albuquerque: University of New Mexico Press, 2000.

Kleinig, John. *Paternalism*. Totowa, N.J.: Rowman and Allanheld, 1984.

Kugel, Seth. "The Latino Culture Wars." *New York Times*, 24 February 2002, 7–8F.

Kury, Farid. *Juan Bosch: Entre el exilio y el golpe de estado*. Santo Domingo, D.R.: Búho, 2000.

La Fountain-Stokes, Lawrence. "De sexilio(s) y diaspora(s) homosexual(es) Latina(s): Cultura puertorriqueña y lo nuyorican queer." *Debate Feminista* 15.29 (April 2004): 138–57.

———. "Entre boleros, travestismos, y migraciones translocales: Manuel Ramos Otero, Jorge Merced, y *El bolero fue mi ruina* del Teatro Pregones del Bronx." *Revista Iberoamericana* 71.212 (July–September 2005): 887–907.

———. "Queer Diasporas, Boricua Lives: A Meditation on Sexile." *Review: Literature and Arts of the Americas* 41.2 (November 2008): 294–301.

———. *Queer Ricans: Cultures and Sexualities in the Diaspora*. Minneapolis: University of Minnesota Press, 2009.

Lair, Clara. *De la herida a la gloria: La poesía completa de Clara Lair*. Ed. Mercedes López-Baralt. San Juan, P.R.: Terranova, 2003.

Lazo, Rodrigo. *Writing to Cuba: Filibustering and Cuban Exiles in the United States*. Chapel Hill: University of North Carolina Press, 2005.

Levins Morales, Aurora. *Kindling: Writings on the Body*. Cambridge, Mass.: Palabrera, 2013.

———. *Medicine Stories: History, Culture, and the Politics of Integrity*. Boston: South End, 1999.

———. *Remedios: Stories of Earth and Iron from the History of Puertorriqueñas*. Boston: South End, 2001.

Lima, Lázaro. *The Latino Body: Crisis Identities in American Literary and Cultural Memory*. New York: New York University Press, 2007.

Lindauer, Margaret A. *Devouring Frida: The Art History and Popular Celebrity of Frida Kahlo*. Hanover, N.H.: University Press of New England, 1999.

Lladó-Ortega, Mónica. "A Community in Transit: The Performative Gestures of Manuel Ramos Otero's Narrative Triptych." *Hispanic Caribbean Literature of Migration: Narratives of Displacement*. Ed. Vanessa Pérez Rosario. New York: Palgrave, 2010. 121–36.

Lomas, Laura. *Translating Empire: José Martí, Migrant Latino Subjects, and American Modernities*. Durham, N.C.: Duke University Press, 2008.

López-Baralt, Mercedes. "Julia de Burgos, poeta de vanguardia." *La poésie de Julia de Burgos: 1914–1953: Actes des journées d'études internationales d'Amiens, 2004*. Ed. Carmen Vázquez. Paris: Indigo and Côté-Femmes; Amiens: Université de Picardie, 2005. 15–34.

———. "Prólogo." *De la herida a la gloria: La poesía completa de Clara Lair*. San Juan, P.R.: Terranova, 2003.

López Jiménez, Ivette. "Julia de Burgos: El talante vanguardista." *Las Vanguardias en Puerto Rico*. Ed. Amarilis Carrero Peña and Carmen Rivera Villegas. Madrid: Ediciones de la Discreta, 2009. 129–41.

———. *Julia de Burgos: La canción y el silencio*. San Juan, P.R.: Fundación Puertorriqueña de las Humanidades, 2002.

————. "Julia de Burgos: Los textos comunicantes." *Sin Nombre* 10.1 (April–June 1979): 47–68.

————. "Julia de Burgos una vez más." *Actas del congreso internacional Julia de Burgos.* Ed. Edgar Martínez Masdeu. San Juan, P.R.: Ateneo Puertorriqueño, 1993. 274–82.

Luis, William. *Dance between Two Cultures: Latino Caribbean Literature Written in the United States.* Nashville, Tenn.: Vanderbilt University Press, 1997.

————. "María C(h)ristina Speaks: Latina Identity and the Poetic Dialogue between Sandra María Esteves and Luz María Umpierre." *Hispanic Journal* 18.1 (1997): 137–49.

Magnarelli, Sharon. *Home Is Where the (He)art Is: The Family Romance in Late Twentieth-Century Mexican and Argentine Theatre.* Lewisburg, Pa.: Bucknell University Press, 2008.

Margolies, Edward. *New York and the Literary Imagination: The City in Twentieth Century Fiction and Drama.* Jefferson, N.C.: McFarland, 2008.

Marqués, René. *La carreta.* San Juan, P.R.: Cultural, 2007.

Márquez, Roberto, ed. and trans. *Puerto Rican Poetry: Anthology from Aboriginal to Contemporary Times.* Amherst: University of Massachusetts Press, 2007.

Martí, José. *Selected Writings.* Trans. Ester Allen. New York: Penguin Classics, 2002.

Martin, Biddy, and Chandra Talpade Mohanty. "Feminist Politics: What's Home Got to Do with It?" *Feminist Studies/Critical Studies.* Ed. Teresa de Lauretis. Bloomington: Indiana University Press, 1986. 191–212.

Martínez, Elena. "An Interview with Luz María Umpierre." *Christopher Street* 163 (October 1991): 9–10.

————. *Lesbian Voices from Latin America: Breaking Ground.* New York: Garland, 1996.

————. "Luz María Umpierre: A Lesbian Puerto Rican Writer in America." *Christopher Street* 163 (October 1991): 7–8.

Martínez-San Miguel, Yolanda. *Caribe Two Ways: Cultura de la migración en el Caribe insular hispánico.* San Juan, P.R.: Callejón, 2003.

————. "Deconstructing Puerto Ricanness through Sexuality." *Puerto Rican Jam: Essays on Culture and Politics.* Ed. Frances Negrón-Muntaner and Ramón Grosfoguel. Minneapolis: University of Minnesota Press, 1997. 127–39.

————. "Female Sexiles?: Towards an Archeology of Displacement of Sexual Minorities in the Caribbean." *Signs* 36.4 (Summer 2011): 813–36.

Masiello, Francine. "Rethinking Neocolonial Esthetics: Literature, Politics, and Intellectual Community in Cuba's Revista de Avance." *Latin American Research Review* 28.2 (1993): 3–31.

————. "Texto, ley, transgression: Especulación sobre la novela (feminist) de vanguardia." *Revista Iberoamericana* 51.132–33 (July–December 1985): 807–22.

————. "Women, State, and Family in Latin American Literature of the 1920s." *Women, Culture, and Politics in Latin America.* Berkeley: University of California Press, 1990. 27–47.

Massey, Doreen B. *Space, Place, and Gender.* Minneapolis: University of Minnesota Press, 1994.

Matos Rodríguez, Félix V., and Linda Delgado, eds. *Puerto Rican Women's History: New Perspectives.* New York: Sharpe, 1998.

McCracken, Ellen. *New Latina Narrative: The Feminine Space of Postmodern Ethnicity*. Tucson: University of Arizona Press, 1999.

Memmi, Albert. *The Colonizer and the Colonized*. Boston: Beacon, 1965.

Méndez, Danny. *Narratives of Migration and Displacement in Dominican Literature*. New York: Routledge, 2012.

Middleton, Peter. "The Contemporary Poetry Reading." *Close Reading: Poetry and the Performed Word*. Ed. Charles Bernstein. New York: Oxford University Press, 1998. 262–99.

Mignolo, Walter. "The Many Faces of Cosmo-Polis: Border Thinking and Critical Cosmopolitanism." *Cosmopolitanism*. Ed. Carol A. Breckenridge, Sheldon Pollock, Homi K. Bhabha, and Dipesh Chakrabarty. Durham, N.C.: Duke University Press, 2002. 157–88.

Mohanty, Chandra. *Feminism without Borders: Decolonizing Theory, Practicing Solidarity*. Durham, N.C.: Duke University Press, 2003.

Montero, Oscar. "La prosa neoyorquina de Julia de Burgos: 'La cosa latina' en 'mi segunda casa.'" http://www.lehman.cuny.edu/ciberletras/v20/montero.html.

———. *Las rutas de Julia de Burgos*. Directed by Memo. Staged reading by Teatro Iati. Lehman Center for the Performing Arts, Lehman College, Bronx, New York, 1 April 2011.

Moraga, Cherríe. "From a Long Line of Vendidas: Chicanas and Feminism." *Feminist Studies/Critical Studies*. Ed. Teresa de Lauretis. Bloomington: Indiana University Press, 1986. 173–90.

Moraga, Cherríe, and Gloria Anzaldúa, eds. *This Bridge Called My Back: Writings by Radical Women of Color*. Watertown, Mass.: Persephone, 1981.

———, eds. *This Bridge Called My Back: Writings by Radical Women of Color*. Exp. and rev. 3rd ed. Berkeley, Calif.: Third Woman, 2002.

Morales, Iris. *Palante: Young Lords Party*. Chicago: Haymarket, 2011.

Moraña, Mabel. "Introduction: Mapping Hispanism." *Ideologies of Hispanism*. Ed. Mabel Moraña. Nashville, Tenn.: Vanderbilt University Press, 2005. ix–xxi.

Moreno, Marisel C. *Family Matters: Puerto Rican Women Authors on the Island and the Mainland*. Charlottesville: University of Virginia Press, 2012.

Negrón-Muntaner, Frances. *Brincando el Charco: Portrait of a Puerto Rican*. New York: Hispic, 1994.

———. "Jennifer's Butt: Valorizing the Puerto Rican Racialized Female Body." *Boricua Pop: Puerto Ricans and the Latinization of American Culture*. New York: New York University Press, 2004. 228–46.

Negrón-Muntaner, Frances, and Ramón Grosfoguel, eds. *Puerto Rican Jam: Rethinking Colonialism and Nationalism*. Minneapolis: University of Minnesota Press, 1997.

Noel, Urayoán. "Counter/Public Address: Nuyorican Poetries in the Slam Era." *Latino Studies* 9.1 (Spring 2011): 38–61.

Nora, Pierre. "Between Memory and History: Les Lieux de Mémoire." *Representations* 26 (Spring 1989): 7–24.

Oboler, Suzanne. *Ethnic Labels, Latino Lives: Identity and the Politics of (Re)Presentation in the United States*. Minneapolis: University of Minnesota Press, 1995.

O'Hagan, Sean. "Ana Mendieta: Death of an Artist Foretold in Blood." *The Observer*, 21 September 2013. http://www.theguardian.com/artanddesign/2013/sep/22/ana-mendieta -artist-work-foretold-death.

Ortiz Rodríguez, Raquel. "Memory Ricanstruction: Literary Portfolios Based on Poetry Created by José R. Alicea." *Centro Journal* 17.2 (Fall 2005): 89–111.

Palés Matos, Luis. *Poesía completa y prosa selecta*. Caracas, Venezuela: Ayacucho, 1978.

———. *Tuntún de pasa y grifería: Poemas afro-antillanas*. San Juan, P.R.: Cultural Puertorriqueña, 1988.

Paredez, Deborah. "Remembering Selena, Re-membering Latinidad." *Theater Journal* 54.1 (March 2002): 63–83.

———. *Selenidad: Selena, Latinos, and the Performance of Memory*. Durham, N.C.: Duke University Press, 2009.

Paz, Octavio. *The Double Flame: Love and Eroticism*. Trans. Helen Lane. New York: Harcourt Brace, 1995.

Pedreira, Antonio S. *Insularismo*. Río Piedras, P.R.: Edil, 1934.

Pérez, Emma. *The Decolonial Imaginary: Writing Chicanas into History*. Bloomington: Indiana University Press, 1999.

Pérez Rosario, Vanessa. "Affirming an Afro-Latin@ Identity: An Interview with Poet María Teresa 'Mariposa' Fernández." *Latino Studies Journal* 12.3 (Fall 2014): 1–8.

———. "Las rutas de Julia de Burgos." *E-misférica* 8.1 (Summer 2011). http://hemi.nyu .edu/hemi/en/e-misferica-81/perez-rosario.

———. "Solidarity across Borders: An Interview with Artist Andrea Arroyo." *Meridians* 11.2 (Spring 2013): 91–111.

Pérez y González, María. *Puerto Ricans in the United States*. Westport, Conn.: Greenwood, 2000.

Plath, Sylvia. *Ariel: The Restored Edition*. New York: Harper and Row, 2005.

Pogrebin, Robin. "Josephine Premice, 74, Actress Who Dazzled on Broadway." *New York Times*, 17 April 2001. http://www.nytimes.com/2001/04/17/arts/josephine-premice-74 -actress-who-dazzled-on-broadway.html.

Portes, Alejandro, and Alex Stepick. *City on the Edge: The Transformation of Miami*. Berkeley: University of California Press, 1993.

Poyo, Gerald E. *"With All, and for the Good of All": The Emergence of Popular Nationalism in the Cuban Communities in the United States, 1848–1898*. Durham, N.C.: Duke University Press, 1989.

Pratt, Mary Louise. *Imperial Eyes: Travel Writing and Transculturation*. London: Routledge, 1992.

Preminger, Alex, T. V. F. Brogan, Frank J. Warnke, O. B. Hardison Jr., and Earl Miner, eds. *The New Princeton Encyclopedia of Poetry and Poetics*. Princeton: Princeton University Press, 1993.

Puebla, Manuel de la. "Julia de Burgos como mito." *Revista Mairena* 7.20 (1985): 81–91.

Puerto Rico Emergency Relief Administration. *The Tariff Problems of Puerto Rico: Report of the Tariff Survey Division of the Puerto Rican Emergency Relief Administration*. San Juan, P.R.: Bureau of Supplies, Printing, and Transportation, 1935.

Quintero Rivera, Angel. *Conflictos de clase y política en Puerto Rico*. 5th ed. Río Piedras, P.R.: Huracán, 1986.

Ramazani, Jahan. *A Transnational Poetics*. Chicago: University of Chicago Press, 2009.

Ramírez, Jason. "Carmen Rivera: Theatre of Latinidad." Ph.D. diss., Graduate Center, City University of New York, 2009.

Ramírez, Yasmín. "Nuyorican Visionary: Jorge Soto and the Evolution of an Afro-Taíno Aesthetic at Taller Boricua." *Centro Journal* 17.2 (Fall 2005): 22–41.

———. "Visual Artists Honor Pedro Pietri: A Pictorial Essay." *Centro Journal* 17.2 (Fall 2005): 134–43.

Ramos, Juanita, ed. *Compañeras: Latina Lesbians*. New York: Latina Lesbian History Project, 1987.

Ramos, Julio. *Divergent Modernities: Culture and Politics in Nineteenth-Century Latin America*. Trans. John Blanco. Durham, N.C.: Duke University Press, 2001.

Ramos Otero, Manuel. *El cuento de la mujer del mar*. Río Piedras, P.R.: Huracán, 1979.

Remeseira, Claudio, ed. *Hispanic New York: A Sourcebook*. New York: Columbia University Press, 2010.

Revista Mairena 7.20 (1985). Commemorative issue on Julia de Burgos.

Ríos Ávila, Rubén. "Víctima de Luz." *La raza cósmica del sujeto en Puerto Rico*. San Juan, P.R.: Callejón, 2002. 211–21.

Rivera, Carmen. *Julia de Burgos: Child of Water*. New York: Red Sugarcane, 2014.

Rivera, Carmen Haydée. "'Language Is Our Only Homeland': An Interview with Luz María Umpierre." *Centro Journal* 20.1 (Spring 2008): 12–21.

Rivera-Valdés, Sonia. *The Forbidden Stories of Marta Veneranda*. Trans. by Dick Cluster, Marina Harss, Mark Shafer, and Alan West-Dúran. New York: Seven Stories, 2001.

———. *Historias de mujeres grandes y chiquitas*. New York: Campana, 2003.

———. *Las historias prohibidas de Marta Veneranda*. New York: Seven Stories, 2001.

———. *Stories of Little Women and Grown-Up Girls*. Trans. Emily Maguire. New York: Campana, 2007.

Rivero, Yeidy. *Tuning Out Blackness: Race and Nation in the History of Puerto Rican Television*. Durham, N.C.: Duke University Press, 2005.

Roach, Joseph. *Cities of the Dead: Circum-Atlantic Performance*. New York: Columbia University Press, 1996.

Rodó, José Enrique. *Ariel*. Chicago: University of Chicago Press, 1929.

Rodríguez Castro, Malena. "Silencio y estridencias: Las Vanguardias en Puerto Rico." *Las Vanguardias en Puerto Rico*. Ed. Amarilis Carrero Peña and Carmen Rivera Villegas. Madrid: Ediciones de la Discreta, 2009. 17–51.

Rodríguez-Fraticelli, Carlos. "Pedro Albizu Campos: Strategies of Struggle and Strategic Struggles." *Centro Journal* 3.2 (Spring 1991): 25–33.

Rodríguez Pagán, Juan Antonio. "Cronología de Julia de Burgos." *Revista Mairena* 7.20 (1985): 163–67.

———. *Julia en blanco y negro*. San Juan, P.R.: Institute of Puerto Rican Culture, 2000.

Roy-Féquière, Magali. *Women, Creole Identity, and Intellectual Life in Early Twentieth Century Puerto Rico*. Philadelphia: Temple University Press, 2004.

Rúa, Mérida. "Colao Subjectivities: PortoMex and MexiRican Perspectives on Language and Identity." *Centro Journal* 13.2 (Fall 2001): 116–33.

Rubin, Joan Shelley. *Songs of Ourselves: The Uses of Poetry in America.* Cambridge: Harvard University Press, 2007.

Ruiz, Vicki L., and Virginia Sánchez Korrol, eds. *Latinas in United States History: A Historical Encyclopedia.* Bloomington: Indiana University Press, 2006.

Said, Edward. *Reflections on Exile and Other Essays.* Cambridge: Harvard University Press, 2003.

———. *Representations of the Intellectual.* New York: Vintage, 1996.

Sánchez, Marta Ester. *Contemporary Chicana Poetry: A Critical Approach to an Emerging Literature.* Berkeley: University of California Press, 1985.

Sánchez González, Lisa. *Boricua Literature: A Literary History of the Puerto Rican Diaspora.* New York: New York University Press, 2001.

———. "Pura Belpré: The Children's Ambassador." *Latina Legacies: Identity, Biography, and Community.* Ed. Vicki Ruiz and Virginia Sánchez Korrol. New York: Oxford University Press, 2005. 148–57.

Sánchez Korrol, Virginia. "The Forgotten Migrant: Educated Puerto Rican Women in New York City, 1920–1940." *The Puerto Rican Woman: Perspectives on Culture, History, and Society.* Ed. Edna Acosta-Belén. New York: Praeger, 1986. 170–79.

———. *From Colonia to Community: The History of Puerto Ricans in New York City.* Berkeley: University of California Press, 1994.

———. "Puerto Ricans in 'Olde' Nueva York: Migrant *Colonias* of the Nineteenth and Twentieth Centuries." *Nueva York, 1613–1945.* Ed. Edward J. Sullivan. London: Scala, 2010. 108–21.

Sánchez Korrol, Virginia, and Pedro Juan Hernández. *Pioneros II: Puerto Ricans in New York City, 1948–1998.* Charleston, S.C.: Arcadia, 2010.

Sandlin, Betsy A. "Julia de Burgos as a Cultural Icon in Works by Rosario Ferré, Luz María Umpierre, and Manuel Ramos Otero." Ph.D. diss., University of North Carolina at Chapel Hill, 2003.

———. "Manuel Ramos Otero's Queer Metafictional Resurrection of Julia de Burgos." *Writing Off the Hyphen: New Perspectives on the Literature of the Puerto Rican Diaspora.* Ed. José L. Torres-Padilla and Carmen Haydée Rivera. Seattle: University of Washington Press, 2008. 313–31.

Santiago, Esmeralda. "Island of Lost Causes." *Boricuas: Influential Puerto Rican Writings—An Anthology.* Ed. Roberto Santiago. New York: One World, 1995. 22–24.

———. *When I Was Puerto Rican.* New York: Vintage, 1994.

Santiago-Díaz, Eleuterio. *Escritura afropuertorriqueña y modernidad.* Pittsburgh: Instituto Internacional de Literatura Iberoamericana, 2007.

Santiago-Valles, Kelvin A. "The Discreet Charm of the Proletariat: Imagining Early-Twentieth-Century Puerto Ricans in the Past Twenty-Five Years of Historical Inquiry." *Puerto Rican Jam: Essays on Culture and Politics.* Ed. Frances Negrón-Muntaner and Ramón Grosfoguel. Minneapolis: University of Minnesota Press, 1997. 95–115.

Schrecker, Ellen. *The Age of McCarthyism: A Brief History with Documents*. New York: St. Martin's, 1994.

———. *Many Are the Crimes: McCarthyism in America*. Princeton: Princeton University Press, 1998.

Silén, Ivan, and Alfredo Mantilla, eds. *The Puerto Rican Poets*. New York: Bantam, 1972.

Small, Mario Luis. *Villa Victoria: The Transformation of Social Capital in a Boston Barrio*. Chicago: University of Chicago Press, 2004.

Solá, María M. "La poesía de Julia de Burgos: Mujer de humana lucha." *Julia de Burgos: Yo misma fui mi ruta*. Ed. María M. Solá. Río Piedras, P.R.: Huracán, 1986.

Sommer, Doris. *One Master for Another: Populism as Patriarchal Rhetoric in Dominican Novels*. Lanham, Md.: University Press of America, 1983.

Spender, Dale. *Man Made Language*. New York: Routledge, 1985.

Sullivan, Edward, ed. *Nueva York, 1613–1945*. London: Scala and New-York Historical Society, 2010.

Thomas, Lorenzo. "Neon Griot: The Functional Role of Poetry Readings in the Black Arts Movement." *Close Reading: Poetry and the Performed Word*. Ed. Charles Bernstein. New York: Oxford University Press, 1998. 300–323.

Thomas, Lorrin. *Puerto Rican Citizen: History and Political Identity in Twentieth-Century New York City*. Chicago: University of Chicago Press, 2010.

Torres, Arlene. "La gran familia puertorriqueña 'ej prieta de beldá' (The Great Puerto Rican Family Is Really Really Black)." *Blackness in Latin America and the Caribbean: Social Dynamics and Cultural Transformations*. Ed. Arlene Torres and Norman Whitten Jr. Bloomington: Indiana University Press, 1998. 2:285–306.

Torres, Arlene, and Norman E. Whitten Jr., eds. *Blackness in Latin America and the Caribbean: Social Dynamics and Cultural Transformations*. 2 vols. Bloomington: Indiana University Press, 1998.

Torres Martinó, José Antonio. "El arte puertorriqueño de principios del siglo xx." *Puerto Rico: Arte e identidad*. San Juan: Editorial de la Universidad de Puerto Rico, 2004. 63–89.

Turner, Kay. *Beautiful Necessity: The Art and Meaning of Women's Altars*. New York: Thames and Hudson, 1999.

Umpierre, Luz María. *En el país de las maravillas*. Berkeley, Calif.: New Earth, 1990.

———. *For Christine: Poems and One Letter*. Chapel Hill, N.C.: Professional, 1995.

———. "Manifesto: Whose Taboos?: Theirs, Yours, or Ours?" *Letras Femeninas* 22.1–2 (Spring–Fall 1996): 263–68.

———. *The Margarita Poems*. Bloomington, Ind.: Third Woman, 1987.

———. "Metapoetic Code in Julia de Burgos' *El mar y tú*: Towards a Re-Vision." *In Retrospect: Essays on Latin American Literature*. Ed. Elizabeth Rogers and Timothy Rogers. York, S.C.: Spanish Literature Publications, 1987. 85–94.

———. *Una Puertorriqueña en Penna*. San Juan, P.R.: Masters, 1979.

———. *. . . Y Otras Desgracias / And Other Misfortunes*. Bloomington, Ind.: Third Woman, 1987.

Unruh, Vicky. *Latin American Vanguards: The Art of Contentious Encounters*. Berkeley: University of California Press, 1994.

Valle Ferrer, Norma. *Luisa Capetillo: Historia de una mujer proscrita*. San Juan, P.R.: Cultural, 1990.

Vargas, Deborah R. "Bidi Bidi Bom Bom: Selena and Tejano Music in The Making of Tejas." *Latino/a Popular Culture*. Ed. M. Habell-Pallán and M. Romero. New York: New York University Press, 2002. 117–26.

Vasconcelos, José. *La raza cósmica*. Mexico: Espasa-Calpe Mexicana, 1966.

Vázquez Arce, Carmen. "Tuntún de Pasa y Grifería: A Cultural Project." *The Cultures of the Hispanic Caribbean*. Ed. Conrad James and John Perivolaris. Gainesville: University of Florida Press, 2000. 86–103.

Vega, Bernardo. *The Memoirs of Bernardo Vega: A Contribution to the History of the Puerto Rican Community in New York*. Ed. César Andreu Iglesias. Trans. Juan Flores. New York: Monthly Review, 1984.

Vera-Rojas, María Teresa. "Polémicas, feministas, Puertorriqueñas, y desconocidas: Clotilde Betances Jaeger, María Mas Pozo, y sus 'Charlas Femeninas' en el *Gráfico* de Nueva York, 1929–1930." *Centro Journal* 22.2 (Fall 2010): 5–33.

Vicioso, Sherezada (Chiqui). *Eva/sión/es*. Philipsburg, St. Martin: House of Nehesi. 2007.

———. "An Interview with Don Juan Bosch." Trans. Lizabeth Paravisini-Gebert. *Callaloo* 17.3 (Summer 1994): 694–700.

———. *Julia de Burgos: La nuestra*. Santo Domingo, D.R.: Alfa y Omega, 1987.

———. "Julia de Burgos: Our Julia." Trans. Lizabeth Paravisini-Gebert. *Callaloo* 17.3 (Summer 1994): 674–83.

———. "The Rival to the Río Grande of Loíza: An Interview with Juan Isidro Jimenes Grullón." Trans. Lizabeth Paravisini-Gebert. *Callaloo* 17.3 (Summer 1994): 684–93.

———. "Testimonio." *The Afro-Latin@ Reader: History and Culture in the United States*. Ed. Miriam Jiménez Román and Juan Flores. Durham, N.C.: Duke University Press, 2010. 262–65.

Whalen, Carmen, and Victor Vázquez-Hernández, eds. *The Puerto Rican Diaspora: Historical Perspectives*. Philadelphia: Temple University Press, 2005.

Wheeler, Lesley. *Voicing American Poetry: Sound and Performance from the 1920s to the Present*. Ithaca: Cornell University Press, 2008.

Wherry, Frederick F. *The Philadelphia Barrio: The Arts, Branding, and Neighborhood Transformation*. Chicago: University of Chicago Press, 2011.

Wordsworth, William. *Poetry and Prose*. Cambridge: Harvard University Press, 1963.

Xavier, Emmanuel. *Americano*. San Francisco: Suspect Thoughts, 2002.

———. *Pier Queen*. New York: Xavier for Pier Queen, 1997.

Zaragoza, Edward. *St. James in the Streets: The Religious Processions of Loíza Aldea, Puerto Rico*. Lanham, Md.: Scarecrow, 1995.

Zavala-Martinez, Iris. "A Critical Inquiry into the Life and Work of Julia de Burgos." *The Psychosocial Development of Puerto Rican Women*. Ed. Cynthia T. García Coll and María de Lourdes Mattei. New York: Praeger, 1989. 1–30.

Zeno Gandía, Manuel. *La charca*. Maplewood, N.J.: Waterfront, 1982.

INDEX

Page numbers in *italics* refer to illustrations.
Plates follow page 122 and are indexed by
plate number.

abstract expressionism, 124–25
Acosta-Belén, Edna, 107
African diaspora: cultural memory and, 6,
  33–35, 112–13, 121–22, 128, 131, 142–44;
  diaspora discourse and, 98; *Latino/a* iden-
  tity and, 97–98, 117–18, 130–31, 161n19;
  Loíza Aldea historical importance, 21,
  118–19; *negrista* poetry and, 33–35; New
  York as site for, 9, 74, 86, 88, 128; *Pueblos
  Hispanos* reports on African Americans, 9,
  86; racial mixing and, 37, 160n28; rhetoric
  of paternalism and, 28–29; *treintista*
  suppression of, 3, 33; *vanguardia* African
  influences, 17. *See also* race; slavery
Afro-Latino identity, 117–18
Agustini, Delmira, 60
"A Julia de Burgos" (To Julia de Burgos,
  1938): Andrea Arroyo references to, *plate*
  7; as anthology selection, 110; Carmen
  Rivera references to, 114–15; double
  consciousness in, 26, 37–40; Juan Sánchez
  references to, 129; Luz María Umpierre
  references to, 104, 107; Oscar Montero
  on, 116; performing femininity, 37–40;
  poetics of presence in, 42; Rosario Ferré
  references to, 109; Sonia Rivera-Valdés
  references to, 108; Yasmín Hernández
  references to, 132–33
A Julia de Burgos (To Julia de Burgos, Arroyo
  installation, 2009), *plate* 7, 138–39

Albizu Campos, Pedro: Burgos writings on,
  31–32; commemoration of, 131; imprison-
  ment of, 30, 54; Juan Sánchez references
  to, 128; Lorenzo Homar references to, 126;
  Pueblos Hispanos and, 73–74; on Puerto
  Rican feminism, 29–30; U.S. relationship
  with, 31; *vanguardia* writers and, 16–17;
  Yasmín Hernández references to, 133
Algarín, Miguel, 94, 96–97
Alicea, José R., 126, 152n28
*All the Women Are White, All the Blacks Are
  Men, but Some of Us Are Brave* (Hull,
  Scott, and Smith, 1982), 106, 108
"Alta mar y gaviota" (High Sea and Seagull,
  1939), 49–50
Alvarez, Julia, 103, 136
"Amaneceres" (Dawnings, 1938), 26–27
Anderson, Benedict, 90
Antillean identity, 17, 18, 33–34, 115
Anzaldúa, Gloria, 68, 103, 106, 108
Aparicio, Frances, 97, 130–31
Arbello, Fernando, 54
Arce, Margot, 34
Arenas, Reinaldo, 99
Arroyo, Andrea, 6, *plate* 7, 137–39
Artes y Letras (monthly cultural magazine), 73
assimilation: Burgos as *Latinidad* symbol and,
  98, 150; cultural identity as defense against,
  84–85; pressure for, 4, 84–86, 96, 98,
  121–22, 150; in U.S. Puerto Rican journal-
  ism, 72–73
atalayismo, 16
Atalayismo/Atalaya de los Dioses (Watchman
  of the Gods), 7

Corazones y flores para Julia (Sánchez, 1994), *plate 2*, 129

Corretjer, Juan Antonio, 30, 73–74, 83, 133, 160n33

Coulthard, George Robert, 35

Creeley, Robert, 148

creolization, 20–21

Crown, Kathleen, 117

Cuba: Burgos period in, 8, 58–64, 158n39; exile by Jimenes Grullón, 64; intellectual culture of, 58–60; Jimenes Grullón's parents' arrival, 63; New York Cuban-American newspapers, 73; reflections on Puerto Rico from, 60–62; Santiago de Cuba boardinghouse, 62–63; University of Havana, 63–64

Cuchí Coll, Isabel, 73

"Cultura en Función Social" (The Social Function of Culture, 1944), 83

cultural identity: Antillean, 17; bi-, 89; cultural nationalism and, 1, 5–7, 22, 33, 86; diaspora, 6, 13, 88–89, 119; double consciousness and, 37–40; José Martí *nuestra América* hemispheric, 24, 30, 58, 84; miscegenation and racial, 20–21, 36; queer, 99–100; racial, in Burgos, 34–35; as resistance to assimilation, 84–85; as resistance to colonialism, 15–16; transnational, and memory, 95, 98, 110–13; triple consciousness and, 117; women's intellectual identity and, 107–9. *See also* diaspora, Puerto Rican; nationalism; nomadic subjectivity; race

Cunningham, Merce, 137

Curie, Marie, 137

Darío, Rubén, 85, 147, 148

Deleuze, Gilles, 3, 65

"Desde el puente de Martín Peña" (From the Martín Peña Bridge, 1938), 24–25, 110

Despierta (Hernández, 2005), *plate 4*, 132–33, 164n27

El Diario de Nueva York, 73

diaspora, Puerto Rican: Burgos biographical narrative and, 4, 6; discourse and, 98, 112; gender and sexuality as components of, 13; identity, 6, 13, 88–89, 119; Institute of Puerto Rican Culture, 125; migration-as-tragedy narrative, 119–20; Puerto Rican heterogeneity and, 18, 34–35, 119; recovery of non-Western life models, 112; triple consciousness and, 117–19. *See also* African

diaspora; cultural identity; nationalism; nomadic subjectivity

Díaz Quiñones, Arcadio, 125–26, 134

Diego, José de, 84–85

Diego Padró, José de, 16, 79–80

diepalismo, 16

Dimas, Marcos, 139–40

Dominican Republic: adoption of Burgos in, 136; Bosch presidency, 158n37; Burgos's "Himno de sangre a Trujillo" (Hymn of Blood to Trujillo), 31, 80; *dominicanidad* and, 59; Jimenes Grullón position on, 8; poems composed on, 31

Duany, Jorge, 69

Duarte Perón, Eva, 123–24, 139

Du Bois, W. E. B., 117

Duke, Anthony Drexel, 140

Durán, Alberto, 75

Edwards, Brent Hayes, 98

Ellington, Duke, 54

epitaphs, 126–27

escape discourse: in Burgos, 1, 3, 12–13, 42, 45, 52, 65–67; New York move and, 46; sexile figure and, 46–48; in Sonia Rivera-Valdés, 109; *treintista* nationalism and, 3

Escudero, Ralph, 54

Escuela del Aire (School of the Air, 1930s), 8, 17

"Es nuestra la hora" (Ours Is the Hour, 1936), 8, 23–24, 135

Espada, Martín, 148–50

Esteves, Sandra María, 5, 94, 95, 98, 110–13

euroforismo, 16

exile discourse, 43–44, 61, 64

Faber, Sebastiaan, 70

"Farewell in Welfare Island" (1953), 12

Faro (1926), 16

feminism: creative women narratives, 107–8, 114–15; double consciousness and, 37–40; early twentieth-century Puerto Rican, 28, 151n6; Frente Unido Femenino, 23, 28–29; *Latinidad feminista*, 106; Luisa Capetillo contributions in, 47; *marianismo* and, 32–33; 1960s literary suicides and, 113–14; nomadic subjectivity and, 3, 37; suffrage movement, 29; in U.S. Spanish-language press, 72–73; women of color and, 68, 103, 106, 108, 123, 139. *See also* gender; sexile figure; sexuality

Vanessa Pérez Rosario is an associate professor of Puerto Rican and Latino Studies at City University of New York, Brooklyn College, and the editor of *Hispanic Caribbean Literature of Migration: Narratives of Displacement*.

The University of Illinois Press
is a founding member of the
Association of American University Presses.

Composed in 10/13 New Caledonia
by Lisa Connery
at the University of Illinois Press
Designed by Dennis Roberts
Manufactured by Sheridan Books, Inc.

University of Illinois Press
1325 South Oak Street
Champaign, IL 61820-6903
www.press.uillinois.edu